CHASING BOCUSE

America's Journey to the Culinary World Stage

PHILIP TESSIER

FOREWORD BY ANDREW FRIEDMAN

CHASING BOCUSE

America's Journey to the Culinary World Stage

Photography by

LARA KASTNER, MEG SMITH, AND DAVID ESCALANTE

PRESTEL

MUNICH · LONDON · NEW YORK

Prestel Publishing Ltd.
14-17 Wells Street
London W1T 3PD

Prestel Publishing
900 Broadway, Suite 603
New York, NY 10003

Library of Congress Cataloging-in-Publication Data

Names: Tessier, Philip, author.
Title: Chasing Bocuse : America's journey to the culinary world stage /
   Philip Tessier ; foreword by Andrew Friedman ; photography by Lara
   Kastner, Meg Smith, and David Escalante.
Description: Munich ; London ; New York : Prestel, [2017]
Identifiers: LCCN 2017017626 | ISBN 9783791383699 (hardcover)
Subjects: LCSH: Tessier, Philip--Awards. | Cooks--United States--Biography. |
   Cooking--Competitions--France--Lyon. | Bocuse d'Or (Competition) (2015 :
   Lyon, France)
Classification: LCC TX649.T39 A3 2017 | DDC 641.5092 [B] --dc23
LC record available at https://lccn.loc.gov/2017017626

A CIP catalogue record for this book is available from the British Library.

Editorial direction: Holly La Due
Design: Level, Calistoga, CA
Production management: Luke Chase
Copyediting: John Son, Amy Vogler
Proofreading: Monica Parcell
Index: Marilyn Bliss

Printed in China

Third printing 2018

ISBN 978-3-7913-8369-9

www.prestel.com

TO PAUL BOCUSE,
FOR INSPIRING GENERATIONS OF CULINARY EXCELLENCE.

CONTENTS

PHILIPPE,

I HAVE JUST LEARNED about the forthcoming book celebrating your culinary achievements. On this occasion, I want to tell you once again how very enthusiastic I am about your wonderful second-place finish at the Bocuse d'Or in 2015. It gave me great personal pleasure to see you awarded for this achievement.

Since 1987, American teams have competed one after the other, and at last we see the results we desired. The whole world knows of my attachment to America. This is why I am delighted to hear of this great step forward, which generates interest in, and suggests a new image for, gastronomy across the cities of your great country.

I send my greetings to your mentor, Thomas Keller, whose contributions—along with those of Daniel Boulud and Jérôme Bocuse, as the three leaders of the Ment'or BKB Foundation—have guided the performance of your team. I am pleased to see America's most renowned chefs continue to work together to develop America's best young talent.

From this point forward, cuisine, as practiced by chefs in the United States, will take on a new dimension, and you have been instrumental as a leader in this venture.

BRAVO!

Paul Bocuse

Stone Ban

Thomas Keller

Daniel Boulud

THE BIRTH OF A
CULINARY TRADITION

MY FATHER, PAUL BOCUSE, has always been a man of incredible vision and charisma, passionately driven to reach beyond the borders of his own Lyonnaise kitchen to embrace the world. That might not seem extraordinary in today's landscape of celebrity chefs, pop-up restaurants, and social media, but in the 1970s and '80s, it was revolutionary. Monsieur Paul, as he is affectionately known, was the first chef of his day to step out of the kitchen, becoming an ambassador of the culinary brigade to his guests, and of French cuisine to the world, around which he frequently traveled.

Those same instincts led him to create a culinary competition for restaurant chefs, the Bocuse d'Or (Golden Bocuse). I remember the first years of the contest, as we struggled to enlist sponsors and even chefs to participate. If that sounds difficult, just imagine attempting it in the days before cell phones and the Internet. And yet, thanks to the global network he had developed, he was able to gather chefs from twenty-four countries together in one place and provide a stage on which they could compete. I'll never forget those formative days when, at the age of eighteen, I helped in any capacity I could, even rummaging through the CDs in my car to find a suitable soundtrack for the competition and ceremony.

Today, more than sixty countries vie for the twenty-four spots in the final.

Over the next two decades, I watched as the Bocuse d'Or developed from those humble beginnings into the most prestigious culinary competition in the world, drawing the world's best chefs to Lyon every two years to compete for gold. Winners of the Bocuse d'Or are now congratulated by their country's political leaders and achieve celebrity status overnight. Nations that have medaled repeatedly, such as Norway, Denmark, France, and Sweden, have created organizations that train and develop chefs from a young age, preparing them for the rigors and intensity of the competition.

Each year I travel internationally, overseeing the continental selections where countries must qualify in order to compete at the final in Lyon. The energy and enthusiasm that even the smallest countries demonstrate—as they compete against the powerhouses that consistently excel—is a tribute to the power of ambition and belief. It is clear how grateful they are for the privilege and opportunity to represent their country before the world. Today, more than sixty countries vie for the twenty-four spots in the final. Once in Lyon, they compete for the chance to mount the podium—an incredibly difficult achievement—where judges award only three teams the bronze, silver, and gold medals.

Technology and new culinary techniques have shaped the competition's recent evolution; it has developed into a trendsetting display of the world's top talent. Many chefs have returned multiple times in the quest for gold, most notably Rasmus Kofoed of Denmark who, in 2011, claimed gold on his third attempt (in two prior attempts he won bronze and silver) with a platter that set the new standard for future competitors.

> Many chefs have returned multiple times in the quest for gold.

In 2008, my father asked me to help organize, in partnership with Daniel Boulud and Thomas Keller, the US Bocuse d'Or effort. The United States had competed since the first Bocuse d'Or in 1987, but had never placed higher than sixth. My father's hope was that the three of us could help elevate the quality of candidates and increase interest across the United States. Over the last twenty years, the food culture in the United States has improved and evolved exponentially, providing a fertile ground for developing young chefs who are poised to compete against the world's best. It has been a steep learning curve over the last eight years, but we are proud to have seen the United States, after nearly three decades of falling short, mount the podium at last in 2015. Philip Tessier and Skylar Stover, with an incredible display of tenacity and determination, made the United States the first country outside of Europe to win silver.

There is now a great expectation in the United States because, for the first time, a winning formula and structure are in place for future candidates to build on. Philip will return as the coach in 2017, sharing his experience and success with the next team in the ongoing quest for gold, much like Rasmus Kofoed put repeated efforts into establishing Denmark as a perennial force. The anticipation of what the United States will do next is higher than it has ever been.

Few of us, Monsieur Paul included, could have imagined the prestige the Bocuse d'Or commands, though I hear his cautionary voice, "Never think you have succeeded; it will be the beginning of your failure." We continue to press on, determined to grow and evolve and yet maintain our identity and relevance within the culinary profession. I look forward to many more decades of discovery as chefs across the world continue to cross borders to compete and, more importantly, develop relationships in a worldwide community.

It is a relief to know I no longer have to provide the soundtrack.

—JÉRÔME BOCUSE, ORLANDO, FLORIDA, MARCH 2016

DANIEL BOULUD

PAUL BOCUSE AND
THE COMMUNITY OF CHEFS

HAD THE PRIVILEGE of beginning my cooking career in Lyon, where the history of food and wine was very well represented at all levels—from beloved local restaurants, brasseries, bistros, and bouchons, to the world-famous temples of gastronomy lorded over by iconic chefs such as Fernand Point and Paul Bocuse. Those legends were driven by a passion for seasonal ingredients and tremendous respect for local traditions while also serving as mentors, imparting their craft to the next generation. I've carried both sides of my hometown's culinary character with me into my professional life—opening both formal and casual restaurants, and always keeping the next generation in mind. (In light of all of this, I'm especially gratified that my protégé, Gavin Kaysen, competed in the Bocuse d'Or in 2007 and has been the heart and soul of the American effort since then, coaching Philip Tessier in his silver-medal-winning effort in 2015.)

> The air was filled with jokes, singing, laughter, and the aura of friendship.

As an apprentice at fifteen, one of my duties in the morning was to go to Les Halles de Lyon, our central market next door to the restaurant. It was there that I first met Chef Paul Bocuse, fondly known in Lyon as Monsieur Paul. He was like a general leading an army of chefs, and everyone respected him for his exceptional talent and his inspiring leadership. He was also beloved for fostering a sense of community and camaraderie among local chefs. The Bocuse d'Or receives worldwide attention for bringing chefs from around the world together. But he achieved a similar, less-publicized feat at home, where I personally witnessed him gathering all his chef friends once a week in a local bistro near Les Halles de Lyon around a *mâchon*. This mid-morning breakfast was composed of *tête de veau* with *sauce ravigote* (calf's head with pickled herb sauce) and many other Lyonnais specialties like lamb feet salad, *cervelas* sausage with truffles and pistachios, *cervelle des canuts* (whipped goat cheese with shallots, tarragon, walnut oil, and aged vinegar), and *le tablier de sapeur* (a steak of tripe poached tender and pan- roasted crispy). Of course, the meal was celebrated with a Beaujolais red and a Mâcon white, and the air was filled with jokes, singing, laughter, and the aura of friendship—this was the chefs' bonding ritual as *confrères*.

With Paul's example as inspiration, I periodically gather chef friends in New York for some real, old-fashioned Lyonnais cooking. On the occasion of Paul's ninetieth birthday on February 11, 2016, while he was in Lyon, we had a celebration at Daniel in New York City, honoring him with a *soupe à la jambe de bois*. He adores this specialty of Lyon and prepares it on special occasions in his restaurant in Collonges-au-Mont-d'Or. It is a majestic dish fit for a king, composed of whole beef and veal shank, a slab of short ribs, rare tenderloin, calf tongue, truffled chicken, partridge, pheasant, cured pork belly, pig's head sausage, boudin blanc, pipe-cut marrow bones, many seasonal root and bulb vegetables, spices, clove-studded blackened onions, and a generous bouquet garni. Everything simmers gently for hours until it falls off the bone, giving the rich stock an unforgettable smell and flavor. The dish is served with a horseradish crème fraîche, pickles, mustard, and shavings of black truffle. It is the perfect vehicle for Gallic and soulful moments between friends and fellow chefs.

> Each serving is a symbol of how cuisine can bring chefs together.

This meaningful dish seems a total opposite of the hyper-precise preparations for the Bocuse d'Or, but they have more in common than meets the eye. Each serving, in its own way, is a symbol of how cuisine can bring chefs together, fostering a sense of community that makes the profession a warmer place for all of us.

—DANIEL BOULUD, NEW YORK CITY, MARCH 2016

THOMAS KELLER

HONORING OUR HEROES

EARLY IN MY CAREER, Paul Bocuse was more of an abstraction than an actual person to me. In the mid-1970s, he was the face of French cuisine, leading a generation of pioneers in his own country and smiling at Americans from a now-famous *Newsweek* magazine cover. The article within heralded the arrival of nouvelle cuisine in France and an unprecedented culinary awakening across the United States, which sparked a new wave of chef hopefuls.

Those were the days when I began cooking for a living, when it was still decidedly unfashionable, if not revolutionary, for a young American to choose a career in the kitchen. In this country, the profession was considered menial, unskilled, and unsavory, and parents confronted with a son or daughter determined to become a chef were, generally speaking, heartbroken, convinced their child was throwing away his or her life. One reason for their dismay was that there were no accomplished American restaurant chefs. They had no reason to believe we could succeed because we young cooks had no homegrown role models to emulate. Today, a young American dreaming of a career in a professional kitchen can build the necessary foundation without leaving the confines of the United States, working exclusively under the tutelage of American mentors. My contemporaries and I, however, had to learn at the foot of a French chef. In New York City, that meant vying for a coveted spot in the kitchens of transplanted toques such as Jean-Jacques Rachou, Alain Sailhac, and André Soltner, among other titans. These men were our Lou Gehrigs, our Joe DiMaggios. They were our heroes. Our gods.

> Today, a young American dreaming of a career in a professional kitchen can build the necessary foundation without leaving the confines of the United States.

But the ultimate learning experience in those days was to live and cook in France, committing to a stint that Americans call a *stage*, an adaptation of the French word *stagiaire* (trainee). The French had set the standard for Western cuisine, and without their example of refinement, as well as a codified vocabulary—established primarily by Auguste Escoffier—of flavors and textures, essential recipes, and classic dishes, we wouldn't have developed the dining culture we have in the United States today. We Americans who came up during those years will always hold the French in the highest regard.

All of which brings me to "the call." One spring day in 2008, Paul Bocuse called and asked me to lead the American effort in the Bocuse d'Or, in partnership with his son Jérôme Bocuse and Chef Daniel Boulud, one of my best friends, with whom I had worked in the 1980s. Chef (as I refer to Paul Bocuse) had always wanted the United States to excel in the competition and specifically, to reach the podium. As a soldier in World War II, he'd been shot in the chest and saved, in part, by a blood transfusion from an American G.I. He likes to say that he still has American blood in his veins; he has been making regular visits to the United States for decades and flies the Stars and Stripes alongside the French flag outside his landmark restaurant.

Of course, we all said yes to his request, but it took a while for us to truly keep our promise and deliver an American to the podium. When the first team to operate under our auspices—led by Timothy Hollingsworth, at the time a sous chef at The French Laundry—competed in 2009, I hadn't yet attended the Bocuse d'Or. I was unprepared for the sheer culinary wizardry on display, and I was surprised and impressed, my sense of ambition stirred. Just as my contemporaries and I had longed to be recognized for our abilities generations ago, I wanted our young chefs to have the resources and support required to distinguish themselves on this unique world stage.

> I was unprepared for the sheer culinary wizardry on display.

Over the ensuing years, Daniel, Jérôme, and I have continued to marshal our professional standing and resources to gather the coaches, sponsors, and creativity to support our team. To give structure to our mission, we founded the Bocuse d'Or USA Foundation, which was renamed Ment'or in 2014. In addition to supporting Team USA every two years, Ment'or establishes and funds opportunities for aspiring chefs to grow and develop outside the competition, and provides the structure for them to do so.

Following Tim Hollingsworth's at-bat came James Kent in 2011 and Richard Rosendale in 2013. Then in 2015, Philip Tessier—a longtime chef within our restaurant group—and his commis, or helper, Skylar Stover, cracked the code and came home with a silver medal. Then in 2017, we achieved what had once seemed like an unattainable goal: the US team of Mathew Peters and Harrison Turone took home the gold, fulfilling the dream of Paul Bocuse, which had become my dream as well.

As gratified as I was by the successes of Phil and Skylar and Matt and Harrison, I am even more humbled and delighted by the close relationship I've developed with Chef. I remember sitting with him in his restaurant on the outskirts of Lyon, in my favorite room, *Salon Fernand Point*—where photographs of French culinary legends line the wall—our hands intertwined. Two chefs, neither of us as young as we once were, were now both using our influence to pay it forward.

Put another way, my commitment to the Bocuse d'Or isn't about me. It's my way of furthering America's reputation on the world stage, of giving a new generation of Americans a chance to attain their dreams, and of honoring the wish of a legend who—improbably, miraculously—became a friend.

—THOMAS KELLER, YOUNTVILLE, CALIFORNIA, FEBRUARY 2017

Chefs Thomas Keller and Paul Bocuse, Lyon, France, 2015.

ANDREW FRIEDMAN

ALL THE DRAMA
IS ON THE PLATE

CASUAL OBSERVERS of the Bocuse d'Or, including the occasional journalist, refer to it as "the real *Top Chef.*"

With no disrespect to Top Chef, or to any televised cooking shows—some of which have introduced genuine talent to the world—the Bocuse d'Or is a different animal altogether. Generally speaking, TV competitions are based on how the "cheftestants" respond to spontaneous challenges, often resulting in improvisational, seat-of-the-pants creativity. It's undeniably entertaining, but has little in common with the Bocuse d'Or, for which candidates know what the challenge will be months in advance, enabling them to meticulously plan what they will cook and serve, with one recent exception. In 2013, the Bocuse d'Or introduced an element of spontaneity by asking candidates to select ingredients from a market on the eve of the competition. My personal theory is that the adjustment was a nod to the pressures of contemporary entertainment; the fundamentals of the event remain intact, but even the Bocuse d'Or has to bend a little to keep up with the times. And besides, what chef hasn't had to make an adjustment "on the fly" when supplies of a particular ingredient are depleted, or to whip up something special for a VIP in the house?

Many televised cooking competitions are also categorized as "reality" shows, with interpersonal dynamics (often heightened by group living situations) impinging on what transpires in the kitchen. By contrast, in the Bocuse d'Or, there are no interviews with the emcees, no ESPN-style biographical videos, and precious little interaction among the candidates save for a welcome reception and group photo. There is nothing but the cooking, the finished product, and the judging.

In short, in the Bocuse d'Or, all of the drama is on the plate. The candidates live and die not by personality or gimmick, catchphrase or getup, but rather by their creativity, technique, organization, and composure—the same things that determine success for any self-respecting chef.

The Bocuse d'Or continues to attract top talent from around the world because it asks chefs to do what they got into the business to do in the first place: cook. That shouldn't be an extraordinary thing, but at a time when success is often determined by style over substance, it's a crucial distinction that makes this competition—which seems antiquated to so many—as relevant as ever.

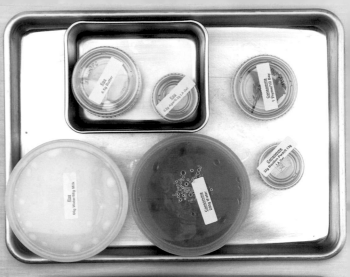

2015

COMPETING TO WIN

THE HOPE OF A NATION

"Success occurs when opportunity meets preparation."

—ZIG ZIGLAR

AS WE PUSHED THROUGH the hotel doors onto the dimly lit streets of Lyon, the damp 5 A.M. chill brought a welcome alertness.

It was hard to believe that "D-Day"—our nickname for the finals of the Bocuse d'Or, the world's most prestigious cooking competition—had finally arrived. Though I'd thought of little else for the past two years, it still felt distant, even in the homestretch. My thoughts flitted between what got us here and what lay ahead. With a history of dashed hopes for American teams, the odds had been stacked against us since the very beginning. The resulting low expectations offered cover if we failed, but our expectations for *ourselves* were high; they had to be because the commitment we'd made was absolute.

We crammed our rental vehicles full of equipment and began the thirty-minute drive to the expo. Our coach, Gavin Kaysen, took the wheel of my SUV so my commis (apprentice), Skylar Stover, and I could try to relax in the back. Completing our convoy, our support team, Will Mouchet and Greg Schesser, followed close behind in the truck with all of our remaining kitchen equipment. The rest of the coaching team and support staff would meet us at the expo.

At the outskirts of the city, the Saône River, lamplight streaking its placid waters, offered a calm contrast to my quickening pulse. The journey to this point had been one of discovery and determination, risk and reward. I thought of everything we had invested in the competition: leaving our full-time jobs, eighteen months of development, ten thousand man-hours of training, and untold resources.

It was all about to culminate in a single meal, a five-and-a-half-hour culinary performance. There would be just one round, one chance, with the world watching. To combat the gathering sense of momentousness, I mentally reviewed our preparation: every list, every recipe, every piece of equipment. We had meticulously planned and rehearsed until we could prepare this meal in our sleep. I had long considered success to be the result of *opportunity meeting preparation*—our mantra over the past two years. We had done everything humanly possible to prepare for this once-in-a-lifetime opportunity: physical training, temperance, French lessons, hours of honing every move in multiple practice sessions. Win or lose, I had to finish knowing that I had left everything in the three-by-six-meter competition kitchenbox that awaited us.

At the same time, any number of things could still go wrong, just as they could in any kitchen during any service: equipment failures or human errors, such as a forgotten ingredient or a cut finger. Then there were the competition-specific pitfalls. Misinterpreted rules were a perennial sore point with many Bocuse d'Or veterans in particular because their subjectivity had derailed past candidates, including the United States just two years earlier. Competitions were a different beast than restaurants; there were no reinforcements or extra ingredients available to remedy a misstep, and there was no opportunity to "make it up" to a customer. Additionally, in sharp contrast to the veterans representing many of the favored countries, some of whose chefs had been practicing for more than a decade, Skylar and I lacked competition chops. Despite all the time we'd spent preparing, we'd never put ourselves on the line this way, and we had never performed together as a team outside of our training. We were, to put it mildly, underdogs.

Two years prior, I had attended the Bocuse d'Or 2013 as a spectator. One moment in particular haunted me: a candidate (Bocuse d'Or-speak for "competitor") was putting the finishing touches on his meat platter when he dropped the tray holding one of his garnishes, sending his composure with it. He stared uncomprehendingly at the culinary wreckage on the floor before turning his attention back to his platter, but by then, failure was a *fait accompli*. A momentary slip had changed and sealed his fate; I bet he still relives it lying in bed at night.

The pressure had been ratcheted up another notch the night before, when Chef Thomas Keller, my mentor and one of the towering figures of American gastronomy, looked me in the eye during a send-off speech and said, "The hopes of the country rest on your shoulders."

The honor of representing the United States had always been a double-edged sword: It was, of course, motivating and imbued the task at hand with privilege and excitement. But if I dwelled on it, the fear of failure could become almost crippling. I call on my faith in times like these—reminding myself that ultimately, nothing was in my control, which allowed

Chef Philip Tessier and team make final preparations.

me to find an inner peace. I recalled a verse I had memorized for moments like these: "Though an army besiege me, my heart will not fear; though war break out against me, even then I will be confident."

It was quiet in the SUV, the calm before the storm. With each deep breath, I visualized a different phase of the competition, imagining myself executing the game plan, relying on muscle memory and the support and camaraderie of Skylar. When I opened my eyes, the lights of the expo were just poking through the thick, predawn fog.

ACTION!

The loading zone was a virtual Babel: a dozen teams, each speaking a different language, unpacking and loading in, everything heightened by the potent alchemy of nerves and adrenaline. The chaos did not reflect the calm, orderly process the organizing committee had depicted during a briefing session the night prior. I directed Greg, who was driving our second truck with supplies, to park off to the side, as far from the drama as possible.

We unloaded our gear and reviewed the checklist, confirming that everything was in order in each of the food boxes. Thankfully all of the food appeared to have traveled without spoilage or damage. A few minutes later, a wiry, bespectacled member of the Committee hurried over, a bit jittery himself, and informed us we could begin unloading our truck. When I gestured toward the equipment already stacked on the carts behind me, his look of surprise was priceless. I guess we weren't the only ones stressed out this morning. He motioned for us to move everything to the internal staging area where each of the teams positioned their equipment before loading into their kitchens. We relocated everything, leaving Will and Greg to stand guard, and then Gavin, Skylar, and I made for the competitors' lounge.

Twenty-four teams compete in the Bocuse d'Or over two days, and the start times for the twelve countries cooking on each day are staggered to ensure a steady flow of finished dishes at the closing bell. In the lounge, we joined several teams anxiously waiting their turn. For all the planning we had done, there was one thing we hadn't organized well: breakfast. Our hotel room didn't have a kitchen, so instead of enjoying Skylar's corn cakes, as was tradition before a practice session back home, I had to settle for nothing but the stale, day-old sandwich I had forced down on the drive to the expo—hardly a breakfast of champions. I was thankful to find a fresh *pain au chocolat* and a bottle of water waiting for us in the lounge, one last hit of sustenance before the marathon ahead. I craved a cup of coffee, but my pre-run limit was one shot of espresso in the morning. I had squandered my daily allotment at the hotel, and the last thing I needed was the caffeine shakes.

There we sat, waiting to be called into battle. We reviewed the small changes we had made to incorporate the market visit and mystery vegetable selection, two components of the competition intentionally added only the night before to test quick thinking and performance under pressure. My buddy Nathan Daulton, our chief supporter throughout training, appeared from around the corner and motioned Skylar and me over. Over the last eighteen months, Nate had organized a support team to pray for the team during stressful times. Now, he offered a final prayer and gave us his trademark bear hug, then headed out to the viewing area. I was pleased that instead of anxiety, uncertainty, or doubt, Skylar and I were both eager to get started. All through our training, excitement and dread had wrestled within us both, but now excitement was winning. We felt as though we had been keeping a secret every day for the past year, one that we couldn't share until

The Bocuse d'Or press pit in Lyon, France, 2015.

Tessier (center) and Commis Skylar Stover (left) begin competing at Bocuse d'Or 2015.

January 27, 2015. Now, finally, we got to reveal the secret we had so diligently kept. The question was, would the world listen?

A committee member, the same fretting man who had met us at the loading dock, called out "USA!" Gavin, in accordance with the rules, headed around to the front of the kitchen-box from which he would coach us during the competition. Will and Greg, who'd been with us for the last five months of training, offered some final words of encouragement and then became the last of our supporters to fall away as we turned and headed in on our own. The Bocuse d'Or is a great metaphor for life: you're prepared for it by those who care about you, but when push comes to shove, you have to stand on your own two feet.

The committee member motioned for us to begin the walk down the dimly lit corridor that ran behind the competition kitchen-boxes. We grabbed our equipment and followed him, stepping over and around cords, random gear, and kitchen equipment cluttering the path. As we approached our own Box 9, the chaos around us took on an air of unreality, especially as we caught passing glimpses of the first few kitchen-boxes, where teams were already cooking at full tilt.

Skylar and I caught each other's eyes. "Here we go!" I said. I will never forget the feeling as I pushed aside the curtain to our kitchen, my eyes adjusted to the blinding stage lights, and we stepped into the box.

There was no turning back now.

WE WERE LIVE.

CHAPTER ONE

THE JOURNEY BEGINS

"Success is never final. Failure is never fatal.
It is courage that counts."

—JOHN WOODEN

A S AN ASPIRING YOUNG CHEF, growing up in Williamsburg, Virginia, I had always been fascinated with France, whose deep roots in cuisine and culture reach far beyond its borders and have influenced the cooking and techniques of chefs around the globe. In 2000, when I was twenty, this fascination led me to move to France for a six-month *stage* (working in a kitchen, for free, in exchange for knowledge) where I would be immersed not only in French food but also in its culture and daily life. Few people would look back on a time when they worked six days a week, over twelve hours a day, unpaid, in an environment where nobody spoke their language, as one of the best in their lives. But I loved every minute of it. Every day was an adventure, a chance to learn a new word or technique, or simply to absorb French culture.

I had pinched every penny to allow myself the opportunity to travel around France for a few weeks after my stage. It was an epic culinary adventure, from the haute cuisine of Alain Ducasse in Monaco to the offerings of street vendors in Normandy. The experience, though brief, was a defining cornerstone in my foundation as a chef.

Returning to the United States in 2000, I overcame my aversion to big cities and landed a position at the legendary restaurant Le Bernardin, New York City's premier seafood temple, where I worked under Chef Eric Ripert. I was a sponge, absorbing every drop of knowledge—from the simplicity and clarity of the sauces to the delicate treatment of fish, and the awe-inspiring efficiency of Chef Ripert's brigade. This was no country kitchen; it was a well-oiled machine engineered to put out world-class cuisine at an unrivaled pace. Over the ensuing three years, I was challenged and pushed until I morphed from a fledgling line cook to an adept and promising sous chef.

In 2004, at Chef Ripert's urging, I set my sights on the next step in my career, which I hoped would be at Per Se. This was the much-anticipated new restaurant Thomas Keller was opening in New York. Long acclaimed as the force behind what was considered at the time America's undisputed best restaurant, The French Laundry in the Napa Valley town of Yountville, Chef Keller was making a daring move returning to Manhattan, and it was all the culinary world could talk about. I assumed it was too late to apply because the restaurant was set to debut in just a few months, but I submitted a resume anyway. I was thrilled to learn that I was just in time to earn the *poissonier* (fish cook) position on the opening team. Little did I know that this was just the beginning of what would become the most intensely demanding trial of my young career. I still vividly remember my first glimpse of Chef Keller. It was on January 15, 2004. The staff of the restaurant was packed into a conference room at the Hudson Hotel on West 59th Street, a block away from what would be Per Se's home, the nearly finished Time Warner Center. Chef Keller made quite the entrance—a tall, lean, commanding figure in a crisp, white chef's jacket. He delivered an impassioned speech detailing his personal journey, his vision for the restaurant, and the opportunity we all had to be a part of its legacy and success. By the end of that day, I realized that whatever I thought I knew about food was dwarfed by the wealth of knowledge in that room. In the months and years that followed, I became not just a part of Per Se but also of the Thomas Keller Restaurant Group (TKRG). The adventure would take me through two states, three restaurants, seven

Michelin stars, and more than one historic moment. I witnessed Per Se earn four stars from the *New York Times* in its first year (a rare accomplishment) and be named Best New Restaurant by the James Beard Foundation, and I was there when Chef Keller became the first American chef to earn three Michelin stars after the world-renowned guide debuted in New York City in 2006.

A few months after opening, my wife, Rachel, joined the Per Se team as a baker. We had met at the Culinary Institute of America and married shortly after her graduation just a year before Per Se opened. It was an exciting and exhausting time for both of us as we worked and learned alongside each other, swept up in the fast-paced and demanding culture of this new culinary landmark. The birth of our first daughter, Naomi, came in 2006 and dramatically changed our lifestyle. Rachel stepped out of the kitchen to care for her and, with one of us perpetually pushing a stroller, the city lost much of its appeal for us. A relocation was on the horizon.

Tessier (second from right) in the Per Se kitchen, New York, 2005.

DAYDREAMS

In 2007 I was named the chef de cuisine of Bouchon, Chef Keller's French bistro, just down Washington Street from The French Laundry in Yountville. Bouchon was a much different animal than Le Bernardin and Per Se—a more casual bistro, but it gave me invaluable experience with the business side of a restaurant and managing my own team. Still, I was always looking for ways to keep a foot in the fine dining realm. Knowing this, a colleague of mine asked what I knew about a competition that took place every two years in France among the world's top chefs called the Bocuse d'Or. The next day, he brought me two documentaries that tracked a few of the competing chefs in different years and told me I should take them home and watch them.

That night, I watched the stories of chefs from across the globe unfold on the world stage at a level far beyond what I could have imagined. Their focus and drive rivaled that of Olympic athletes; the grandeur of the event was substantial; the food was stunning, inventive, and breathtaking in its ambition and execution. And the involvement of the fans—screaming for their national teams and hanging on every revelation during the awards ceremony—gave me goose bumps.

Over the ensuing years, I kept tabs on the Bocuse d'Or, occasionally wondering what it would be like to compete. But with a growing family and a full-time job as a chef, my interest was unlikely to develop into anything more than a daydream.

ONE TEAM, ONE NATION

Still, living and working in Yountville, I had the chance to observe Chef Keller as his involvement with the Bocuse d'Or deepened. I watched as Keller, along with superstar chef Daniel Boulud, a Lyon native who had apprenticed for Bocuse as a teenager, and Paul Bocuse's son Jérôme Bocuse, CEO of Les Chefs de France restaurant at Orlando's Epcot Cen-

ter, took the reins of the Bocuse d'Or USA in 2008 and began the slow process of building a foundation to train American candidates.

The United States' first at-bat with Chef Keller at the helm was in 2009, and when the team failed to earn a medal, he understood it as a learning experience. When he returned, he regaled me with stories of the team's efforts. He also pulled a large shiny object from his bag, his eyes widening with an excitement and awe that I rarely saw in this usually reserved, deeply private leader. It was a Bocuse d'Or trophy. Paul Bocuse had given him a replica of the coveted prize. If Monsieur Paul's intent was to inspire Chef, it worked, fanning the flame he had stoked when he first asked Chef Keller to lead the US efforts at the competition.

That Paul Bocuse could have such an effect on Chef Keller impressed me because Chef was a living legend himself. It really tells you all you need to know about Monsieur Paul. There are few culinary figures whose influence is worldwide, and spans generations, and he is one of them.

But beyond that, Chef Keller has always felt a sense of camaraderie with his fellow toques. It was that which led Monsieur Paul to create the Bocuse d'Or competition in 1987 to bring chefs and countries from around the globe together. No other event in the culinary field mingles collaboration, determination, tenacity, craft, community, and patriotism so effectively. One team. One nation.

Over the next few years, I observed firsthand the cycle of emotions as a new team was chosen: hope abounded, anticipation built, and the team left to compete with our dreams trailing them overseas. It was difficult, for those following the US effort, to watch chef-candidate James Kent and commis Tom Allan return empty-handed again in 2011, placing tenth. Many had assumed that with such powerhouse backing, success would be inevitable. When the 2013 campaign began, expectations were again high as

Richard Rosendale, a longtime culinary competitor with Culinary Olympic experience, won the US selection event and became the new US candidate for the 2013 finals. Everyone felt he was the missing link; if anyone understood competition and could overcome the odds to reach the podium, it was Richard.

During Richard's training I had a closer glimpse of the Bocuse d'Or ramp up because Richard periodically trained at the Bocuse House, two doors down from The French Laundry where Chef Keller's father had lived until he passed away. By then I had become the executive sous chef of The French Laundry and had regular interactions with the team when they were in town. I observed as Richard and his commis Corey Siegel prepared their meat platter and fish plate for the tasting where Chefs Keller, Boulud, and Bocuse would be present. It was fascinating to observe the intensity and detail with which they composed and assembled everything. I listened in as the board of mentors and other consulting chefs tasted the food and provided feedback and direction. Watching all of these chefs work together toward a goal outside of the walls of their restaurants was incredibly rare, and I felt fortunate to be able to observe the process.

It was a great honor when, a few months later, Chef Keller asked if I would be a part of his team preparing a course for Le Dîner des Grands Chefs du Monde, held in Lyon during the Bocuse d'Or competition. Not only would I have the chance to be a part of that incredible event, but I would also have the opportunity to actually attend the Bocuse d'Or. I was eager to witness firsthand what I had only been able to observe from a distance. Little did I know that the trip would become the first step in a journey that would change my life.

CENTER STAGE

We hit the ground running, setting up camp at l'Abbaye de Collonges, Paul Bocuse's private event space just down the road from his eponymous restaurant. We set

to work preparing a *pavé*, a terrine-like presentation of lamb with spinach and black trumpet mushrooms that we would serve at the Grands Chefs dinner.

We prepped during the day, only pausing to enjoy the lunch from Paul Bocuse's restaurant, an unexpected and memorable treat. For three days leading up to the main event, we would sit, enjoying some of the most iconic dishes of Western cuisine offered up as staff meal: *poulet au crème*, tarte Tatin, and the legendary black truffle soup that Chef Bocuse created in honor of the French President in 1975. In the evening, if we were free and had enough energy left, we ate at the unassuming bistros that lined the streets of Lyon. It would be impossible to replicate the experience one has at a true Lyonnais bistro: communal tables, hosts who might (as ours did one night) spontaneously begin strumming a guitar and singing, sharing of plates, and the owner cooking and then sitting down with the guests. It was quintessential France at its best.

On one of these nights, we were invited to the send-off dinner for Team USA, who were already in town for the competition. As plates of pig's feet, foie gras terrine, onion soup, and calves' tongue were passed around at the bistro Daniel et Denise, I looked around the room at the group assembled about me. Thomas Keller, Daniel Boulud, Jérôme Bocuse, Chicago's Grant Achatz of Alinea and Next, Roland Passot of San Francisco's La Folie, former Daniel restaurant chef de cuisine Alex Lee, Next restaurant chef Dave Beran, Gavin Kaysen, and others were all assembled for one purpose—to support Team USA. At that moment, a seed of possibility was planted for me. "Maybe I should actually be a part of this. Why *wouldn't* I want to be a part of this?"

After the event, we were ready to put our knives away for a few days and discover firsthand what the Bocuse d'Or was all about. After all I'd heard about the event, and observed in those documentaries, nothing prepared me for the spectacle I encountered

WHAT IT TAKES TO COMPETE

RICHARD ROSENDALE

COOKING IN THE COMPETITIVE ARENA requires the relentless dedication, drive, and discipline of an Olympic athlete. Only the candidate and commis compete, but everyone in their lives feels the ripple effect of their commitment. Family, friends, and coworkers all play a role, building a network of support like that which springs up around those preparing to run a marathon. But before you can race, you must train, and train hard. When you submit your application, it's hard to imagine how that simple task can change your life. Earning the right to compete in Lyon is just the starting point; it's after the tryouts that the real work begins. For someone on the outside looking in, it may appear that the hard work is summed up only on the plate, but the training also takes a mental and emotional toll. That's why many teams follow physical training programs to keep them mentally sharp and prevent fatigue during the rigorous schedule. After a long day of practice, it is not uncommon to ponder how your performance can be better the next time. Those fortunate to compete at the level of the Bocuse d'Or point to these moments as the ones that made them a better chef.

GETTING INTO THE ZONE: THE COACHING PROCESS

GABRIEL KREUTHER

PREPARING FOR THE BOCUSE D'OR is a journey, one that requires a candidate and a commis who share a chemistry with each other, as well as with the coaching team. One of the first steps is for the candidate to share his vision with us; it needs to come from him so that he can cook with passion. The coaches are there to give advice and support, but the candidate must be at the center of the process, driving his own ideas forward. Our services as coaches focus on sharpening an idea or honing execution, helping the candidate identify the very essence of food and technique.

The ultimate goal, for both coaches and candidate, is to introduce the unexpected, perhaps even hitting on a groundbreaking method that has never been done before. That method might impact taste, presentation, and/or service, if not all three. You know you are on the right track when people scratch their heads and say, "How come I didn't think of that?"

upon entering the competition hall. To my right were twelve identical open kitchen-boxes where the chefs worked; over each box, the names of each country's candidate and commis were emblazoned on signs. In and around each kitchen was a flurry of white coats as candidates, judges, commis, assistants, and coaches intensely focused on the task at hand: creating an elaborate meat platter and fourteen equally intricate fish plates over five and a half hours. The pace and determination as each team raced against the clock to put their best food forward was mesmerizing.

To my left, stadium seating bulged with two thousand spectators organized by country, cheering and screaming for their teams as deliriously as soccer fans, dressed to the hilt in their country's colors, their faces painted, a variety of noisemakers in hand. The sound was deafening. The United Kingdom had even brought their own five-piece marching band, which would play nearly nonstop for the next six hours. In my mind, their trumpets, tuba, trombone, and drums provide the soundtrack for that memory.

The carpeted expanse between cooks and crowd belonged to the press, an international gaggle of journalists, video crews, and photographers representing more than five hundred media outlets. Throughout the competition and especially as the platters and plates were presented, this section became a mosh pit as everyone jockeyed for the best positions, especially the camera crews televising live around the globe.

In the center of that carpeted area, long tables were set up. This is where the twenty-four judges—the heads of each competing nation's Bocuse d'Or organization—would sit and taste the food, twelve evaluating the meat offerings, the other twelve judging the fish. Additionally, five kitchen judges prowled the competition floor, making notes on the working habits of the teams, noting such things as kitchen cleanliness and efficiency.

I got swept right up, chanting "U-S-A!" at the top of my lungs along with the hundred or so supporters from across America who had traveled to be here. We just hoped Richard could hear our meager contingent above the thousand Norwegian fans right next to us. Whether he could hear us spurring him on or not, he seemed steady and methodical as he knocked down the action items on his task list. We sat with anticipation as each of the fish plates and meat platters were presented and displayed in front of the judges and the audience before being served to each of the judges to taste—the true test. We held our breath as each kitchen dispatched food, wondering who could be better than us. We all knew that although taste made up forty percent of the score, presentation was a huge part of winning this competition.

Every year, one team seems to own the presentation phase of the competition. On this day, that team

France's winning platter: Bocuse d'Or 2013.

was France. When they put their meat platter up in Box 7's window, those two thousand rabid fans went dead silent, the reverent *absence* of sound conveying their awe. France's platter—a contrast of elegant white porcelain and gleaming gold, the food arranged to mimic the gardens of Versailles, with the word *Versailles* emblazoned across the front, no less—told a story with roots in the earliest days of haute cuisine. It seemed a sure bet that they'd win high marks both for presentation and for representing their country's heritage.

Sitting atop that beautiful platter amidst the "gardens" was the *pièce de rèsistance*, a filet of beef layered with foie gras and truffles and wrapped in a perfectly round, patterned crust so shiny it was almost reflective. Chef Keller once famously said that there is no such thing as perfection, but—from a visual standpoint at least—the French team's technique and presentation were flawless. Whether or not they'd win gold was anyone's guess, but everybody in that room who understood the Bocuse d'Or knew that France would "make the podium." They had already won a personal victory; they had caused every other chef in the hall to wonder, "How did they do *that*?"

It was an out-of-body moment for me. Something clicked and suddenly I felt a part of the Bocuse d'Or, and I understood something deeply, instantly, and with the same clarity I had seen on the French platter. You had to deliver *the moment*—the moment when the judges first lay eyes on your food and presentation. You had to hit the high note.

WE'LL BE BACK

Richard Rosendale and Corey Siegel, Team USA, had performed well that day, finishing strong with hopes that they would reach the podium, despite the high level of creativity and finesse displayed by some of the other countries. But we all knew it would be difficult to break through to the top three and earn a medal—the best we'd ever done as a country was two sixth-place finishes in 2005 and 2009. There was a mix of emotions as France, Denmark, and Japan were respectively awarded first, second, and third place. We knew the right teams had won, but the disappointment stung, not just personally but also patriotically.

As we left the stadium, I texted Chef Keller asking what place we had taken, hoping that we might at least have done better than sixth place. His short reply said it all: "Seventh." I knew this would be a hard loss for Chef. He was the general, and he was keenly aware of how many resources, and how much time and effort, had gone into getting the team there. We spent the rest of the night and part of the next day licking our wounds, but our team from TKRG also had something to look forward to. We were going to eat at Paul Bocuse's restaurant that night, a dream come true for each and every one of us. They invited us in through the kitchen and we were soon joined by Monsieur Paul himself, who graciously posed for photos with us in the very kitchen that had ignited a culinary revolution so many years ago. As we sat with him at our table, we took in our surroundings and basked in the moment, looking at each other in disbelief.

We had a meal to remember that night: *pâté en croûte*, rouget with potato scales, *poulet en vessie* (heirloom chicken gently steamed in a pig's bladder . . . the original sous vide!), local cheeses, not one but three dessert carts, and some of the finest Chartreuse on planet Earth. As we exited through the front door, I looked down a pathway where every Bocuse d'Or medalist's name is engraved. Arriving at the row marked 2013, I saw the names of the competitors we had watched just the day prior, freshly engraved in the walkway. Beneath them were three empty slots with the year 2015 stenciled above them. I slowly brushed my foot over them, and thought of the reply I'd texted to Chef Keller the night before: "We'll be back."

CHAPTER TWO

THE GREATER THE RISK

"Life is either a daring adventure or nothing at all."

—HELEN KELLER

N THE FOLLOWING MONTHS, a couple of persistent questions nagged at me: *"Why couldn't that be you? Why wouldn't you want the privilege of representing your country?"* I'd had no trouble dismissing the notion in the past, but with the support of Ment'or—the organization set up by Chefs Keller, Boulud, Bocuse, and others—that argument was no longer valid. I was in a transitional period at The French Laundry and looking for the next thing. With the team of coaches assembled, the financial resources firmly in place, and the support of Chef Keller available to me if I chose to make the leap, I allowed myself to dwell on the dream and consider the possibilities.

There was no shortage of ready-made excuses, both personal and systemic, to plant seeds of doubt in my mind; unfortunately, they were all valid. Though I was an accomplished chef, I wasn't a *competition* chef, and so had no foundation to build on. In addition, the initial confidence and excitement in the seeming dream team of Boulud, Keller, and (Jérôme) Bocuse were waning in the face of a third straight disappointing result; and Richard's seventh place finish was especially dispiriting. If this competition veteran couldn't bring home some hardware, then what business did I have thinking I could? Also, since moving to Yountville, our family had expanded to three kids—our son Justin was born in 2009, daughter Ariela in 2010—so family was a weighty consideration as well.

At the end of service one night, a few weeks after returning from Lyon, Chef pulled up a stool next to me at the sous chef desk just off the breezeway, an interior corridor through which servers walk back and forth from The French Laundry's kitchen to its dining room. I was writing the menu for the following day. Chef often was in the kitchen at night, to keep an eye on the team and greet guests who visited the kitchen. I always looked forward to those moments because our discussions were unfailingly engaging and he always challenged me to see things from a new perspective. That night, we began talking about the 2013 Bocuse d'Or effort. He took on an unusually somber tone as he recounted the time, effort, resources, and frustrations of trying to shape the team to reach the podium. His voice trailed off as he came to the moment of disappointment in Lyon; the wound of defeat was clearly still fresh and would take time to heal.

In nearly a decade of working for Chef Keller, I had rarely seen him so vulnerable. As a cook, you are trained to make your number one priority whatever the chef needs at any moment to maintain the vision and values of the establishment. "Whatever it takes," was our constant philosophy. So the first thought that ran through my mind on seeing his frustration was, "What do I do? How do I solve this?"

That was the moment I knew I was going to apply to be the candidate for the Bocuse d'Or. It might sound corny, but I wanted to give my all in the name of my country and especially our cooks and chefs. And I wanted to do it for *my* chef. At the end of the day, it was as simple as that. A few weeks later, after talking through the commitment with my wife, I approached Chef and told him I intended to apply. We had a few more discussions about how we could make it work and still keep me engaged in the company, then he gave me his full support and encouragement to apply.

The journey had begun.

THE COMMIS

They say that the first important decision a presidential candidate makes is choosing a vice president. By the same token, the first test of a Bocuse d'Or candidate is selecting the right commis, or apprentice. The rules of the competition require that the commis must be twenty-two or younger at the time of the competition. In Europe, culinary aspirants begin their apprenticeship at age fifteen, so a twenty-two-year old cook is already practically a chef. In the United States, where most cooks don't finish culinary school until age twenty or older, finding a cook with the chops for this competition who was also young enough would be quite a challenge. The commis would also have to be not only highly skilled but mentally strong enough to withstand the pressures and scrutiny of the training and competition.

I immediately turned my thoughts to which cooks at The French Laundry had the qualities and character to handle this level of pressure and the internal drive to commit to the journey ahead. After a quick survey, I discovered that only one of them was young enough to

even qualify: Skylar Stover, a blond-haired, blue-eyed, twenty-one-year-old man with a baby face and stocky physique.

Skylar was not the obvious choice to anyone in the kitchen, including me. He'd only been with us for a few months, having recently moved from a Seattle restaurant where he had worked with a former colleague of ours. Young chefs who step through the doors of The French Laundry find themselves instantly in culinary boot camp. Not only are the hours long, the work demanding, and the standards high, but there is also a very strong, almost militaristic culture of discipline, with a clearly delineated chain of command. It's not for everybody, and some adjust better than others. Skylar didn't adjust very well at first. Having been largely independent from a young age, he had developed an air of confidence that many mistook for arrogance, but which I recognized as a defense mechanism, a shield from hurt and disappointment. Despite his obvious love for food, competent knife skills, and natural kitchen sense, it would take time for Skylar to fit into the deeply entrenched culture surrounding him.

But understanding somebody and believing in them are not the same thing. I was about to put my own neck on the line and had to be sure that I could count on my commis to do whatever it took to get there. So I began to observe Skylar as a potential commis. Two factors gave me the confidence he could perform the task ahead: when given a specific project or technique, he showed an underlying technical skill as well as an ability to follow directions and produce high-quality work. And his confidence could be a plus; you had to believe in yourself to make a run at the Bocuse d'Or. Anything less, I believed, would cause you to crumble or underperform when the moment of truth arrived. My decision made, I arranged to speak with Skylar after service one night. After "shaking out" (shaking hands with the entire kitchen brigade, a decades-old tradition at The French Laundry), we took a seat at the picnic table tucked behind the restaurant and next to Chef Keller's house, a popular spot for impromptu meetings.

"What do you know about the Bocuse d'Or?" I asked Skylar.

"I mean, I've heard of it, but I don't really know anything about it."

I told him that I had my eye on him to be my commis, that I thought it would be the opportunity of a lifetime and also the hardest thing he would have done up to that point in his life.

I explained to him my experience at the 2013 finals and why I was applying, describing the competition and what it required. I gave him a list of websites to visit and a book on the Bocuse d'Or that Chef Keller had given me, and I told him to get back to me after the weekend.

A few days later I asked him, "So, did you study the stuff I gave you?"

"Yes, Chef, I did."

"You ready to talk after work?"

"Yes, Chef."

We returned to the picnic table and I let him have the floor. "I've looked at everything you gave me and it certainly looks intense. I'm honored that you would ask me to be the commis for you. I'd like to do it."

I spent the next few minutes playing devil's advocate. He affirmed that he understood what was at stake and that he was eager to be a part of the team. I stood up and shook his hand to congratulate him, adding, "Well, Chef (everyone is called "Chef" at The French Laundry, a sign of mutual respect), from this point the only thing that matters to you in life is the Bocuse d'Or. Welcome to the team."

I often wonder how many times over the next year and a half Skylar looked back on that conversation.

Nothing could have prepared him for the road ahead and what it would require of him.

LIVING THE DREAM

Every two years, US candidate hopefuls submit essays, letters of recommendation, and resumes as part of an extensive application process. Ment'or then selects the best potential candidates for the honor of representing the United States in Lyon. I had submitted my application, naming Skylar as my commis, and now had to wait months for the selection process and final decision, just enough time for those nagging doubts to resurface.

Still, the potential to work with the coaching team Ment'or had assembled was not only irresistible, but seemed to offer a buffer against failure, or at least embarrassment. When I read through the application packet and saw the all-star list of chefs who would be involved in coaching and guiding the team, a sense of calm and confidence washed over me.

After several months, I at last received word that the finalist was selected and that soon I would learn of the decision. Indeed, that turned out to be the case and the news came quicker than expected.

I had just finished my shift in the kitchen running the morning crew and making sure the dinner team was ready for the night's service. After placing the last orders for the next day's menu, I headed out for my "commute" home, a fifty-yard walk across Washington Street. I always took a moment to detox from work mode, taking in the beauty of the late evening sun as it cast a warm glow across the garden. I hurried across the street to beat an oncoming car, when I recognized that car as Chef's BMW. I turned to wave when he stopped in the middle of the street and motioned me over. Before I could even say hello, he said, "Congratulations, you are the candidate!" It took a moment for it to sink in. Before I could reply, he continued: "The board reviewed the approach to the coming year and you are the guy. I'm excited. I think we have a great opportunity in front of us." Slowly the reality set in: I was now officially representing the United States at the Bocuse d'Or. I thanked Chef for his faith in me, and we began to discuss what was next when we both realized traffic was gathering behind him. "Let's talk more soon," he said. We shook hands and he sped off. I stepped onto the sidewalk, looking out over The French Laundry's culinary garden with its array of colors. The warm glow of that evening sun shone a little brighter, just for me.

Years earlier, when I was the newly appointed executive sous chef at The French Laundry, Chef gave me an etched, brass paperweight. Its inscription read: "Having a dream is hard, living it is harder." As the importance of this moment washed over me, the truth of that inscription came home. Because I wouldn't just be living *my* dream. All of the hopes and expectations that had been invested in the previous candidates was now on my shoulders.

As thrilled as I was to be selected without having to compete in a public competition, I was also disappointed. I had never competed in a major event, and I wanted the experience to test our abilities, nerves, systems, and techniques. I was faced with going to the 2015 finals against seasoned competition veterans. Several of the leading candidates were returning for their second Bocuse d'Or and hailed from countries with a winning history. Like so many other teams, we were in a David-versus-Goliath scenario.

For the next few months I would have the same vivid, recurring nightmare: I was at the finals in my kitchen-box, surrounded by judges and media, lights glaring, the crowd cheering. The official timekeeper counted, "Three, two, one: *Go!*" I looked down at an empty cutting board with no idea what I was supposed to do. What was the program? Where was Skylar? What proteins were we working with? I woke up in a cold sweat every time.

Stover and team prepare for a coach's tasting.

THAT FIRST CONVERSATION WITH CHEF PHIL about the Bocuse d'Or came out of the blue. I had no idea what was coming. He had asked me when my birthday was about three times that day, mentioning that we needed to talk about something after work. I asked him if it was a bad thing and he replied, coyly, "Has it ever been?" The answer to that question was "no," but all I could think was that there is a first time for everything. At the end of the day, we walked out to the picnic table where many of The French Laundry business meetings took place. Chef Phil didn't waste any time asking me what I knew about the Bocuse d'Or.

Chef Phil asked me to consider applying with him in the role of commis, or apprentice. I was incredibly honored and surprised, but also ready to reply with an emphatic, "Yes!" I knew right when he asked me that this was the opportunity of a lifetime I could not pass up. As a young chef, you learn early on that if there is one thing you don't say to the Chef, it's "No." That night, my excitement at being given this opportunity was overwhelming. I set out immediately with a determination to prove that he had chosen the right person.

SKYLAR STOVER EARLY DAYS

CHAPTER THREE

ONE TEAM, ONE NATION

"By failing to prepare, you are preparing to fail."

—BENJAMIN FRANKLIN

F THERE WAS ONE FEELING I did not want to have after the competition, it was wondering whether I could have done more or trained harder. I could live with failure, but not if it was founded on any "what ifs."

The same "whatever it takes" mentality that had seen me through the last decade would be tested as never before in the Bocuse d'Or. In a restaurant, if you have a bad service or something goes wrong, as much as you regret it, you have the opportunity to come back the next day and do better. With the Bocuse d'Or, you only have one chance. There is no tomorrow. That reality would make me more determined than ever to strengthen every aspect of my preparation: mental, physical, technical, and spiritual.

One of the first commitments I made was to not drink any alcohol until after the competition was over on January 28, 2015, a date that was fixed in my mind. Though I didn't have any issues with alcohol, I knew that my focus was better and my energy higher when I abstained. I also adopted a regular regimen of CrossFit, cycling, and soccer to enhance my physical and mental toughness, especially during the high-stress moments leading up to the finals.

I continued to work at The French Laundry through the fall. At the end of the year, I would resign my position as the executive sous chef and transition into a project-based role, developing a shared recipe database for the company's restaurants. It was a big job, but one that offered precious flexibility, carving out room for training and travel. Until that day came, I spent my off hours studying the history of the competition and what food had done well there, reviewing themes and ideas, and drawing up calendars. I was eager to push forward.

I made time to travel to Chicago to visit Martin Kastner at his culinary design studio, Crucial Detail. He would design the platter for our meat dish, the pièce de résistance of the competition. Martin would be my chief collaborator in hitting that elusive high note, so I scheduled a meeting with him to begin discussing the project ahead of us. The visit to Chicago also allowed me to visit Chef Grant Achatz at his famed restaurant Alinea, as well as his Next restaurant, where Chef Dave Beran was serving a Bocuse d'Or-themed menu.

THE TEAM

On a cold, rainy, December day, a cab delivered me from my hotel to an industrial neighborhood on the outskirts of Chicago, the city skyline receding behind me. Martin met me at his studio, overstuffed with shipping boxes containing his latest creation, the Porthole, a creatively designed infuser that had received immediate acclaim. He showed me around and then described the new studio space to which he planned to relocate the following month, an old bicycle shop that had been abandoned decades earlier. We got to work: I showed him pictures and videos on the Internet to help emphasize my points. As Martin asked questions and expressed his thoughts, it struck me that this guy saw the world through a different lens than I did. What I saw as food, technique, and colors, he perceived as forms, materials, and dimensions. It would take several months working together before we connected and hit on what Martin called a "common language."

Come January, with my new job underway and the ability to focus more fully on the Bocuse d'Or, Martin and I engaged in a long-distance dialogue to define our approach, theme, and design direction. I wanted to understand his design process, and he needed to see my style of food and presentation. Our first conversation was very much a "What do you want to do?" "I don't know, what do you want to do?" back and forth. We needed a unifying theme and "story" to shape the creative process, something that would focus my food

and his design elements and set us on our way to a winning score. I had a vague notion that I wanted to do something related to my spectacular Napa Valley surroundings but hadn't fleshed it out yet.

In early February, Skylar and I flew to New York City to meet with the entire coaching team for the first time. I began to see myself in the third person, as the protagonist in a caper movie, jetting across the country and the world; gathering with co-conspirators in design studios, empty restaurants, a training house; and even casing the competition in crowded European stadiums. And, as in most caper movies, we had our eye on treasure—the Bocuse d'Or.

The New York weather was less than welcoming—Skylar and I trudged through the slush and ice-covered sidewalks to Bar Boulud, Daniel's bistro-style restaurant across Broadway from Lincoln Center. There, we descended the stairs to the wine-cellar-like private room and were face-to-face with a Mount Rushmore of culinary royalty. In addition to Chefs Keller and Boulud, there were Gavin Kaysen, Gabriel Kreuther, Grant Achatz, and Dave Beran.

The team on an inspirational hike overlooking Napa Valley, California. From left to right: Gabriel Kreuther, Dave Beran, Martin Kastner, Monica Bhambhani, Gavin Kaysen, Tessier, and Stover.

That caper-movie feeling deepened. I began to realize that each person in the room offered a unique skill that would be crucial to achieving our joint mission. Chefs Keller, Bocuse, and Boulud had been working together collectively for the past five years to build Ment'or, the foundation that provided support to train and develop a winning candidate. They had learned much through those years and now had a greater understanding of what it took to win. Their insight, guidance, and support would be crucial to building my confidence.

Gavin Kaysen, in 2007, had been the last candidate for the United States before chefs Keller, Bocuse, and Boulud took on leadership of the US teams. His personal passion for the event had helped inspire their involvement because his own experience had been so disappointing. When Gavin competed, he had to support himself through the training process, raise his own funds, and design all of his service pieces. He subsequently made it a personal mission to ensure that future candidates received more backing. Gavin had also coached both Richard Rosendale (2013) and James Kent (2011). His firsthand experience would help prepare me for the intangibles of our mission.

The assistant coaching team of Grant Achatz, Dave Beran, and Gabriel Kreuther would offer their creative energies as well as a fresh perspective when we came together intermittently during my training. Grant and Dave had followed the 2013 campaign as part of their research for the Next restaurant's Bocuse d'Or menu, so they had an informed perspective on the training process. They also brought an avant-garde style to the table, one that would be balanced by Gabriel's classical European leanings. Gabriel had also been an assistant coach for the 2013 campaign.

Then there was Richard—former captain of the US Culinary Olympic team and previous Bocuse d'Or candidate himself. Cast as Team Organizer, Rich's knowledge of systems, organization, and structure made an

OCD sufferer look spontaneous by comparison. His skills would no doubt help me alleviate stress and save time in the kitchen.

Young Yun, Ment'or's then recently appointed executive director, and Monica Bhambhani, the director of competition and events, rounded out the team that kept us moving forward. It takes a tremendous amount of effort, creativity, and energy to raise the funds to compete on this level. Young was determined to exceed expectations. If there was anything the team needed, Monica made sure we had it. She would also wear two hats: as "one of the guys" and also as team "Mom," providing crucial moral support as the pressure ratcheted up.

Over the next few hours, we reviewed the past successes and failures of the US efforts, as well as what distinguished past winners. The consensus was that we had to create a compelling story that would clearly represent not only myself but the United States, and we had to do it differently than we had in the past. We needed that elusive X factor that made the food leap off the platters and plate and capture the imagination of the judges and audience.

When the time came to present my ideas, I shared the theme I had in mind: Napa Valley, an internationally recognized food and wine destination that the world could relate to, as well as my current home and a daily source of inspiration. I explained that I needed a box to live in, an idea that would help focus my food and thoughts. I couldn't think of a better source of inspiration than where I had lived for the past seven years, in the postcard-pretty town of Yountville. There my small house, nestled between a few rows of trees across the street from The French Laundry, had the most incredible backyard—the restaurant's garden. A few years after I arrived, I had watched as it was transformed from a few rows of tomatoes and mustard blossoms to the expansive, picturesque landscape—more farm than garden, really—it is today.

LEFT MY HOTEL ROOM around 5:45 A.M. It was chilly, the frost was still on the ground, the sun had not yet risen. Birds were chirping, and I was in no mood to hear it. But this was the morning run, a routine that I had become accustomed to, realizing that building routines leads to consistency.

About a half mile into my run, I met up with my companion. Phil was ambitious and far more eager than I was at this time of day. We started off quietly, no conversation, simply squinting into the shadows to make sure we weren't going to trip over an animal or turn an ankle.

Our conversation began around the time the sun lit the path. Small talk at first, anything to take our minds off the fact that it was cold and dark, and we still had five more miles to go. Eventually conversation loosened up with our legs. Pace picked up; we talked about family, friends, aspirations.

Running is a release, a way to build a routine that offers both mental and physical results. I fell in love with running because the scenery inspired me. Some of the best things I have done in the kitchen were inspired by things that came to me in moments along the path. Some of the best friendships I've made were forged in moments of complete fatigue and distress.

The restaurant industry is very difficult. You are always working at your limit. It requires a constant level of focus and intensity in order to maintain a certain standard. The harder you work and focus, the greater the result. Our pace rose, and sank, and rose again. Conversation stabilized it. That run led to the start of our friendship, and the start of my understanding who Phil really was as both a chef and a person. The morning run became a metaphor for what Phil was going to do with the competition. Every day, Phil did the same thing. He put his head down, he focused, and he pushed. Every day he did the same thing, but he put in just a little more effort, improved a little more. And he inspired people.

THE MORNING RUN DAVE BERAN

That evening, Williams-Sonoma hosted a reception for the team at their flagship store in the Time Warner Center at Columbus Circle in midtown Manhattan. It was exciting to see the enthusiasm of the supporters and press who came. We took photographs, held interviews, and gave speeches. But the truth was that I could scarcely focus on where I was or what anybody was saying. The meeting earlier had brought home how far we had to go and how much was resting on my shoulders. In all the kitchens of TKRG, there's a plaque that reads "Sense of Urgency," and that's what I felt. I couldn't wait to get home to California. To Napa Valley. To the garden. To the work at hand. I couldn't get back fast enough.

GETTING STARTED

Back home, as I continued to think about my platter, Gavin and I exchanged phone calls and emails as the first coaches' session, scheduled for March, approached. The view out my window of the garden, and the vineyards of Napa across the highway, had inspired ideas based on our beehives, garden beds, and wine service. I also shared my thoughts about some of the flavors and ingredients I felt would best represent America to the world, such as corn, huckleberries, local mushrooms, and the flavors of the California wine world. That was one of our biggest challenges because the American palate isn't necessarily in sync with the judges' predominantly European sensibilities.

My challenge was to transport the magic of the Napa Valley to Lyon through our food in such a way that twenty-four judges from as many countries would recognize the United States for culinary excellence. In March, when Gavin, Monica, Dave, Gabriel, and Martin arrived for the coaches' session, I invited them on a hike up the steep hillside overlooking the whole valley. It was a perfect day, cool and damp from the morning fog. If there were any skeptics in the group, the view from the top of that hill converted them.

Returning to the Bocuse House, I presented the initial concepts I had been working on for the meat platter: a consommé poured over a custard, a pea crepe made to mimic the garden bed, and a sausage set in a beehive mold. One of the highest mental hurdles I had to clear was presenting "unfinished" food to such respected advisors; every tasting would prove to be an exercise in humility and trust.

Martin's role in the 2015 American campaign was to design the platter and possibly a few service pieces. But that all began to change during that coaches' session, as he first saw what Skylar and I were up to. Martin is a passionate creator, craftsman, and artist who simply doesn't know any limits once he's engaged in a project. For example, as I was working on the pea garnish he asked me, "Would you want me to make a mold for that? You wouldn't have to cut it; you could just lay it in and set it. You would save time and produce less waste." Before we knew it, he had analyzed each process and began to offer ideas and suggestions for tools and equipment he could make to bring a higher level of efficiency and precision. By the end of the day, Martin had a long list of things to create from scratch: beehive molds, consommé glasses, and cutting tools, some of which would require considerable research.

Skylar took all of this in stride as he continued to divide his time between work at The French Laundry and Bocuse d'Or development and training. One of the things he didn't take in stride, however, was his introduction to CrossFit, which took place around this time. Physical exertion was quite a departure from his "sport" of choice: fishing. I took him out for our first workout together and prepped him on what we would be doing and how to pace himself. The workout was three sets of fifteen burpees (a jumping push-up) with two 800-meter runs in between, a good beginner session. He struck out with confidence on the run and, despite my reminder that we had 800 meters to go, settled in on a quick pace. It at was around 600 meters when I first heard him gasping for air like a horse being run too hard. I encouraged him to take a few minutes to catch his breath and helped him labor through a set of burpees. After the slower-paced run back, I asked him how he felt. "I thought I was going to die!" he winced. Over time, our daily workouts would become a cornerstone of our training, a daily test of our mental toughness and determination.

INTIMIDATION

In May, we headed to Stockholm to watch the European Continental Selection for the Bocuse d'Or, where twenty countries would compete to qualify for twelve spots. (Similar competitions take place in Asia and the Americas, while the United States and Canada have a coveted, standing invitation to participate.) I wanted to size up the competition for myself. I also thought it was essential that Martin see the environment in which his creations would be displayed and judged, and that Skylar gain an understanding of what we were up against. Our coach and guide Gavin would come along, and my wife Rachel would join us to get a sense of what it was I'd gotten myself into. En route to Stockholm, we stopped off at Per Se in New York City to prepare the current iteration of our meat platter for Chefs Keller and Boulud, as well as Chef Gabriel Kreuther, and Chefs Eli Kaimeh and Matt Peters of Per Se. This was the first time Skylar and I felt the pressure of preparing our food for an A-list audience, and it didn't go well. We had planned to set the mushroom base for the pea garnish with Martin's new silicone molds. It was an undercooked disaster (a result of our not anticipating the insulating properties of silicone), creating a domino effect that made applying micro-flowers and greens to the garnish at the end a trembling affair. A new rule was born that day: test all molds and tools before any official tasting.

Despite those misfires, I presented the garnishes we had prepared and shared my vision of how to bring the spirit of Napa Valley and The French Laundry's culinary garden to life through cuisine. Martin followed, describing potential platter concepts and materials to frame the story I wanted to tell. Surprisingly, after the struggle in the kitchen, Daniel nodded approvingly, "Well done. This is a great story and an excellent start and direction." The board shared his sentiments, adding their approval. It was a welcome confidence booster that sent us off on our whirlwind visit to Stockholm.

In Stockholm, we were lucky enough to procure VIP access passes, meaning we could roam the competition floor and look right into the kitchen-boxes rather than view them from the remove of the spectator seats, which was invaluable to me, Skylar, and Martin for different reasons. While Skylar maintained an air of youthful cockiness, I could see in his eyes that it was just a façade. There was fear as well, his first sense of what we were up against. Martin's reaction was more pragmatic and analytical. He was taken aback by how long it took for the platters to be served to the judges from the time they left the kitchen-boxes. It was inevitable that the food would get cold during that time (a constant battle for Bocuse d'Or competitors), so Martin astutely perceived that the platter didn't just have to impress visually; it had to be able to maintain or even *introduce* heat as it was presented.

My personal goal was to observe how the teams organized themselves, what equipment they were using, and the overall level of creativity. The divide between the top countries and some of the traditionally weaker ones struck me. The best candidates were operating without so much as a task list; the weakest had, and presumably needed, pictures of their finished platter and food to guide them.

The techniques were impressive, especially Sweden's creative use of potato skins. After cooking the

Tessier harvests pea shoots and blossoms from between the vineyard rows in Napa Valley, California.

carefully selected and identically sized potatoes, they scooped them out, turned the skins inside out, fried them to a golden crisp, and used them as a shell over another garnish. But what made the greatest impact on me had nothing to do with the food. It was instead the awe-inspiring, Zen-like mastery that Sweden's candidate, Tommy Myllymäki—a past silver medalist who was on the hunt for gold this time—displayed for the entire five and a half hours. With a crush of media bearing down on him, Myllymäki was a study in calm focus and efficiency as he methodically transitioned from task to task in a way that suggested he was cooking dinner for friends rather than competing in the qualifying event for the world's most prestigious culinary competition. I

had always imagined myself sprinting through our final routine, but Myllymäki showed me a new ideal, that of a marathon runner, pacing himself for the long haul. His example would serve as a North Star.

During the awards ceremony at the close of the second day, as we watched countries with Bocuse d'Or pedigrees pick up their prizes (Sweden—first; Denmark—second; Norway—third), Rachel turned to me, eyebrows raised, and with a smile offered an unconvincing, "Good luck."

Her tone said it all. We'd all have to push ourselves to another level, both in food and design. To compete with what we'd just seen, we had a steep mountain to climb.

Tessier in The French Laundry culinary garden, Yountville, California.

THE JOURNEY TIMELINE

2013

JAN	FEB	MAR	APR	MAY	JUN	JUL	AUG	SEP	OCT	NOV	DEC
Philip Tessier attends Bocuse d'Or with Team USA in Lyon				Application sent in			Tessier selected as US Candidate				Martin Kastner and Tessier meet in Chicago

2014

JAN	FEB	MAR	APR	MAY	JUN	JUL	AUG	SEP	OCT	NOV	DEC
	Nespresso machine delivered		First team trip to Crucial Detail in Chicago	First Ment'or Board garnish tasting; European Finals in Stockholm		Duck carcass first design	First round platter design (first prototype of final design)	Meat announced: guinea hen	Fish plate assigned; Greg Schesser joins the team; Will Mouchet joins the team	Lyon practice trip; Fish announced: brown trout	Final Ment'or Board tasting

2015

05	17	21	24	27	28	29
JAN	JAN	JAN	JAN	JAN	JAN	JAN
Crucial Detail's fish plate design rejected	Team departs for Lyon, France via New York City	All boxes stuck in customs	Final practice run	D–DAY!	SILVER!	

USA

Forever engraved in front of Paul Bocuse restaurant

24 Months   **1** Team

I WAS EATING LUNCH WITH A FRIEND AT Odge's, a quintessential Chicago hot dog place near my studio where cops gather and gangbangers get takeout. Buy four hot dogs, get one free. It's a place with soul. My phone rang. It was Gavin Kaysen, then the executive chef of Café Boulud in New York City and the coach of Team USA for the Bocuse d'Or 2015. His pitch was simple and direct: "The United States has never placed. I feel this time, with this team, we have a real chance, and we'd like you on board. The competing chef will be in Chicago soon. Meet with him." I am pretty sure he added, "This competition is like a drug." But that may have been later on.

"What makes you think I could be helpful?" I asked Phil when he came by a couple of weeks later.

"I'm a traditionalist at heart. I have a feeling I know what my food will look like. I'm looking for someone who will challenge that," he answered.

I often say that when someone approaches me knowing exactly what they want, I don't take the project. I see design as a process, one that begins with a stare into an abyss, and then a jump in. It's a risk. If we believe we know what the concrete end result of a collaboration should be, then we're not approaching the problem we're facing with a truly open mind. Sometimes the best solution is not doing anything; other times it is changing the path midway as we recognize that something isn't working.

Phil was serious, organized, composed. In this sense, the exact opposite of me. And he was asking for a challenge. Sometimes a long journey starts with soggy fries and a Polish sausage with everything, two sport peppers and all.

SOGGY FRIES AND A POLISH WITH EVERYTHING

MARTIN KASTNER | CRUCIAL DETAIL

Tessier and Martin Kastner at the Crucial Detail studio in Chicago.

CHAPTER FOUR

THE X FACTOR

"There is no creativity in comfort."

—MARTIN KASTNER

T HE TEAM RETURNED from our trip with a healthy fear and renewed zeal and determination. This was especially true of Skylar, who, though he tried to hide it, was clearly intimidated by the performance of our competition. To add to the fuel, I would occasionally show him pictures I had taken during the Euro Finals of the best commis and ask him, "Are you better than this guy?" I watched as over the next few months Skylar slowly overcame his dislike of exercise and discovered the benefits of fitness. Though he would never love our workouts, they came to shape his mental attitude and endurance.

MOMENTUM

The start of summer brought a sense of urgency as we continued our work on the garnishes and set our sights on the next challenge: the protein. All candidates are assigned the same proteins (meat and fish) to work with, but they are not announced until well into the training timeframe, and the announcements are staggered. In 2014, the meat would be announced in September, which would be too long to wait; we had to get started now. I began to search for direction by first reviewing the proteins from the last decade of competition, discovering that no poultry had been selected since 2007. So rather than work on a variety of meats to be ready for anything—the approach favored by many other teams—I decided to focus our development work on poultry, specifically duck.

My gamble was that if we ended up with beef, veal, pork, or lamb, we would be getting out of the blocks at the same time as our competition; if a bird was assigned, we'd be miles ahead. To me, it was a no-brainer. We started developing different techniques for cooking duck, rolling terrines, developing skin crackers, layering the breast meat with sausages and other farces (stuffings), and examining how to best use every part: necks, gizzards, livers, skin, legs, breast, tenderloins, bones—everything. One of the things I had decided early on was that whatever the protein was, I wanted it to be the focal point of the platter and present it with as "natural" an appearance as possible. I had seen numerous competitors over the past years present some pretty wild food, but often it looked more interesting than it did delicious. I wanted the judges to ask themselves how I prepared the protein, not why.

We continued our work with the first three garnishes and began adding in other elements as well.

Inspired by the summer season, I began focusing on corn as an ingredient, exploring numerous ways we could preserve its flavor and present its many different textures. Looking at every part of the corn as a viable product we isolated the silk, juice, kernels, popcorn, and even the cobs, examining how we could use each of them. This, too, was a gamble because corn is largely disdained in Europe. If we could present it in a creative way, however, it would not only be impressive, but it would help us earn those precious points allocated for representing one's country.

One of the elements of Napa I needed to make sure I captured was its world-renowned vineyards. I had a vision of a wine trellis or lattice made from some kind of crisp, with greens woven through it. We had presented a version of this to the board in New York, but it was too rustic—not refined enough for the competition—and we couldn't figure out how to elegantly divide it into portions. We continued to work on this concept and slowly began to put together ideas for the fish plate as we prepared for our next goal: our first platter presentation to the board.

In mid-June, just as the World Cup kicked off in Brazil, we returned to Chicago for a board tasting, at which we could share our new ideas and concepts. Gabriel, Gavin, Monica, and the team returned to meet Dave and Martin, and together we took our first look at a prototype of the valley-shaped platter Martin had constructed out of a thin pressed wood and embellished with a unique use of one of his trademark materials, polished wire, forming a bridge over the "valley." We lined the platter with aluminum foil and placed the food on it to try and replicate the shiny finished surface we eventually would use. It looked horrible. There is a reason platters aren't lined with foil in Lyon. Despite its rustic appearance, the valley with the wire suspended over it offered a promising direction, and we agreed we should continue to

refine the concept. I presented some of the new garnish ideas, such as a "nest" made of corn silk cradling a corn purée, a terrine of duck leg and horseradish, and the current iteration of the duck. I had spent the last several weeks exploring different forms and presentations of the bird and had settled on refining the process of roasting the duck "on the crown," meaning, whole with only the legs removed. It was far from finished, but the idea was clear: form an even layer of duck breast with perfect layers of sausage on the breast, reassemble it with the skin, roast it so it appeared whole and untouched, and finally, have it yield twelve identical portions.

Our tastings always brought out each chef's personality, especially when it came to presentation and flavor. "I think you should look for a more 'organic' plating style, not so contrived and regimented," Dave commented, adding, "I like the idea of the duck being an unexpected presentation. You definitely need an element of surprise."

Gabriel always brought a sense of tradition, focusing on flavor. "You should use the liver in the sauce; it adds a nuance and depth that will enrich it." Nothing was in a finished state, but the direction we were headed was well received, especially the corn garnish.

We finished the session at Martin's studio, by working with some new materials and molds he had developed for the beehive and pea garnish. These collaborative moments were the highlight of the training period for me because they spawned new ideas and inspiration, which were essential to keeping focus and momentum throughout the year. They were also a welcome antidote to the intense feeling of isolation that took hold of me from time to time.

Martin and I had developed a common language and a unique relationship, a far cry from our "What do you want to do?" period six months earlier. We had settled into an efficient process of creativity, development, problem-solving, and refinement that was allowing us to achieve some exciting results, and none too soon. The next board tasting was just a few weeks away.

FROM A TO X

I had continued to work through the duck concept with some success but struggled to achieve the ultimate result I sought, with every iteration yielding too much waste and the duck resembling a football rather than its natural beauty. I had a solution in mind that would allow me the control I needed, but it required a different approach. I needed Martin. Over the phone I explained my idea to him, emailing along some photos of what I had done thus far. As I explained the type of mold I was looking for, he emailed me some quick renderings in the hope that one of them might work. After about an hour and a dozen modifications, he sent one through that fit what I was looking for. It was essentially a wooden frame resembling a carcass with a cutout on top that would produce

the shape and volume I needed to yield six perfect portions out of each bird. When complete it would appear as a beautiful, whole-roasted duck. This was it! We worked through some of the details. Within a week, I had a working prototype in my hand and was beginning to bring our duck to the next level. I was convinced this was a giant step forward—but would it be enough to earn a medal?

Our next tasting was in July, with Chef Achatz in attendance along with Chef Keller and the other coaches. This time we held it in the kitchen of Ad Hoc, Chef Keller's family-style restaurant on Washington Street. This tasting was a milestone for us, our first full-platter presentation. The plan was to use the valley-shaped platter finished in two different colors, one black and one silver, to see which we preferred.

The buzz in Ad Hoc's kitchen was gratifying as we began final assembly of each of the garnishes and the "duck." A crowd had slowly been forming all afternoon as members of our team, Ad Hoc's kitchen

Tessier (right) and Stover (left) present the first full platter at Ad Hoc, Yountville, California.

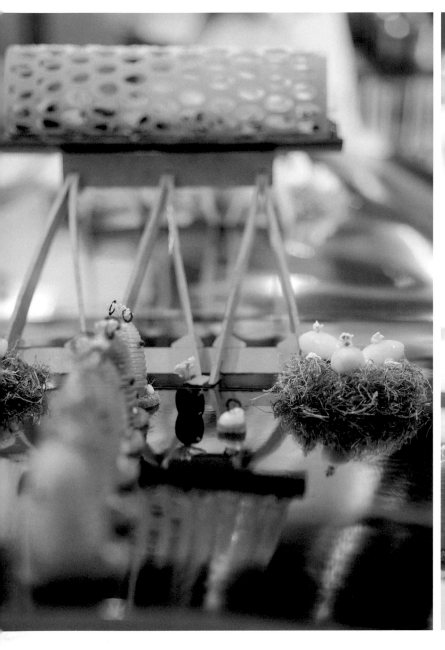 

2015 platter silhouette.

SYNERGY

THOMAS KELLER

TALENTED CANDIDATES represented the United States in the three prior attempts at the Bocuse d'Or since Ment'or had become involved, but in hindsight, each campaign lacked that elusive something special required to make the podium. I first recognized the potential for the United States to medal in 2015 when I saw an alchemy developing between Phil and Martin Kastner. Early in the ideation process, Martin showed us all the excitement and energy he was capable of conjuring, an apt match for Phil's culinary savvy. Martin delivered a sense of wonder through his brilliant design talent. He combined visual panache with technical and culinary utility—from small touches like the technique for plating peas in a straight line to the audacious originality of the guinea fowl preparation and presentation. I knew that Phil had the requisite taste and talent, but it was when I first saw how their abilities complemented each other, adding up to more than the sum of their parts, that the whole enterprise lifted off into space and I could feel that we had a real shot at the podium.

VERSATILITY VS. SPECIALIZATION

MARTIN KASTNER | CRUCIAL DETAIL

AT CRUCIAL DETAIL, we believe in the culture of making. We have an itch to get our hands dirty, and we combine that with a conceptual approach to the meaning of objects and the way they come into our lives. We explore various reproduction methods, in a variety of materials, on a variety of scales. And in this dimension, there are many similarities between the studio and a kitchen. Our medium might be different, but we're still looking at mixing, cutting, heating, cleaning, joining, molding.

In our conversations with Phil, we very quickly realized that there are many similarities between our world and his, and we could not only design a platter for the Bocuse d'Or, but also make some of the specialized tools he could use in the kitchen. Usually, designing tools has to tread carefully around the notion of versatility. Things can't be too specialized; they need to do many things reasonably well. But when devising a single-purpose tool, many of those restrictions disappear. And when we consider the context of a competition, it becomes especially exciting. Can we shave some minutes off? Can we take nine person-hours using conventional tools and reduce them to five by making specialized ones? Can we achieve something that, in the context of a competition, might at first glance even seem impossible?

staff, and the coaches filed in to see our progress. I was surprised to find that, despite there being more people in the room than we had ever had, I wasn't nervous. I had learned a great deal from our first board tasting, and this time we had planned meticulously for the moment, our prep list stretching across six pages.

Martin had just arrived with the "platter," so this would be the first time any of us would see all of the pieces come together. After six months of individual ideas, they were finally melding into a cohesive whole. When we finished, Gavin and Martin carried the platter into the Ad Hoc dining room so the crowd that had gathered could view it and the team could begin our discussion. As we gathered around the table and took a few pictures, there was a long, uncomfortable silence. Too long. Chef Keller finally broke the silence: "Well, it's rather quiet. What do we think?" It was obvious that everyone's thoughts reflected my own. The concepts represented were compelling, but taken together, they fell flat, adding up to less than the sum of their parts. As the team shared their feedback, I tried to put my finger on what was missing. Why did I have this anticlimactic feeling?

We pushed some garnishes around, trying different ways of laying things out, but nothing we did gave us that moment, that X factor we were looking for. We had work to do. The duck did deliver the element of surprise we had hoped for, so at least we were on the right course there. We presented my first pass at the fish plate, exploring the use of aromas, dry ice, and a beautiful tumbler that Martin created and which I had turned into a cloche. Chef Keller was impressed with the direction and progress we had made, and the plate even generated some unexpected applause.

Still I couldn't get past the disappointment of the platter. It just wasn't at that jaw-dropping level that was a prerequisite for the podium. So, despite enthusiasm from the board, Martin and I went back to the drawing board, and decided the valley needed to be more dynamic with more aggressive slopes and steeper, more soaring edges. Over the next month we tried several approaches, but no matter which way we spun it, the platter always came out looking like either a boat or a UFO. At least we were making good progress on the food itself. The corn became a more cohesive presentation of eggs in a nest, and the lattice evolved as a delicate crisp, easily portioned and presented. We had also developed a puffed cracker that we intended to serve on the side of the fish plate. While all of these concepts took time to develop, the food could be adjusted relatively quickly as the competition required. Once the platter was set, however, there would be no changing it. The clock was ticking; we were a week away from our next coaches' session, and the expectation was that we would have a near-final design of the platter. It would take several months just to work out the design details and requirements, and then we would have to manufacture it. If we wanted time to practice on the finished platter, we needed to make decisions very soon.

Martin had sent through a number of renderings of ideas, some meant to conjure a "valley" while others were more abstract. Chef Keller and I looked through them together, but they seemed to be moving in more of an avant-garde direction, something that hadn't always been well received at the Bocuse d'Or. I spoke with Martin on the phone one evening and expressed our concern about the new designs.

"I've got a design that I really like," Martin replied. "Actually, I've already started building a prototype." At first I was a bit skeptical, but I heard something different in Martin's voice as he explained his thoughts—an excitement and confidence as he switched over to FaceTime so he could show me what he was working on. There on his worktable was a traditional round platter, with one crucial difference:

the center was missing! He explained his plan to suspend the wire frame we had been working with over the center and then find a way to suspend the "nest" we had developed underneath it, giving the platter a sense of weightlessness, of magic.

Over the last seven months I had learned two things about Martin. First, working with him, you will always fly by the seat of your pants. He waits until the final moment before committing to a design, allowing the maximum amount of time for the ideas to take hold before digging in and making the piece he is working on. The method works for him, but from a practical, user standpoint, it creates enormous stress.

The second thing I had learned about Martin was that I could trust him. I might have to wait till the last minute, or even past it, for the things I needed to come through, but when they did, it was worth the wait. *Always.* That night as we spoke over the phone, I sensed that this new direction could be the answer. The fact that Martin had committed to an idea and began building it meant that there was something compelling enough about the path he was taking that he could begin immediately. Had he found a solution to our platter dilemma? I was eager to find out and encouraged him to continue on the path he was on; I also encouraged him to finish the latest "valley" rendition he was working on as well, just in case.

A week later, Martin arrived at the Bocuse House in Yountville, and we set to work assembling our food so we could see it displayed on the two platters: the new valley and the circle. We planned a smaller, more intimate tasting, this time with just Gavin, Gabriel, and Chef Keller in attendance. We decided to try the round platter first since we had seen a previous version of the valley already. We began to lay out the food as Martin had envisioned it, alternating the three garnishes around the outer rim, using the lazy Susan he had rigged to spin the platter as we plated, eliminating the need to walk around it—a nice touch. We rigged the wire frame to suspend over the void in the center of the platter and attached the ducks to it. We put the final touches on it, lifted it gently off of the Lazy Susan, and set it on the table.

Stepping back and taking in the presentation, I had that feeling I hadn't had since twenty months earlier, when I was sitting in the stands as France's Versailles platter was unveiled. It was the aha moment. That same audible hush I had heard in France filled the room. The food sang like a beautiful painting elevated by the perfect frame. A chatter of excitement soon broke the silence as we snapped pictures with our phones and took it in from every angle. I smiled to myself. Martin had done it. The X factor was here. Suddenly, the podium didn't seem so far off.

Team USA's 2015 meat platter.

CHAPTER FIVE

THE BREAKING POINT

"Give me six hours to chop down a tree

and I will spend the first four sharpening the axe."

—ABRAHAM LINCOLN

SEPTEMBER WAS A TRANSITIONAL MONTH. Martin had struck upon a beautiful wooden plate for the fish, and with the platter design now confirmed, we were pushing forward on every front. And this was the month the most eagerly anticipated information would soon be in our hands: the release of the Bocuse d'Or's tech file—the document that outlines several key details and specifications for the competition and, at long last, reveals the meat each of the candidates would be assigned to use.

We had put all of our eggs in one basket with the duck—pun intended. What if it wasn't duck, or wasn't even a bird? The anxiety of that lingering question plagued me constantly. When the tech file was finally released in late September, Gavin got ahold of it first and immediately texted me the protein: guinea hen. Duck would have been a bull's eye, but we were only one ring away on the target. I was, in fact, *ecstatic* that it was a bird and that the concept we'd been working on so diligently could be modified quite simply. I breathed a huge sigh of relief as it sank in that we had a clear path forward.. The main task before us now was to make all of our recipes, techniques, and ideas conform to the five-hour-and-thirty-five-minute competition timeframe. Just as an Olympic gymnast or figure skater perfects jumps, spins, twists, and other elements, then assembles them into a free-flowing "dance," we had perfected our moves; now it was time to dance together.

DIGGING IN

As I considered our practice schedule, which would eventually have us performing three full runs per week, I quickly realized that we couldn't do it alone. Each run required a full day of prep followed by the five-and-a-half-hour practice, then clean up and reorganization. We also had to further develop the fish dish, exploring new techniques and ideas between runs. We needed support in a big way. What we needed was a bigger team.

You lean on your friendships at times like these. I called Greg Schesser, a former colleague from The French Laundry, and asked him if he'd be willing to come on board and support me personally, helping out with organization and logistics. Linebacker big, he was actually a teddy bear of a guy with a kind face, known to my kids as "Uncle Greg." We hadn't spoken in months, but I could hear the excitement in his voice when I asked for his help. The only possible wrinkle, a rather significant one, was that he was getting married in a few days and his wife, Yvonne, was going to be attending nursing school in New York. I told him I understood, but within a few weeks, he'd worked out an arrangement to be in Napa to help our team. Talk about sacrifice; I still owe her one.

Next I asked Ross Melling, chef de cuisine of Bouchon, if he had anybody on staff who could assist Skylar with ordering, prep, recipe development, and the mountain of dirty dishes we generated every week. Over the weeks, I'd observed that while Skylar's attitude had improved, he was beginning to show signs of fatigue and pressure. Ross recommended Will Mouchet, a tall, broad-shouldered Southerner with a hearty drawl and intense blue eyes. After a few questions, Will signed on. Both he and Greg would be on board by October, and I couldn't have been more reassured.

And then there was Richard Rosendale, who had taken on more responsibility since Gavin had moved to Minneapolis to focus on opening his own restaurant. If there is ever a natural disaster, unexpected crisis, or alien invasion of planet Earth, I want to be with Richard. He is one of the most prepared and organized individuals I have ever met. He taught us the importance of knowing every detail of the space we would be working in, the challenges of working in Europe versus the United States, and how to organize our equipment before and during the competition.

Richard offered a wealth of knowledge, especially regarding the competition itself, sharing his own Bocuse d'Or experience. He put the fear of God in us when it came to our ingredients and equipment, recounting his harrowing set-up hour before the competition in 2013. The kitchen judges had nearly derailed his entire effort when they questioned how he had arranged some of his ingredients. He also warned us that they would probably be especially strict this year due to a controversy that had swirled around France's win at the last competition. In a spectacularly witty display, the French team paraded a giant soup terrine behind

One of many team planning sessions, Lyon, France.

their platter during the presentation stage, a touching tribute to Monsieur Paul's iconic black truffle soup. Everybody was charmed except fellow competitors, who complained that the rules stated that everything had to be presented *on* the platter itself.

Come October, we began timed training runs, upped our schedule to six days a week, and introduced bi-weekly French lessons to ease our time in Lyon and, I hoped, facilitate communication with organizers and judges. That was the whirlwind Greg and Will entered. Not only did they quickly fulfill the roles we had outlined for them, but they offered Skylar and I moral support and encouragement and eased our almost suffocating focus on each other.

A MOMENT OF PAIN

I think it's the nature of any enterprise like this that every gain seems to be offset with a loss. Richard's affirmation of my approach gave me confidence, but Skylar didn't take the same strength from our new support team as I did, and was becoming closed off and defensive. Meanwhile, drama was brewing in Chicago where Martin was struggling to find a metalworker who could spin the platter with the precision he required. We were behind schedule and in danger of not having the practice platter we hoped to use in Lyon during our November run.

In addition to our platter struggles, our fish plate was at its own cliff-hanger. For the last six months, Martin and I had worked on developing a stunning plate concept that would allow us to release an aromatized "fog" from a glass cloche at the table. It was meant to evoke the San Francisco Bay Area and the Napa Valley. It was brilliant, elegantly combining wood, ceramic, and glass. We were excited for the direction it was taking until I opened an email from the organizing committee with an amendment to the original technical file.

The amendment stated that all teams had to use one of the assigned service pieces from sponsor Villeroy & Boch, a standard, nondescript off-white bowl or plate. Martin and I had just spent three hours the night before finalizing the design of the plate and how the fog-release would be activated. It was a tough pill to swallow, but we remained optimistic that we could find a solution.

I prioritized our platter and fish plate woes over Skylar's morale and hopped on a plane to Chicago to huddle with Martin, leaving Skylar to do a solo meat run with Will and Greg's support.

I arrived at Martin's studio around 8:00 A.M. on a cool, crisp fall morning with my list of urgencies: platter layout, platter heating elements, guinea mold, lattice support tray, beehive mold, fish plates, and cracker cutter. We worked through the day and into the evening, pausing only for a quick lunch out. As evening descended, we didn't even consider leaving again, instead making "dinner" in his ceramic kiln, baking some of the cracker dough I had brought to test the cutter. Before we knew it, it was four in the morning and Martin was falling asleep on his feet, literally. We hashed out a revised schedule for the coming weeks, knowing that it was going to be a race to the finish. Pressure mounted when I came back, exhausted, to California the following afternoon and learned that Skylar's frustration had finally boiled over in a heated exchange between him and Greg after his practice run. I spoke to everybody involved, and it became clear that Skylar was reaching a threshold. The transition from development to training runs had been difficult for him, and the long days and weeks, constant pressure, stress, and intensity were taking their toll. The four of us (Will and Greg had eagerly joined in) were in the gym every morning at 6:00 A.M., training all day, and then working on our organization sheets through the evening six days a week. Skylar had never worked at such a pace for so long, and he craved a reprieve from the grind.

I knew I was pushing him to his limits and though I sympathized, I was also frustrated. I mean, what more could I do than bring on a dedicated helper, as I had in Will, to support him? Didn't he get it? This was the opportunity of a lifetime, and we only had one chance to succeed. D-Day was just three months away, and there was still so much to be done. Why wasn't he asking, "What else *can* I do?" instead of "What do I *have* to do?" Where was the "whatever it takes" attitude?

Shortly after Greg started, he began telling me about a new book that had come out, the story of an Olympic runner who joined the Air Force in World War II, was shot down, and floated across the Pacific for nearly fifty days, only to be captured by the Japanese. After two years of horrific abuse as a POW, he returned home and fought through nightmares and personal struggles to put his life back on track. The book was *Unbroken*, the Louis Zamperini story, and we began reading it as a team. We soon borrowed our team motto from Zamperini—at every difficult juncture we would state, "A moment of pain was worth a lifetime of glory."

Over the next few weeks, our schedule only got more taxing as we prepared for a practice trip to Lyon in mid-November. There was a daunting amount of development and organizational work still to be done between full, timed runs twice a week. We were only a week away from leaving for Lyon, and the final was only a few months away. Skylar wasn't the only one feeling the mounting pressure. The possibility of a medal often felt far off.

BOILING POINT

Previous US teams had traveled to France for a casual practice run, giving them an opportunity to organize equipment, acclimate to the French products and language, and become familiar with Lyon and its surroundings. I had a different plan, treating the trip as a full-scale dress rehearsal for the actual final. We would approach everything exactly as we planned to in January. We would ship or bring the platter, food, and equipment, and even travel on the same days of the week—a real-life visualization that would, I hoped, imbue the actual final with a sense of "been there, done that."

To minimize any surprises or variance in ingredients, we packed up and shipped equipment and food ahead, even eggs, butter, and dairy. We tapped The Chef's Garden, an artisanal grower with an expansive offering of greens and petite vegetables, to send us some greens and flowers from their farm in Ohio. They had been a constant source of support and collaboration and were even growing wild fennel from seeds we sent them in the hopes that we would have them in January, when they were otherwise out of season. Richard and Gavin had set up a storage unit in Lyon two years prior to store the larger equipment, plus pots, pans, and so on, which gave us a leg up. Richard would meet us in Lyon a few days after our arrival and mentor us throughout the week.

After a quick stop in New York to pick up Monica, we were in the air again, bound for Lyon. The boys had never been to this culinary mecca, and their anticipation was palpable. Upon landing, we were pleased to see that everything had arrived safely, including the practice platter, although the TSA agent examined it several times over as we tried to explain what this large, donut-shaped silver object was.

We set up camp at the Institut Paul Bocuse, the culinary school where we rented a kitchen space for the next few days. We made all of the stops we had planned: the butcher for the guinea hens, Les Halles de Lyon Paul Bocuse for local produce, the rental vehicle outpost where we'd rent a truck to transport our equipment. When Richard arrived, he updated the inventory of the storage unit he had created the year prior; it was arranged like a mini Williams-Sonoma, clearly labeled and organized, making our jobs that much easier. Despite the long list of tasks and logistics, I gave the team some time to wander around Lyon's Old Town—a magical labyrinth of narrow streets and alleyways that led up the hill to the iconic Basilique de Notre Dame de Fourvière overlooking the city—and take in the legendary bistro fare in the evenings.

Though traveling had been tiring, the team was in good spirits as we made the final preparations for our full trial run. Everything had arrived safely and in good condition, and all of the equipment we needed was accounted for. We placed "Do Not Disturb, Team USA" signs on all of the doors to our kitchen and taped parchment paper over the kitchen windows to deter any curious onlookers or "spies" hoping to catch a glimpse of what the Americans were up to. We were ready to go.

We made several tweaks to the run, as we always did, and planned to use a few new pieces from Martin for the first time. We reviewed the sheets, and I made sure Skylar understood each of the changes. We high-fived as we always did before beginning, started our watches, and were off.

I set about my first tasks, butchering and preparing the proteins, and was cruising through my list when we hit the first-hour mark, our first check-in. I asked Skylar how he was doing and there was a mumbled response, "Uh, okay."

"What does that mean, Skylar?" I demanded. Greg stepped in for him and responded with a hesitant, "He's thirty minutes behind, Chef." Thirty minutes! In the first hour? This was not a response I was prepared for. The first hour was traditionally our strongest. What was going on?

I walked over and saw Skylar struggling with the new lattice cutter Martin had sent, but instead of asking for help or simply pushing through the challenge, he was approaching it casually as though we were back home on a development day.

"Skylar, we are in a run. We don't have time to play around with this. Get back to the list. We can finesse this later," I told him.

"Yes, Chef."

I reminded him that he had a thirty-minute hole to dig out of, then returned to my station and tried to shake my frustration by refocusing on my tasks.

Things went from bad to worse. Not only did Skylar not make up any time but he actually slipped further and further behind. Hour two: thirty-five minutes. Hour three: fifty minutes. Hour four: seventy-five minutes. I took several tasks off his list and tried to fit them into my schedule, but it seemed that for every leak I plugged, another two sprang. By the time we were done, we had slipped a staggering ninety minutes behind. We had never been more than thirty minutes late; if this was a real-life visualization of the actual final, then we were well on our way to failure.

I had my own frustrations, as I always did, with some of the new fish garnishes I had planned. But being this late was not only unacceptable, it was also embarrassing. I tried not to look at the expression on Richard's face as we self-destructed, almost terminating the practice mid-run. I summoned all my willpower to overcome my internal fury as we plated the fish and regrouped to plate the meat, nearly seven hours after we had started.

Most alarming to me wasn't how far behind we were, but Skylar's nonchalance. When Richard asked him how he thought it went, he responded with a casual, "Yeah, it was a bit tough. I spent a little too much time figuring things out." A bit too much time? Try *two hours* of time. I had expected, at minimum, "Man, Chef, I'm so sorry. I totally let you down and

ONE OF THE TRAITS in Phil that I feel was an asset in the Bocuse d'Or was his tremendous discipline. I recall speaking with him at the very start of his training. Usually when I tell people the level of preparation needed they say, "What? Is this really necessary?" Or sometimes it sounds intimidating to them. I spoke to Phil about color coding equipment on the station so the dishwasher knew where to put the tools after they cleaned them, starting a fitness program to keep up stamina, making sure the pot handles were all facing the same direction, or even playing crowd noise and deafening music during practice sessions to mimic the intense environment of the actual competition. I stressed relentless organization with an almost military approach toward training. Phil was wired the same way and it was not foreign to the way he already worked. You cannot say that about many chefs. Sure, there are great cooks out there, and there are some very organized people, but when you hurl a chef into the energy-charged cooking arena of the Bocuse d'Or and shove cameras in their faces, yelling, techno music blasting on the speakers, a lot of people will fall apart. One of my early fears was that he and Skylar were going to be facing this for the first time in Lyon so I talked about it every chance I got to get them in the mindset of what it was going to be like. It was evident as we progressed that Phil "got it." I knew he had a chance to win the Bocuse d'Or.

THE WORLD STAGE

RICHARD ROSENDALE

didn't communicate with you." Nothing. The casual air that had given me pause when I first selected him was coming back to bite me.

I was so angry I had to start cleaning up just to collect myself. It was nearly 11:00 P.M. when I turned to Monica and Richard.

"We need to find a new commis," I said. "This isn't going to work. He just doesn't get the magnitude of all this."

Richard looked me right in the eye. "I know what you're feeling," he said. "But changing now would do more harm than good."

We shut the kitchen down and headed into Lyon. Miraculously, we found a small bistro, La Gratinée, that served all night. It was a real discovery, a place I would have loved on a normal night, with local classics like *tartiflette* and steak frites. I kept waiting for Skylar to express some remorse. Not only did he not do that, but he chowed down and laughed through dinner, as though we had crushed it. I was at a loss.

I don't know that I've ever felt more alone than I did sitting in my hotel room that night. I hadn't set aside my career, given all of this effort and taken such risk to let it all hinge on a twenty-two-year-old. I sat on my bed and prayed, acknowledging that all of this was out of my control as it always had been. I opened my phone and found the verse of the day was a well-known passage of encouragement: "For I know the plans that I have for you . . . plans for welfare and not for calamity to give you a future and a hope." These were the words I needed to hear at that moment. I didn't have the answers, but I had a reassurance that despite the dark valley we were in, we would come through this and be stronger for it. It was at that moment I decided to invest everything I had into Skylar and continue our commitment together to the finish line.

The trip wasn't the confidence-building dry run I had planned, but it proved to be the moment we would look back on as the turning point. The next day, Will and Greg were driving to the storage unit with Skylar when he asked them why I seemed upset. Will explained to him why this run was so important, reiterated that we only had one chance at this and that now we were returning with our tail between our legs. Slowly, Skylar began to comprehend the value I had placed on this trip and the recognition that this could happen at the finals fell on him like a ton of bricks. He realized, at long last, the magnitude of what we were doing and the fact that he could let everyone down: the board, Martin, Ment'or, the team, and every young chef and supporter back home. We brought the team together at dinner that night and openly discussed the challenges we had faced, how we could be better and the most important factor: rebuilding a sense of *team*. For the first time in months, Skylar seemed open, receptive, humble, and ready to listen.

Though it would still be a slow process, requiring a great deal of firm coaching and encouragement, Skylar began to transform. Over the coming weeks he began to evolve from a tired and frustrated commis to a confident, eager, and dedicated wingman, ready to do "whatever it takes." Within two weeks, that fateful Lyon run would be a distant memory as we began consistently finishing runs on time, sometimes even ten minutes early. Whenever Skylar found himself struggling with a technique or timing he would, on his own initiative, practice it over and over until he was a master at it. His motivation now came from his own desire to succeed.

CHAPTER SIX

UNBROKEN

"All I want to tell young people is that you're not going to be

anything in life unless you learn to commit to a goal. You have to reach

deep within yourself to see if you are willing to make the sacrifices."

—LOUIS ZAMPERINI

WITH LYON BEHIND AND AHEAD OF US, we shifted our focus to the next hurdle: adjusting the fish plate based on the new requirement of using a pre-assigned service ware. Fortunately, when we received the new bowl, we discovered that the ceramic insert we had been planning to use fit inside. We would lose the beauty of our own custom-made wood vessel, but our concept would remain intact, a palatable compromise.

In addition to reworking the plate, over the last few months we had been working with various types of fish, developing specific techniques for each one—a blini-wrapped salmon, a delicate, steamed halibut crusted in truffle—in the hope that we would be ready to adapt quickly when the fish was announced. Traditionally, the committee selects a larger fish such as turbot, sea trout, halibut, or cod, supplementing it with secondary proteins such as shellfish and crustaceans. This time, my gamble betrayed me when it was announced the day after Thanksgiving that the fish would be ten brown river trout . . . and nothing else. I was tempted to panic. Not only had I not planned on a small fish, but we'd have to source it from France, which would take time. And the absence of a secondary protein meant throwing out a lot of our work and changing several of the garnishes in only two months. We were already doing two full training runs a week, and our final board tasting was less than two weeks away.

A SEA OF CHALLENGES

Around this same time, a month later than I had hoped to receive a finished practice platter, we learned the company that had been trying to spin the metal couldn't get it right. Even worse, the only other company that could spin it didn't have an opening in their schedule until Christmas, and even then, there was no guarantee they could do it better. But we were out of options. We would have to continue practicing with the wooden replica we'd been using for the last four months and pray we could get the real one finished on time.

The number of training runs intensified to three a week. We began treating every run like a final, timing our setup the night before, the morning of, and—in an effort to be prepared for the deafening noise of the stadium environment—played techno and rock music at full volume in our cramped training kitchen.

It took Skylar and Will a full day to set up the food and equipment for the training run while I continued to develop the food and Greg worked on all of the peripheral logistics and planning. The day of the run, we would hit the gym at 6:00 A.M., eat breakfast (prepared by Will or Skylar, whose corn cakes were a team favorite) at 7:15, begin our official set-up at 8:00, and start at 9:00, finishing around 3:00 P.M. We would invite guests to try the food, their expectations upping the pressure in the kitchen. Sometimes those guests were my wife and kids, a special moment when they could feel involved and snack on all the yummy crackers and "those creamy things," as one of them called the truffle custard.

After a long cleanup, we would finally close the kitchen down around 10:00 P.M. and then sit down to reassess and plan for the next run, finishing around midnight.

Rinse. Dry. Repeat.

Skylar was showing great progress, his drive and determination blossomed before my eyes, and it was reflected in his work. We pushed right through Christmas and New Year's, taking a brief pause to enjoy family and catch the theatrical release of *Unbroken* together. The timing of Zamperini's story couldn't have been more appropriate because the biggest test for me lay just around the corner.

PERSEVERANCE

The questions we had fired off when the second tech file was released were a distant memory as two months had passed since we had sent them. I honestly thought they were a formality, as it seemed like nothing we were doing contradicted the rules. Were we ever wrong.

On the morning of January 5, twelve short days before we would leave for France, we were about to begin a full run when I received an email from the competition organizers. They had just finished a meeting to answer questions various teams had asked about what would and would not be allowed. The news was bad. We wouldn't be able to use either the new fish plate or the box with the puffed cracker on the side. The plate they considered an inedible ornament. The cracker served in the box on the side was not allowed—all the garnishes had to be on the plate.

I couldn't believe it. First we lost the wood bowl, and now the whole plate was gone? All of our food was designed around that plate and the garnish. How would we incorporate it? A thousand questions raced through my mind. I even thought about canceling the run. How could I work over the next six hours knowing that every move I made for the fish dish—the fog, the insert, the cracker—would all change tomorrow? I gathered myself and decided we had to press on and simply focus on the task at hand. We began the run as planned, and six hours later it proved to be our best training run to date—an important lesson for me on the value of mental strength and fortitude.

The next day, a Tuesday, Gavin and Monica arrived for the last group tasting before Lyon. It was the first time we had seen Gavin in months and the circumstances and timing couldn't have been worse. We were in the throes of reinventing the fish dish and were ill-prepared for the run, scheduled for Wednesday at Ad Hoc. We gave it our best effort but the fish, very much in transition, fell flat on the plate. It could have been a breaking point for us—last-minute changes, embarrassment in front of our peers, and the loss of so much effort. I met with the team that afternoon and assessed the situation with them: "Okay, boys, obviously this is not where we wanted to be at this point, but this is our reality. We can't

GREG SCHESSER **ZAMPS**

THROUGHOUT TRAINING, we as a team were always looking for ways to keep ourselves grounded, whether it was by working out together, or taking twenty minutes away from training to spend time with Phil's kids. Sometimes it was something as simple as taking an hour off to get a haircut. That might sound silly, but we were so focused on the task at hand that separating reality from the Bocuse d'Or was sometimes difficult. We literally ate, drank, and breathed the competition day and night for weeks and months on end. For balance, Phil suggested reading a book together as a team. I remembered months back that I had seen a *60 Minutes* special on a World War II POW hero about whom Angelina Jolie was making a movie. It moved me, and so I looked it up and found *Unbroken*, by Laura Hillenbrand. Looking back now, it's amazing how much that book brought the team together and helped us during our darkest hours.

More than anything, the book put the competition, training, and life itself into perspective. Every failure, bad day, disappointment, and struggle that beset us paled when compared to the stories in *Unbroken*. Louis Zamperini's story made us all realize how truly lucky we were to be in the position that we were. The Bocuse d'Or is the most intense cooking competition in the world, demanding its own relative sacrifices, and the life and stories of Louis Zamperini taught us to never give up and always believe there is a way. I honestly don't know if we would have placed if it weren't for that book.

GLOVES GAVIN KAYSEN

IT WAS MY FIRST CHANCE to be with the team after opening my restaurant, Spoon and Stable. The vibe in the Bocuse House was edgy because the team had received some tough news about the fish plate just the day prior. When I walked in, Phil was clearly distraught, Skylar was getting things packed up, Greg was as serious as a heart attack, and then there was Will . . . blowing up latex gloves? I was shocked. What the hell was he doing, and how was this supposed to help the team? We all have funny things we do— some of us like to put our shoes in the same spot every night; others throw them in a corner. It turns out that Phil likes to have his latex gloves pre-separated before putting them on because it saves him a few seconds. I burst out laughing. It might not have been the right thing to do, but the team needed it. Sometimes I feel that as serious as this is, we also have to have fun and enjoy the journey of the Bocuse d'Or, and this was my outlet. It was something we all laughed about; in fact, we had tears coming down our faces. It still cracks me up.

focus on what we've lost. We have to focus on what we *have*, and that is a talented and determined team, and I am confident that we can turn this around in spite of the short time frame. We have trained well for this and together we are talented enough to be able to adapt to this change." We all had the same thought: "We didn't come this far to give up now." We set about reworking the fish dish only to have a new twist added to the process. We received word via email from the Bocuse d'Or committee that the "mystery vegetable" we would be required to feature on the fish dish would be one of four vegetables: celery, leek, fennel, or butternut squash. We began working on a variety of techniques for each of these vegetables so that we'd be ready to incorporate any of them, though we were pressed for time to adequately practice everything we devised.

In fact, there would be several components on the dish the day of the final that we would do for the first time, a testament not only to our competition training but the versatility that comes from working at The French Laundry, where the menu changes every day.

We would never regain the X factor the plate design had given us, which nagged at me, and still does. The food had always been the primary focus; now it was the *only* focus, and there simply wasn't time to design and manufacture something comparably stun-

ning. So we pushed even harder to elevate the flavor profile of the fish dish, determined to make it better than it had been before. We would remain *unbroken*.

PACKING UP

The two weeks preceding our departure for Lyon blurred together. In addition to the fish changes and continued training runs, we had to nail down every last detail and organize how we would pack and ship everything to Lyon. Our last training run was set for Tuesday, January 13, leaving just two and a half days to clean, organize, pack, and ship our entire kitchen to France. Every item, down to the last gram of salt and piece of parchment, was on a list. There was a list for Skylar's rack, my rack, the fridge trays, under the counter, on the counter, the dishwasher, and on and on. We actually had so many lists that I had Greg write a list of all the lists so we wouldn't forget any.

We had a quiet send-off dinner at Bouchon with the team and my family, the kids holding me tight, knowing I was leaving for two weeks. At the close of the meal, we walked up to the Bocuse House and, with a fresh Sharpie, and at Chef Keller's insistence, we signed the wall where previous candidates had inscribed their signatures in years prior. Then we shook out and headed home for our last night of sleep in our own beds; it was time for the last leg to begin.

CHAPTER SEVEN

DAVID AND GOLIATH

"Never give up, for that is just the place and time where the tide will turn."

—HARRIET BEECHER STOWE

THAT WAS IT. January 17. Time to say goodbye to the comforts of home and round the final bend to the finals. I packed the last few things that morning and prepared to give one last hug to my wife and kids. As I zipped my suitcase closed, I felt more and more anticipation tinged with that ever-lingering fear of the unknown. I had learned to live with this fear. It was a healthy emotion, and I had come to consider it a friend. It gave me my edge, tenacity, focus, and, ultimately, courage.

After the last checklist was complete, we huddled together as a family and said our final prayers for Papa's big competition. I felt a great sense of comfort and, surprisingly, excitement, that what lay ahead was out of my hands, as it always had been—in bigger hands than mine. Four hugs, kisses, and goodbyes later, I loaded my last bags into the car and set out on the first leg of the trip, the fifty yards across the street to the Bocuse House.

WHEELS UP!

The boys were waiting for me when I arrived, and their faces showed eagerness and anticipation, almost but not quite off-setting their air of exhaustion. We grabbed the final elements we had left to pack, did our final walkthrough to ensure we hadn't left anything behind, and prepared to head out for the final time. As they loaded the car, I allowed myself a solitary walk through the space that had been my working home for the last year, passing my hand over the counters, saying goodbye. The last thing that caught my eye was our signatures on the wall. Would they merely blend into the others or become symbols of a historic achievement?

We had a layover in New York City and then were bound for Lyon. With Beethoven flowing through my headphones and melatonin coursing through my veins, I slept my way across the Atlantic. The only problem was that I'd let my guard down too much. After boarding our connecting flight from Zurich to Lyon, I realized I'd left my computer at the boarding gate. Though a flight attendant assured me I could recover it in Lyon, I never saw it again. I was luckier that my mobile phone—my main means of communication with vendors, the team, suppliers, and home—which I left on the connecting flight, was retrieved for me after we landed. The fact that our crucial files were stored in the cloud and retrievable by

Greg was reassuring, but I took the necessary lesson from my slip-ups: there was no room for relaxation. Like that old expression, "I'll sleep when I'm dead," it hit me that I couldn't lose focus, even for a moment, until after we'd competed.

DARK CLOUDS

On the ground in Lyon, we picked up our rental SUVs, and I tried to mentally reset myself only to receive an email from Lauren Van Ness, The French Laundry's concierge, saying that our boxes would be delivered a day later than planned. She explained their unexpected delay in their leaving Napa, but when I scanned the FedEx tracking report, my focus quickly shifted away from the one-day delay to something far worse—the dreaded phrase *"Clearance delay–Import"* next to the location, Charles de Gaulle, Paris. Our entire kitchen, a year's worth of effort and planning, was stuck in customs.

Before I could get on the phone and begin sorting out the circumstances surrounding our boxes and how to get them cleared, we made a quick stop to pick up a few items we had arranged to be delivered for us. We began to grab the boxes we needed—our Kitchen Aid, insulated warming box, and the insulated box that was to be our dry-ice freezer. It didn't take long to realize that the freezer box was missing. We scoured the entire property for the better part of half an hour before conceding that the delivery invoice was wrong. It was a deceptively big problem because that freezer had been measured down to the last millimeter, making it all but impossible to simply procure a new one. The sinking feeling I'd had for the last twelve hours deepened.

I was thankful for our investment in French lessons at that moment because I was able to get on the horn and sleuth out what had happened to the box, dealing exclusively with agents who spoke no English. It took

more than forty-five minutes and six phone calls to finally convince them that we hadn't received the box, despite what the invoice said. I'm not sure if it was the pleading tone of my voice or the prestige of the Bocuse d'Or that finally convinced them, but at long last they agreed to send a new box and have it there by Thursday. A ray of hope in the midst of a dark day perhaps, but I wasn't going to be reassured until I saw that box with my own eyes.

I was less optimistic about our chances of getting our boxes cleared through customs in a timely manner. A flurry of emails and phone calls yielded questions, automated answering machines, and worse: silence. My last hope was that we could push things through customs in Paris.

As we drove through the outskirts of Lyon, I peered out through the window at the gray, wintry sky. I was overwhelmed by a mind-numbing potion of jet lag, intense stress, and an acute sense of discouragement. Had we come this far, through all of those trials and challenges, just to have the wheels come off when we landed in Lyon?

Somewhere in that moment, I found the clarity to ask God to guide me through this trial and grant me peace despite the chaos. I didn't understand why all of these trials were taking place, but I was acutely aware of my inability to control the outcome. In that dark moment, I homed in on the parallels to David and Goliath that I had drawn nearly two years prior. Nobody expected us to attain victory. Was all of our courage and determination to confront the giant to be met with defeat before we even set foot on the battlefield? At that moment, I felt a reassurance that there was somehow a purpose in all of this, and I took courage that I wasn't alone.

Finding some peace, I realized I should check to see how our food shipment was coming along. I very quickly wished I hadn't called, as they informed me that the boxes of food, like those filled with equipment, had also not arrived. They had met the same fate in customs. At this point in the day, nothing surprised me anymore, and I simply added it to the proliferation of challenges. We never imagined winning a medal was going to be easy.

I was relieved when we arrived at our last stop of the day, an impressive catering location outside of town that had offered us a space to train with the equipment we needed, a vast improvement over the shared culinary school space. All we had left to do that day was meet up with Greg and Skylar, who had driven the rental truck ahead to unload the few pieces of equipment we had. I scanned the parking lot for our truck but there was no sign of it. Perhaps they had driven into the loading dock to unpack the equipment closer to our kitchen space. We walked

inside the chilly loading dock only to find that there was no sign of them there either.

Back at the SUV, I checked my phone to see if Greg and Skylar had been in touch with their whereabouts. No texts; no voicemail. I was exhausted, frustrated, and admittedly angry. It had been hours. Where were they? I just sat there stewing until, a few minutes later, my phone finally rang.

It was Skylar. "Chef, can you come and get us? We're lost."

I had quite a few other things I wanted to say at that moment but fortunately only asked, "How did you get lost? Where are you?"

After a brief pause he replied, "Um, we're at Domino's Pizza."

The day couldn't end soon enough.

Lyon, the gastronomic capital of France.

Team USA, Ment'or Board, and supporters at the final send-off dinner. From left to right: Kaysen, Stover, Dave Bernahl, Tessier, Keller, Boulud, Bocuse and Young Yun.

CHAPTER EIGHT

THE LAST MILE

"The pessimist sees difficulty in every opportunity.

The optimist sees the opportunity in every difficulty."

—SIR WINSTON CHURCHILL

AFTER THE CHAOS OF THE PREVIOUS DAY, I was ready to start fresh, hoping that it would be a downhill race moving forward. The day's agenda was full: retrieve and organize equipment from our storage unit, purchase guinea hens from a local butcher, shop for any outstanding ingredients, and receive and unpack our slew of boxes. The chances of our boxes arriving that day were slim, but we could still accomplish a lot of work without them if we had to, and if they arrived the next day, Wednesday, we would still be in good shape for our planned training run on Friday.

We got an early start and worked through the morning, retrieving the equipment we needed from storage and transporting it the twenty-five-minute drive to our practice space, which had a near-perfect replica of an actual Bocuse d'Or competition kitchen. The only downside: it was bitterly cold. We were stationed right next to the loading dock, which was constantly open to accommodate the flurry of activity the expo demanded. We did our best to mitigate the conditions, hanging rolling rack covers over the entryway and using the oven as a makeshift space heater. If Martin was correct that "there's no creativity in comfort," this was going to be a very creative week.

ONWARD

The delayed release of our boxes continued to be a source of stress. There is simply no predicting customs; they could come tomorrow or the next week. Of course, "next week" meant "game over." I redoubled my prayers but Wednesday brought no boxes and an onslaught of rain. We were as prepared as we could be without our food and equipment, so there was nothing we could do but wait.

I was glad I had arranged for Bouchon to send us new shipments of the flowers and greens we needed, as well as fresh dairy, bread, and eggs as back-ups in case the customs issue persisted. They planned to send a shipment every day for the next week, which might sound extreme but was prudent to ensure we had a steady supply, especially since some of the food we had shipped ourselves was likely spoiled by now. In addition, The Chef's Garden, our devoted sponsor, would be sending daily shipments of the flowers and greens they were growing in their greenhouses. As for the wild fennel blooms they were trying to grow, progress had been steady but slow. It seemed unlikely we'd have what we needed in time for the competition; I had no choice but to accept that it was out of my hands, like everything else.

We took advantage of this pause to engage in a group workout, meet to review the week ahead, and recharge. Nevertheless, it was impossible to contain my gathering stress and returning doubt. I retreated to my hotel room and read through the messages of encouragement from friends and family back home who knew of our predicament. I was thankful for their support and took strength from their encouraging words, verses, and messages of confidence, reinforcing my belief, even certainty, that nothing would stand in the way of what we had come to achieve and that all of this was happening for a reason.

And then, the next morning, I opened my email to find, finally, the blessed word I had been anticipating for the past three days: *Dédouanement*. Customs cleared!

Later that same day, Gavin, Dave, and Martin arrived, along with Martin's brother Lukas, who had been helping him in the mad rush to finish everything. Martin and Lukas (who had flown in from Madrid) had been working for thirty days straight, including six all-nighters—an amazing and touching sacrifice and commitment to our cause. Together we raced to set up the equipment, organize the food (the dairy box we had shipped ourselves was completely rotten, validating the reserves we had sent behind it from Bouchon), and finalize the platter. I found myself thankful for the rest we'd been forced to take.

Because so much of what we needed arrived late or had been held up, we pushed our final practice run back from Friday to Saturday and went into a flurry of activity to make sure everything was in place. With the new schedule, there would be just one day between the practice run and the first day of the finals—not a minute to make changes.

As we began our final practice, I don't know whether our last Lyon run was in the back of Skylar's mind, but if it was, he never showed it. The strongest part of our run was now that foundational first hour, and we flew through it effortlessly, setting the tone for a smooth, confidence-building practice. The unfamiliar environment and the stress of the previous days hadn't fazed us; we were laser-focused.

Skylar and I were now one unit. We could execute the entire run without notes or checklists, having full confidence in each other's every move. Gavin and I discussed a few minor changes afterward, but for the most part, we were locked in. It was the first time we'd had a chance to use the finished platter, and it was stunning. We were poised for the final ahead and brimming with confidence.

Another relief arrived just as we finished our run: my wife Rachel. She was full of excitement and encouragement, fueling us with fresh energy. She also pitched in—understanding that there was no time for sentimentality—and got to work shucking peas fresh from California. We shut down the kitchen one last time and made it to our send-off dinner that evening in the nick of time. There, sponsors, friends, chefs, and supporters were waiting for us. It was a surreal feeling arriving to such fanfare. We had been in the trenches, in our own little bubble, for so long that we had nearly forgotten there was a nation of people behind us. We embraced the moment and welcomed the encouragement even though, in reality, we were consumed with the coming competition and our desire to get on with it.

That said, I was deeply touched when Chef Keller toasted the team, wishing us success, and then turned to me and said, "We believe in you and the team. The hopes of our nation rest on your shoulders." It was a flattering yet heady sentiment. To ward off the doubt it threatened to unleash, I focused on the tasks ahead, all the little steps that would get us through the competition. One step at a time would be the only way to proceed. Like a mountain climber or high-wire artist, looking down—allowing myself to consider how far we could possibly fall—was the biggest mistake I could make.

FINAL STEPS

We set out early Monday morning to pack everything up and receive the final shipment of greens from The French Laundry culinary garden and The Chef's Garden. I opened The Chef's Garden box to inspect the delivery. Removing the insulated lid, I couldn't believe what greeted me: the most beautiful fennel I had ever seen was arranged within, like a bouquet. It was a radiant sight, like the first ray of sunshine as the storm breaks. This was a good sign. I embraced it.

We moved everything into position on the truck, triple-checked the lists, and set off on the twenty-minute drive to our first meeting at the official team hotel, the Novotel Lyon Gerland Musée des Confluences, where most of the teams were staying. The

hotel was a mini Olympic Village, with flags from the many competing countries embossed on jackets, shirts, and gear, and teams gathering and hustling about. We queued up to enter the meeting room and I introduced myself to Adam Bennett from the United Kingdom, who was making another go at the gold after a fourth-place finish in 2013. Though we were competitors, I wished the best for him since he had missed third place, and the podium, by just six points. We took our seats in the room and looked around, sizing up the competition. A few minutes later, Tommy Myllymäki strode in with Team Sweden, exuding alpha-male energy. Having won silver in 2011 and gold at the Euro Finals in 2014, he was the favorite, and he knew it. After a short debriefing we gathered our bags and Skylar and I departed with the other teams on the team bus for the expo center.

Upon arrival, we received our official jackets and posed for official team photographs. It was exciting to be among the other teams, and while some maintained

Tessier and Stover shop at the official Bocuse d'Or market.

I N PREPARATION for the Bocuse d'Or 2015, the team adopted a strict physical regimen that included working out at least five days a week, starting at 6 A.M. We'd meet in front of the Bocuse House in Yountville, run to the local gym, and have a one-hour, fast-paced, and strenuous workout before we began the day's kitchen training. It was something of a religious effort that could not be skipped. When the time came for the team to travel to Lyon, one of the pressing issues for Phil and me were where we were going to work out once we were in Lyon. Arriving the week before the competition, we checked out a local gym, but it was lacking in basic equipment. So we continued our 6 A.M. ritual jogs through the streets of Lyon. One morning, on one of these jogs, we passed by a construction site where an old structure was being refurbished. We looked at the scaffolding across the front and without hesitating, we turned the scaffolding into our gym, creating an impromptu circuit of sit-ups, pull-ups, chin-ups, push-ups, and squats. While in the middle of a circuit, I couldn't help laughing at the thought of what the passersby might be saying as Team USA hung off this scaffolding. All I knew was that it was the best workout of the week.

THE WORKOUT WILL MOUCHET

a steely distance, most were eager to meet and chat. We sat through the next round of meetings, and then prepared for the final step before we would receive our kitchens: the market. The rules stated that any produce we used on the fish plate had to come from the market, which added spontaneity to the competition. And the mystery vegetable, which each of the candidates had to feature on their fish plate, would not be selected until the eve of the competition.

I could have feared the unknowns of the market, but instead I welcomed them. After all, this was how we worked at The French Laundry, using the garden's bounty to create the next day's menu. Rather than panicking, we took inspiration from all of the different greens and blossoms, salsify, Meyer lemons (a surprising nod to California so far from home), and apples. We put our selections in a basket that was then sealed and set aside until the next day, when it would be delivered to us in the competition kitchen. We checked out with a "cashier" who gave us a receipt for everything we had ordered so we could dou-

ble check it the next morning. I had to take a picture of how the register's screen ID'd me: "Mr. United States of America." Pretty sweet.

The vegetable assigned to the twelve candidates who would compete on the first day was celery. Not my first choice. How many people showcase celery, ever? And with trout, no less? I had to stifle an impulse to feel aggrieved that the teams competing on Day 2 would certainly have a more inspirational vegetable, but those were the rules. Back on the competition floor, the Coupe du Monde (the Bocuse d'Or's sister pastry competition) was just finishing up. The Italians had just won and the United States placed third, ecstatic to have medaled. Another good omen for our medal chase?

After waiting for the Coupe du Monde groups to clear out, we were assigned our kitchen box, Box 9. It was the same box the Italians had occupied for their winning effort. I took that as yet another good sign, even though they must not have been judged on kitchen cleanliness; the floor and walls resembled something out of Willy Wonka's chocolate factory.

After a quick clean up, we loaded in our equipment and set up the kitchen, only to discover another potential setback. The worktables didn't have shelving, which was an issue because we couldn't just stack our stuff on the floor. Skylar rose to the occasion, retrofitting our push cart and removing its handles so it would fit under one of the tables. For the other table, we improvised a shelf out of a baking tray and milk crates. This wasn't ideal and certainly was something that would have given the The French Laundry team fits in our kitchen back home, but if that was the worst thing in store for us, we'd be more than fine. Martin applied a few finishing touches to the platter, and we sealed the box and loaded it into the back of the kitchen. I looked around the kitchen space at our equipment surrounding us and smiled to myself. For the first time since we'd left California ten days earlier, it felt like home—a reassuring feeling.

Back at the hotel, I typed up our final run sheet, incorporating the new vegetables we had selected as well as the assigned celery into the schedule: celery root purée, hazelnut-celery mousse, and trimmed celery branch. Skylar and I hadn't needed to use lists for more than a month, but Gavin would have a list to track our progress and act as a safeguard to human error, making sure we didn't forget anything. It was nearly 11:30 P.M. and I knew it was important for Skylar and me to get some rest, so we headed off to our rooms, leaving Gavin and Greg to finalize and print the menu, incorporating the new elements.

I was surprised at how relaxed and confident I felt. Moments later, there was a knock at the door. It was Greg. "Chef, I can't find the files for the menu that we need to print." I looked up at him, put my hand on his shoulder, and said, "Greg, I know the files are there, and I am confident that you will find them and do a great job printing these menus. I need to get some rest. I will see you in the morning."

I said goodnight and closed the door. I knew they would figure it out, and I knew the best thing I could do for the team was to be as rested as possible on game day. Within minutes, I was sound asleep.

From left to right: Richard Rosendale, Roland Passot, Greg Schesser, Bhambhani, and Will Mouchet on the competition floor.

CHAPTER NINE

BOX OF NERVES

"A creative man is motivated by the desire to achieve,

not by the desire to beat others."

—AYN RAND

D-DAY HAD ARRIVED. That morning, we loaded up our rental vehicles, and our core team made its way to the expo, Gavin driving the SUV, allowing Skylar and me to relax in the back, and Greg and Will following behind in the truck. At the expo, we unloaded our equipment and supplies, said our goodbyes to our support team, and Gavin, Skylar, and I cooled our jets in the Competitors Lounge, waiting until it was our turn to enter Box 9 and start cooking. Finally, one of the committee members summoned us, and we followed him to the staging area, where we met up with our assigned student-assistant, Pablo. We then headed down a dark corridor to the box, pulled aside the curtain, and entered.

As we walked into the box, we were like thoroughbreds scratching at the starting gate. We sprang into action, and dove into our set-up lists, filling pots with water, firing up the oven, and setting out our cutting boards, trays, and tools. After months of training at the Bocuse House and Ad Hoc, taping down tables to replicate the competition setup, we at last found ourselves in the actual space we had planned for. Everything was where we had mentally pictured it. We methodically worked through our lists while receiving and organizing our market produce, celery, trout, and guinea hens as they were delivered to our kitchen. The last hurdle between us and the smooth, organized start we had planned was the kitchen judge inspection. We had worked diligently to follow the rules and guidelines, but their generalized nature left room for doubt. The cautionary tale Richard Rosendale had shared of how, in 2013, the judges had penalized him for the way in which some of his products had been processed—and then proceeded to put the rest of his kitchen under the microscope—lingered in my mind. It had cost them twenty points and set them off on a rocky start.

SCRUTINY

The five kitchen judges entered our box, the lead judge taking charge and inspecting all of our containers, pots, bowls, trays, and equipment. I removed everything from the refrigerator and they continued, examining every container, asking questions about anything that wasn't immediately recognizable. I was just about to breathe a sigh of relief when the lead judge pointed to the bag of foie gras terrine on my tray.

"Qu'est-ce que c'est?" he asked. What is that?

In French, I explained to him that it was foie gras terrine to finish my sauce. He responded with a frown and turned to confer with another judge.

"This is cooked. You can't use it," he said. I calmly replied that it wasn't cooked but simply cured, a process that took twenty-four hours but no heat, thankful that my French allowed me to explain this well. That seemed to alleviate his concern for the moment but he walked away, bag in hand, to confer with one of the other judges. I followed him, afraid to let him, and my foie gras, out of sight.

My mind was racing, forming a plan in case the foie gras wasn't returned. It wouldn't be a game changer, but the two sauces into which it would be whisked would lose their nuance. Watching the exchange between the two judges, it was evident that even they were unclear as to whether the rules permitted this or not. Finally, he turned to me and said that because it had been "processed," we couldn't use it, but that we could replace it with some of the sponsored foie gras. I didn't have the time, or the bandwidth, to argue. After replacing our foie gras with the sponsor's, the judges shook our hands, wished us luck, and left for the next candidate's box. We had survived the inspection relatively unscathed.

READY, SET . . .

In seven minutes, we'd be off to the races. I put the guinea hens on my board, double-checked my fridge trays, and turned to confirm that Skylar was ready and nothing was missing. For weeks I had asked myself what I would say to him in these final moments. One last time, we reviewed the set up together, the initial steps, key points, and Pablo's responsibilities. I then grabbed his shoulders, looked him in the eyes, and said, "Skylar, I want you to know, there is no one I'd rather have in my box today than you. You've trained hard for this moment and have proven yourself. I am confident that today we are ready to do our best work. Let's do this one last time." A grin spread across his face and he responded with the usual, "Oui, Chef!" He was eager and ready, and most importantly, confident.

I meant every word. All of the challenges, conflicts, and disappointments we had worked through had made both of us stronger and more determined than ever. The transformation that Skylar had gone through over the two months since our first trip to Lyon had been incredible. He was self-driven, motivated, and brimming with a new kind of confidence.

I allowed myself a glance at the immensity of the stadium and thought how eerily quiet it was, the calm before the storm. A few kitchen-boxes over, France was already well under way, their box barely discernible behind a sea of cameras, judges, and other media. It was a different scene at our kitchen. Surrounding our box was our core team of coaches and support: Will, Greg, Gavin, Monica, Young, Nate, Rachel, Dave, Martin, and Richard. The lack of media attention was a stunning reminder of how low the expectations were for the United States. After all, for all the hard work in the past, we had never even come close to gaining the podium.

I took a moment to gather my thoughts and express my gratitude to God for bringing us this far, and I prayed for strength and clarity of mind for the six hours ahead. Skylar and I high-fived one last time as the clock ticked down and the official timekeeper approached us. Spain's candidate was already humming away just a few meters away. The timekeeper held out the official clock, *"Un minute!"* I envisioned my first moves, repositioned my cutting board, and made sure Skylar was ready.

The timekeeper counted down from ten and then gave the command, *"Bonne chance!"*

THE RACE

I grabbed my knife and quickly went to work on the guinea hen, the first task on my list. I felt an incredible surge of excitement and adrenaline course through my body, and the world around me fell away.

We set about that all-important first hour, seeking to ensure that it was, again, the most efficient part of our routine. I flew through the guinea hen, trout, and sauce work. The constantly circling kitchen judges were a new piece of atmosphere to factor in, but the stadium was so empty this early in the morning that compared to the deafening music in our training kitchen, we had an easy time keeping focused and blowing through our tasks. My only misstep was forgetting to start my stopwatch, but Gavin let me know when the first hour was up. I called out to Skylar, "One hour, Chef!" He replied, "Oui, Chef! I'm right on time!"

We were off to a good start but the most difficult part of my list was next: assembling the guinea hen, a super-technical process that demanded full focus. This would be the first curveball of the day. As I began to unmold the mousse and sausage layers the breast would rest on, I found that the frozen layers of sausage had softened under the bright stage lights and ambient heat. I had no choice but to return the sausage to the freezer. This proved a challenge for two reasons. First, any deviation from the schedule could prove catastrophic if I didn't successfully adjust my other tasks and timing accordingly. The second held even more implications if I got it wrong. The entire run was built around the guinea hen. The process involved butchering, pressure-cooking, making two forcemeats (stuffings), freezing, assembling, cooking, chilling, and roasting, which occurred literally moments before we served it. Anything that derailed this intricate process threatened the overall timing of the program.

Team USA in the middle of their final run at Bocuse d'Or 2015.

HAVE BEEN to every Bocuse d'Or competition since 2005. Inevitably, the night before the competition was when I had always looked back and thought how unprepared we really were. But 2015 felt different. Not only did we have a plan of attack, but we were prepared to execute it with ease, confidence, and a singular goal.

One of my favorite books is *Tribal Leadership* by Phil Jackson, which describes the highest level of leadership as a feeling where the tribe approaches life with an attitude of "life is great." That is the stage we were in, both the night before and the morning of the competition. There is no doubt that we had fear, especially of the moment when we had to go through our kitchen inspection. Once that hurdle was cleared, the countdown began, our hearts raced, and fear turned into excitement. This year felt different, however, as Phil and Skylar's excitement still seemed laced with fear, and to me, that is why they made it to the podium. They had just enough fear to keep them going, just enough fear of failing to keep pushing harder with each cut. When they worked, it was like a dance—each knew exactly what the other was doing throughout the entire competition. It was magical. They had the dance, they had the fear, and they had the "life is great" mindset. Little did they know, it would get a whole lot better in about five hours and thirty-five minutes.

THE DANCE

GAVIN KAYSEN

I reluctantly put the mousse and sausage back in the freezer and moved on to making one of the sauces, hoping that the mousse would be refrozen by the time I finished. I had to force anxious thoughts aside as I whisked the sauce. I knew that if I pushed my luck and tried to assemble the guinea hen while the mousse was warm, the definition of the layers would be compromised. I strained the sauce, put it in a thermos and pulled all the guinea hen molds back out.

Providence was with me. The mousse was just frozen enough to proceed. But where was the sausage mold? My heart sank. I checked the freezer: no dice. Neither was it in the fridge. I retraced my steps and realized, in horror, that I had put it in the dish station to be washed. A flurry of prayers flew through my mind as I walked over to see if it was still there. Thankfully, it was. (Skylar had been keeping Pablo so busy he hadn't had a chance to wash it.) Amazingly, after all that drama, the only hit I'd taken was a slight loss of time, and I was confident I could make it up.

As the third hour came, we were both fifteen minutes behind our respective schedules due to a couple of hiccups: the new pistachio mold was sticking, requiring me to spend nearly five minutes unmolding it to prevent breakage, and Skylar had forgotten to make a celery root purée we had discussed the night before for the fish garnish. We hadn't been this late in weeks. Fifteen minutes might not sound like much, but come the fourth hour, that represented our entire allotment of time for the fish plate-up.

"Don't panic," I told Skylar. "We'll make it up. Stay focused and we'll make it happen."

I was flowing on instinct and adrenaline now and decided to make up some time during my next preparations—three sauces—all at once. Working saucepots like a DJ, I whisked, stirred, seasoned, tasted, and strained each of them into the thermoses that would keep them warm until service.

Presto—five minutes regained! Onward!

With just thirty minutes until fish service, I checked in with Skylar: "Are you on track yet?" I yelled over the din.

"Chef, I'm still ten minutes behind," he replied. "What is Pablo doing? Is he helping you?"

"I don't have anything for him to do. He's done his list."

I dropped what I was doing and walked over to him. "Have him do the apples, get the greens ready, all of the little things you need to do to get organized for service." He nodded and set Pablo to work. I had nearly forgotten that because celery was the mystery vegetable, I had a few minutes available at the end of my list since the celery preparations were less time consuming than those we had developed for the other possible vegetables. I was pretty sure I only had two tasks left but wanted to make sure I hadn't missed anything. I asked Gavin, the only member of the team following a written list.

"Chef, you're good. You're more than good: You're fifteen minutes *ahead*! Did you get angry or something?" he asked.

"Maybe," I smiled back. I took a few tasks from Skylar and, just like that, the team was back on track, if not a few minutes ahead.

Though I never once looked up at the crowd, which by now was at full capacity, I could feel, and hear, the gathering presence around our box as the morning wore on. One camera became three, two jury members became four, and a crowd of onlookers began to form. Gavin fended off a few overzealous camera people and kept watch around the box to ensure that no one invaded our space. By this point, the adrenaline had built up to the point that my body was on fire, a battery on overdrive. I was amped—a good thing, since the most difficult and intense part of our program had arrived: service. The time had come to stick the landing.

THE FINISH LINE

Skylar and I double-checked the list and location of every item while arranging the heat lamps, table warmer, plates, and service pieces. Every minute was precious. If we started too early, the food would be cold. Too late and we'd miss the three-minute window where we had to serve all fourteen dishes at once. And with points deducted for each minute of tardiness, you simply don't win if you are late.

"Let's go!" I called to Skylar as the first garnish hit the fish plate. Ten minutes. That was the time we allotted ourselves for the process: two chefs, fourteen plates, sixteen steps per plate, 224 moves to make. We often talked about "the dance" at The French Laundry, the choreographed movement of kitchen, dining room, and guests required for impeccable food and service. This was our dance—quick, efficient, rhythmic, and meticulously timed.

"Two minutes!" Gavin called, sounding the warning for the fish plating. I gave Skylar the last few greens to arrange on the plate and pulled the glass cloches out of the warming box, setting them over the skin and apple tart. I double-checked the plates and turned to Skylar, "Ok, let's go—smoke!" He grabbed the smoke gun and we lit her up. Skylar carefully lifted the cloches and I directed the smoke under them. "Let's start. We're ready, Chef." We handed the plates forward and Gavin directed the service team to pick up the plates. I poured the mushroom consommé and passed them off to Gavin. Fish was out.

"Okay, let's clean up. Grab the platter and get set for meat." I directed Skylar and Pablo. I moved to the back station and set about getting the guinea hens in the oven; they needed every moment in the oven to get the skin to brown correctly. We reset and returned to a steady methodical pace. We had practiced the meat platter twice as much as the fish and had become proficient at each of the steps.

I assembled the lattice and beehives while tending to the guinea hen, glazing it with a honey-soy glaze every four minutes. At this point, I didn't have to look up to see the crowd that had gathered around our box. They pressed in on all sides, and it felt like at any moment they would pour over the divider and into the kitchen. I could hear Gavin explaining things to those closest to him. Everyone was intrigued with the platter, its heating elements, and design.

"Seven minutes, Chef." I turned to Skylar, "Finish the platter and I'll plate the two plates." We had to serve two plates separate from the platter, one for the table where Jérôme Bocuse sat with the previous competition winner and the honorary chef, and one for the media photo. I finished the plates and Gavin called out, "Three minutes."

As he said this, some confusion broke out. The official timekeeper was standing next to him and said, "No, no, you have one minute." Gavin pointed at the clock, "The official time clock over the box says three minutes." She looked at him and said, "Yes, but that clock isn't right."

There was no time to dwell on fairness: "Skylar, we have to move!"

We went into overdrive, and Skylar fully blossomed before my eyes, taking charge and directing the service staff and everyone around the box. The once-timid soldier had turned into the commander.

Racing to beat the clock, my hand began to shake like a leaf as I poured the guinea hen consommé into the tiny glass service pieces. I grabbed the container with my left hand to steady it, somehow managing to get by without spilling a drop. We lifted the guinea hens onto the platter and were finished. I reached for the platter to send it out when Skylar called, "Wait, Chef, we forgot the lattice tray," pointing to the tray still sitting on the table. In the midst of the confusion, I had left it sitting on the table behind me.

Tessier under scrutiny from Coach Kaysen (right) and a Bocuse d'Or committee member.

I quickly grabbed it and set it in place at the top of the platter, between the two guinea hens. We lifted it onto the ledge and it walked. Thirty seconds to spare.

We changed into clean aprons, grabbed our service kits, saucepots, and warming elements and hustled out onto the service floor where we would disassemble the platter and transfer it to plates for the twelve meat judges. As soon as the platter had paraded past the judges, it was delivered to us and we went to work on it, Skylar plating the garnishes and me breaking down and slicing the guinea hens. A few minutes into it, the next candidate's meat platter was announced and presented to the judges. The head maître d' panicked and said, "Okay, okay, we have to help them!" The staff around us began to descend on the table,

hoping to get our plates out before the next candidate was ready.

"*Attend!*" I demanded. Wait!

I hadn't come this far to let this turn into a free-for-all. I gave each server a task and direction and made sure they understood.

With each step, the maître d' tried to start the service and direct his staff to pick up the plates. I had to fend them off until the last strand of frisée was down.

"Ok. *Allez-y!*" Go ahead.

The plates walked, delivered to the judges by a team of servers, as another squad of servers followed with the glass vessels containing the custard and consommé.

And just like that,

WE WERE **DONE**.

BOCUSE D'OR

2015

Location
Lyon, France

Dates
27 & 28 January

2 Chefs

1 Oven

4 Burners

18 Square Meters in Box 9

Team USA
Philip Tessier | Skylar Stover

5h/35min

Race to Victory

40 Recipes

130 Ingredients

1 Platter

28 Plates

Official photo of Team USA meat platter.

Opposite: Placing the lattice. | Above: Final Team USA meat plate.

Above: The original Crucial Detail-designed fish plate and "fog concept." | Opposite: Final Team USA fish plate.

I HAD BEEN a close friend of Phil's since he first arrived in the Napa Valley in 2007, and I had followed his progress through the kitchens of Bouchon and The French Laundry before he submitted himself to the rigors of training for the Bocuse d'Or. Though I am a wine chemist, not a chef, I love food and found myself immersed in supporting the team, even stepping in as the commis/dishwasher for one of the practice runs. Because of my connection to the team and desire to help in any way I could, Young Yun, executive director of Ment'or, asked me to help acquire the customary paraphernalia for the American rooting section at the Bocuse d'Or finals in Lyon.

I organized all of the gear, arrived early in the morning with the team, and helped claim a section of the stadium seating for the American fans, directly in front of Box 9, already marked with "USA: Philip Tessier/Skylar Stover" above. Walking through the loading bay doors into the exhibit hall at the expo, the gravity of the moment hit me: we were *here*. I helped the team as much as I could, then attended to my duty of getting the fan gear ready, setting a shirt, poster, flag, and noisemaker on each seat.

Before the competition began, I took my place in the front row of the stands with my wife, Phil's family, our friends, and fellow Americans. The rest of the other countries' fans filtered in, as did the noise and excitement. Not to be outdone by the other cheer squads, we proceeded to sing, scream, and blow our noisemakers for the next five and a half hours. We didn't know if the team could hear us, but we behaved as if our energy could fuel them. More than a few passersby shot glances our way as we cheered, "USA! USA! USA!"

The most magical moment of the day was when the meat platter was presented for the first time. Cameras immediately panned over to capture it on the big screen in all its glory. An audible hush fell over the crowd, like the gasping silence that might follow a gunshot. Time stood still. Then, just as abruptly, there was an eruption of applause and cheers. Tears of joy ran down my face. At this point, I had no voice left to express my excitement, so I just blew my noisemaker as hard as I could, again turning heads. I didn't care. The USA had just hit the Bocuse d'Or like a bolt of lightning, and everyone in that stadium knew it. Afterward, as we cleaned up the remaining supplies, a dozen strangers asked me if they could have an extra poster, or shirt. This was a good sign; they wanted a piece of memorabilia from a team to whom no one had previously given the time of day.

NUMBER ONE FAN NATHAN DAULTON

Schesser, with Nathan and Carolyn Daulton, cheer on Team USA.

CHAPTER TEN

THE VERDICT

"I've said all along that God is in control."

—TONY DUNGY

AS SKYLAR AND I hustled back to the box, I turned to him and said, "We did it!" He turned to me with the biggest smile I had seen in a long time. We both knew that we had just put out the best food we had ever done. We gave each other a high five and headed back to clean up our kitchen space.

We had given everything we had; only time would tell if it was good enough, but it wasn't long before a buzz began to build for what we had put out.

Gavin, who'd seen it all in Lyon, came over with an irrepressible, "Dude, I just had two chefs walk over to me and say, 'Congratulations.' That's never happened before."

It got better. The Danish Bocuse d'Or president told me the fish was the best he'd tasted all day. Moments later, one of the committee members pulled me aside, lowered his voice, and told me what a pleasure it had been to watch us work, how we never let up for the entire five and a half hours, and how organized he thought we were.

What more could I ask for? Well, maybe a medal and a trip to the podium. Clearly, we had won the day, but it was far from over. The other twelve teams would compete the next day, including some of the countries with the strongest track records: Denmark, Sweden, Norway, Japan, and Finland.

WATCHING AND WAITING

That evening, I gathered the coaches and my parents and friends, who had traveled from Singapore, Virginia, and California to support us, for a quiet dinner together. Young had managed to secure a suitably large private room at a local restaurant where we could share a moment of calm after the tumult of the past year. A reserved optimism filled the room as everyone shared the same exhaustion, excitement, anticipation, hope, and uncertainty.

Nate was the quietest of everyone, having lost his voice cheering all day, earning him the nickname "Number One Fan." Throughout the evening, everyone shared their experience of the day. Martin asked why the stadium went quiet when our platter was lifted from the lazy Susan and revealed to the crowd. This was the first I had heard of that detail, and it sent a chill down my spine. Had it? My

USA's meat platter is paraded before the examining eyes of the judges' table.

mind flashed back to two years earlier when France's Versailles meat platter was presented and the crowd emitted that deafening silence. Greg described a similar moment when I sliced into the guinea hen and everyone realized it was more than just a roasted bird. I was pleased to hear the effect that we had sought so hard to achieve had been realized. Toward the end of the evening, I raised a glass to toast those around the table who had all sacrificed much to be there: "Today was an incredible day, the culmination of thousands of hours of dedication and focused commitment. Skylar and I would never have been who we were today without your presence, support, and hard work. I don't know what tomorrow holds for us, but I do know that I will be forever grateful to each of you for all you have done to get us to where we are today. From the bottom of my heart, thank you." After recognizing each of them individually, we returned to the hotel for some much needed rest.

The next day, I was a bundle of nerves. I climbed into the SUV with Gavin, Monica, Richard, and Greg. "I think it was easier yesterday when my mind was filled with everything I had to do," I told Monica. "This waiting is killing me!"

Adding to the suspense, I spent the next three hours watching the other countries' presentations, holding my breath as each fish plate and meat platter was released, wondering if one of them would steal the show. Finland's fish was beautiful, a stunning mosaic of colors on a uniquely designed tray. A flawless-looking meat platter rose from Norway's kitchen, an exquisite balance of color and technique. It was going to be close. As the presentations came to a close, I was headed down to meet up with the team backstage when I overheard someone say in French, "*C'est les Etats-Unis, alors.*" It's going to be the United States, then.

The next few hours were brutal as we waited, waited, and waited for what seemed like days. I had man-

aged to gather all of the US supporters and bring them, with Daniel's help, up to the front VIP area where they would have better seats during the awards ceremony. Our little contingent huddled together and took pictures until, at last, they motioned for us to head backstage, where we waited some more.

Backstage, we received participant medals that each of the candidates, coaches, and presidents would wear during the awards ceremony. Gavin tied mine around my neck, and when I looked up, there was Chef Keller tying Skylar's on, only *his hands were shaking*. I froze where I stood. In the eleven years I had worked for Chef, I had never seen anything even close to nervousness; his air of confidence and experience defined him. Yet here he was, his hands shaking, an expression of concern on his face.

After a moment of disbelief, I walked over and said, "Chef, I can get that for you." I tied it on for Skylar and then turned to tie on Chef's.

"Are you okay, Chef? Can I get you anything?"

"No, no, I'm fine, just nervous."

He smiled. It struck me then what the source of his nervousness was. Every other year for the last six years, Chef had stood behind these curtains, waiting and hoping to break through to the coveted podium. At that moment, I saw how deeply personal this journey had been and how much it meant to him. We knew all too well that the smallest of margins could separate us from victory. The organizers assembled us in the order we would be called out and gave us a US flag to carry. We decided Skylar should carry the flag. Chef Keller spoke to him firmly, "Don't let that flag drop, Chef. Keep it high no matter what!" It was evident from the look in Skylar's eyes that he had no intention of doing anything but that, and he replied emphatically, "Oui, Chef!"

When we were finally called out, Skylar began the most incredible flag-waving display ever witnessed at the Bocuse d'Or, beginning by nearly decapitating me with his first over-the-head pass. I walked across the competition floor, taking in for the first time the crowd in front of me. Over 2,500 fans cheering, waving flags, dressed to the hilt. It was a sight to behold.

HISTORY

We took our place in line along the front and waited for the lengthy awards ceremony to begin. Before the medal stage of the ceremony begins, there are a slew of awards given out: Best Promotion, Best Poster, and Best Commis are selected separately from the final scores of any of the teams. Two additional ones, however, Best Fish Plate and Best Meat Platter, are essentially consolation prizes to the best in each category that fails to medal; basically, the equivalent of fourth and fifth place.

We waited through the first three awards as Hungary, Argentina, and Finland claimed those prizes. When the announcer revealed that the Best Fish Plate went to Finland and Best Meat Platter went to Japan, I knew we were in the running for a medal because two of the top contenders wouldn't make the podium. Combined with the overwhelmingly positive reaction to our food, it seemed more than plausible that our goal was in sight. I met Gavin's eyes. Could this really be happening?

This was it. Bronze, Silver, Gold. I held my breath. "Now for the moment we have been waiting for. The podium," the announcer teased. "Let us find out who will claim the *Bocuse de Bronze!*" He passed the envelope to Thibaut Ruggeri, who won for France the year before. Thibaut opened the envelope and read it: *"Le Bocuse de Bronze: La Suede!!"* Sweden. Tommy had been the favorite to come back to win gold after his silver in 2011. I couldn't believe it. Could we have beaten them? They took their place on the podium and the audience quieted, collectively holding its breath.

Only two non-European countries had ever made the podium in the history of the competition, and they had both taken bronze, Singapore in 1989 and Japan in 2013. If we placed now, we would not only be making American history, but we would be making Bocuse d'Or history. The announcer turned to Grant Achatz, the *Président d'Honneur* for this year's competition, and asked him to read the name of the winner of the *Bocuse d'Argent* winner, the silver medal.

Grant opened the envelope, read it to himself, and turned to the announcer. "Okay, Monsieur Achatz, have you read the contents of the envelope?"

"I have." Grant replied.

"Will you tell us who is the winner of the *Bocuse d'Argent*?"

Grant replied coyly, "Let me just double check." He pulled the card out of the envelope. I held my breath. Gavin, having seen a cameraman turn his camera in our direction, whispered to me, "Get ready." Grant paused a moment longer and then, with an emphatic voice, declared, "The United States!"

We let out a roar and embraced each other in a flood of unbridled, emotional release. I don't know how long that embrace lasted, but what I do know is that at that moment, time stood still and we disappeared into another world. All I could hear was Chef Keller saying, "I love you guys!" over and over. As we came back to earth I realized, "We need to get to the podium!" We broke the huddle and raced together to the podium, still in a partial embrace.

An incredible weight fell from my shoulders that I hadn't realized was there. For the last two years, I had carried the pressure of pursuing this moment. It had been there so long that I had grown accustomed to bearing it. Now that it was gone, I felt like I could fly. It was all I could do to hold back my tears of joy. I had come through so much to get to this point and I thanked God for giving me the

Team USA awaits the verdict.

The silver medalist is announced: "The United States!"

Team USA's historic walk to the podium.

strength, wisdom, and support to achieve this moment.

I accepted the trophy, found Skylar, and together we acknowledged the crowd, trophy in my hand, flag in his. I was so proud of him, up there in front of the world waving our flag—the very picture of patriotism. We mounted the podium together and I passed the trophy to Chef, who ran his hand over it, gazing at it, turning it in his hand. He looked to our relatively small section of supporters and held it up, triggering a cheer.

Gavin turned to me and said, "I'm so proud of you, man. You did it!" and then added, "So this is what it feels like to stand up here!" I shook hands with Tommy and congratulated him, and we waited for the Bocuse d'Or winner to be announced. Jérôme made the big reveal, opening the envelope and announcing, "*Norvège!*" Norway had won. Well deserved. Ørjan was a talented chef who had devoted over half a decade to getting here, an incredible commitment.

The Norwegians took the podium, received the gold medals and statue, and then Ørjan turned to me. "I want you to know, I thought you had won." It was a huge compliment. The scorecard would eventually show that'd we'd missed gold by a mere nine points out of a possible two thousand, but just to be standing on this podium—with two return competitors from countries with long winning histories—was extraordinary. As soon as I could, I jumped off the stage, found Rachel, and hugged her tight. That was the moment that I finally was able to release all the tension, allowing tears to stream down my face. She had sacrificed and given so much to support me, and I never could have done it without her. "*We* did it!" I told her.

Then I found Will and Greg, and my two bodyguards embraced me in a massive hug, lifting my feet off the ground. I handed the trophy to Martin and told him, "We wouldn't be here right now without you. Thank you."

Tessier, Chef Ørjan Johannessen of Norway, and Chef Tommy Myllymäki of Finland celebrate their wins.

THOMAS KELLER VALIDATION

THERE'S A PLAQUE that hangs in all kitchens of the Thomas Keller Restaurant Group, inscribed with the words: "Sense of Urgency." It's a constant reminder for the team to stay on their toes, to be constantly moving things forward, and to complete each task as quickly as possible.

Waiting for the results of Team USA's effort at the Bocuse d'Or 2015 *felt* urgent to us, but because we competed on Day One, we had no choice but to wait overnight and to find a patience that runs counter to that plaque.

I knew that Phil and Skylar had done well. I was one of the meat judges, but because I was so familiar with our presentation, I didn't watch the platter go by, instead observing the surprise, joy, and amazement of my fellow judges. It was immediately apparent that we had dazzled them all. One of the chefs carrying the platter even winked at me. There was such a strong sense of accomplishment that I slept fine that night, even though many of the strongest European teams were set to compete the next day.

When Day Two was done, and we were waiting for the results, it finally hit me. We'd gone home empty-handed before, but this year I knew we had a chance, and that upped the emotional ante. It would have been much harder to pick ourselves up off the canvas if we didn't make the podium this time.

As the moment of truth drew closer, my stomach was in turmoil. My heart was pounding. I tried to tie a ceremonial ribbon around Skylar's neck, but my hands were shaking so badly that Phil had to take over for me. I focused on controlling what I could, assigning Skylar the honor of waving the American flag when we stepped out onto the competition floor for the awards presentation. "No matter what happens, don't ever let that flag fall below your waist," I told him. "I want everybody to see the pride we have in our country and our effort."

I meant it. The effort Phil and Skylar put forth that year filled me with enormous pride, especially since they came from my organization. But I wanted that accomplishment, and all the work that went into it, validated. I almost couldn't believe how much I wanted it.

FULFILLMENT DANIEL BOULUD

WHEN GRANT ACHATZ read the words "United States" from the card containing the name of the silver medalist country, it was deeply meaningful for me. I had, of course, been very familiar with many cooking competitions in Europe, but always thought the Bocuse d'Or was the most important one. It is a true representation of a team's ambition, culinary talent, and ability to master the balance of taste, technique, presentation, and creativity within the exacting confines of the rules.

Sure, like many countries that compete every year, we had our struggles along the way. But we always believed that we could improve each time and make it to the podium one day. When that day came in 2015 and Team USA won silver, I felt a rush of pride, for the team and my adopted home country, and also a feeling of a mission fulfilled. For me and for many American chefs, who, for the last three decades had been trying to succeed at this competition, it was a symbol of how far American cuisine and chefs have come in the same timeframe. Of course, we remain hungry. Our passion, discipline, creativity, and reverence for tradition are stronger than ever as we continue our push for the next prize: gold.

An unforgettable moment in Paul Bocuse's kitchen at L'Auberge du Pont de Collonges.
From left to right: Boulud, Keller, Tessier, Paul Bocuse, Stover, Kaysen, and Jérôme Bocuse.

CHAPTER ELEVEN

IMPACT

"A moment of pain is worth a lifetime of glory."

—PETE ZAMPERINI

THE NEXT MORNING, at the winners' breakfast at Paul Bocuse's restaurant, I looked down at the names newly inscribed in the brass walkway with a deep sense of pride and patriotism. The script that had unfolded over the twelve hours since the trophy presentation had been a whirlwind of celebration: a gala dinner, the breaking of my twenty-two-month abstinence with a parade of toasts celebrating the medal, a plaque presentation by the mayor of Lyon. And, just moments before, posing for pictures with Paul Bocuse, and the trophy fashioned in his image, right in his own kitchen. It was a pinch-me moment if ever there were one.

Now, in front of the restaurant where fifteen years earlier, as a young cook, I had timidly peered through the windows, were inscribed the letters USA, and next to them my name. I knelt down and ran my hand along the plaque to convince myself that this wasn't a dream. I was imbued with such warmth that I didn't even register the cold, gentle rain falling around me. I stood as we were ushered inside for the legendary winners' breakfast—a feast of pâté, *saucisson en brioche*, tripe, calves' head, red wine, and crêpes suzette. A true breakfast of champions.

Later that evening, we returned for a memorable team dinner, our final moment together before we would head our separate ways the next day. With the silver statue in the center of the table and historic photos of Lyon's culinary history surrounding us, we shared stories, recounted memories, and toasted to the role each person had played. Chef Keller gave an especially moving toast, speaking of the importance of one decision, my decision to compete, and how one decision can change the lives of so many. At the end, he turned, raised his glass and said, "The decision you made has impacted so many of us and brought us here to this historic moment. Thank you for taking the risk, dedicating yourself to the task, and overcoming all the odds to bring us here. This will always be one of the greatest moments of my life. Thank you."

ONE OF THE AMAZING THINGS about this experience is how much like a family you become. My mentor Chef Peter Timmins, who had recently passed away, had always talked to me about the Bocuse d'Or when I was his apprentice. I think he always wanted to compete in it so you can imagine how wonderful a feeling it was for me to bring him with me to Lyon when I competed. It was a real joy to see how much it meant to him and how meaningful it was. It was the same feeling for me after helping and supporting Phil. After spending so much time with him and Skylar, we all began to form a family-like bond, and when they competed and reached the podium it felt like we had all won. It was amazing.

But one of the most telling things about Phil that I think really says a lot about the kind of person he is happened after the team reached the podium. As soon as I got home I got a call from Phil, who was still swept up in the whirlwind of media activity following the win. He called to simply say, "Thank you for all your help and support; it was great to work with you over the last year." I thought here is this guy who just did what no American has ever done, and despite his hectic schedule, he is so grounded and humble that he made time to call me. It meant a lot the way he shared this win with all of us.

OBSERVING THE TEAM
RICHARD ROSENDALE

I MAKE THE TRIP TO LYON every two years to support the US team, but in the end, the mission is all about Paul Bocuse. The entire Bocuse d'Or experience has been distilled down to a single person and his wish to have the American team succeed in his namesake competition. That focus deepened my disappointment in our three attempts prior to 2015, and it amplified my joy at finally winning silver. The headline of the regional French newspaper, *Le Progrès*, said it all the day after the competition: *"Les États-Unis sur le podium: le rêve de Paul Bocuse se réalise"* ("United States on the podium: Paul Bocuse's dream comes true"). It was the fulfillment of a promise I'd made seven years prior: that we'd make him proud of the United States. Just as Phil—out of loyalty and respect—had stepped up to help me, his chef, achieve a goal, I had the satisfaction of coming through for a man who, quite literally, changed our world. Like any great chef, he immediately set a new goal for me. When I visited with him at the pass of his restaurant kitchen the day after we won that precious silver, he leaned in close and whispered a single word, one more wish for himself, for the United States, and for me: "Gold."

GOLD THOMAS KELLER

PHIL TESSIER'S TALENT as a chef blends a dedication to perfection, tireless testing and training, a deep focus on organization and precision, and a creative approach to taste and texture with a passion for technique and presentation. Every time I visited with him and Skylar during their year of recipe development and practice, I was struck by how driven they were and by the vision Phil brought to his role as the candidate. It wasn't just their food that evolved every few months—it was also their rapport, organization, and, of course, their energy level, no doubt thanks to the physical regimen Phil insisted on. If the Bocuse d'Or is, in fact, a metaphor for the professional kitchen, and its ultimate test, then Phil distinguished himself as a chef par excellence throughout the entire process, not just on the big day when he and Skylar brought home the silver for the United States.

PAR EXCELLENCE DANIEL BOULUD

Tessier and Stover on the Winners' Walk outside the legendary Paul Bocuse restaurant in Lyon, France.

CHASING BOCUSE

2015

ROAD TO LYON TRAINING DAY

4:45 AM	Rise and shine
5:15 AM	Morning devotion
6:00 AM	Workout
7:15 AM	Arrive at Bocuse House
7:45 AM	Breakfast
8:20 AM	One-hour setup begins
9:20 AM	Kickoff!
2:20 PM	Fish plate served
2:55 PM	Meat platter presentation
3:10 PM	Meat plate served
3:15 PM	Tasting and review of fish plate and meat platter
4:00 PM	Cleanup begins
7:00 PM	Dinner
7:30 PM	Reset and organize tools and equipment
9:00 PM	Review and analysis of run
10:00 PM	Next day planning and organization
11:00 PM	Final cleanup
11:30 PM	Kitchen closed

Time commitment on training run day **18h/45 min.**

2,650	8,050	2	30	100+	900+	22
Tessier's training hours	Total team training hours	Team assistants	Training runs	Recipes developed	Nespresso pods used	Months no alcohol

2017

COACHING TO WIN

CHAPTER ONE

UNFINISHED BUSINESS

"Ambition is the path to success.

Persistence is the vehicle you arrive in."

—BILL BRADLEY

I SAT IN THE BACK OF A NEW YORK CITY CAB, deeply exhausted after my return trip from Paris. The days following our historic win in Lyon had been a series of celebrations from the breakfast and dinner at Paul Bocuse to a dinner with Chef Keller at the US Embassy in Paris and finally a few welcome days touring through Paris with family and friends. We had rerouted my trip home through New York for a lineup of media interviews, further celebrations, and a victory tour with the trophy. As we twisted our way through the streets of Manhattan, I subconsciously watched the flickering advertising screen typical in New York City cabs. The local news channel was covering all the buzz about the Super Bowl between the Patriots and Seahawks. "That must be coming up soon," I thought to myself. A few moments later it dawned on me that the game was actually on right then! Shockingly, the world had continued moving despite my "absence" over the past months of intense training; I was slowly coming back to earth. I arrived at my destination, Cafe Boulud, and reunited with the Ment'or team as we enjoyed a quiet dinner together—aside from the occasional cheers from the kitchen team as they took in the game toward the end of service.

Over the next two days we wound through the streets of Manhattan rolling from interview to interview at USA Today, Yahoo, Saveur, and Food & Wine, sharing our stories, the journey, and the historic moment itself. After the first few interviews, it became clear that our story took each of them by surprise and that they weren't sure how to capture our unprecedented accomplishment. I couldn't help but draw comparisons between our achievement and the 1991 Women's World Cup soccer team that took gold and returned home to a surprised and unprepared media reception. No one had expected us to win anything. Few had followed our journey and even fewer had been in Lyon to see it. I hoped that much like the 1999 World Cup that eventually followed the women's victory, with 90,000 American fans in attendance at the final, much would change in the coming years for Bocuse d'Or USA. But there was a lot of work to be done in order to create a similar degree of excitement.

Between interviews we took the trophy on an extended tour of Manhattan and visited a few of the flagship culinary landmarks: Daniel, Per Se, Eleven Madison Park, Dominique Ansel Bakery, Gramercy

Tavern. I was deeply honored to walk into each of these establishments and receive a hero's welcome with hugs, congratulations, and at times, glasses of Champagne! These chefs knew what our performance meant to us and to our country on the culinary world stage. After engulfing me in a prolonged bear hug, Chef Daniel Humm of Eleven Madison Park held the trophy in his hand, turning it over with a childish gleam in his eye. That gleam revealed what all of us felt. Despite the silver finish on the trophy, it was gold to each of us. After nearly thirty years America had made its mark on the Bocuse d'Or for the very first time. This trophy was a symbol of achievement, respect, and honor among our culinary peers across the world, a shot heard around the world that America belonged among the world's culinary elite.

It would take a few weeks for the fog to lift after the flurry of interviews, dinners, and celebrations following our victory lap through New York. As exciting as all of these celebrations were, the most rewarding moment was reuniting with the team back at the Bocuse house in Yountville. For the past year I had questioned our approach every day, wondering whether it was the right path, if it was it good enough to win, what I was forgetting. Now, with success behind us, we had the opportunity to reflect on the moments we had shared together. We had given it everything we had and it was rewarding to relive the memories and moments that had transpired. We looked around at the empty space that had been our home for over twelve hours a day for so many months and smiled to ourselves. "It worked!" we said. And it had been worth it.

In the past two years I had been consumed by thoughts of the Bocuse d'Or: preparation, training, and at last, competing. I had meticulously prepared for every moment, mapping out each and every detail. But the one thing I hadn't prepared for was life after the finish line. Within a few weeks after our trip

to the podium in Lyon, Greg had returned home to New York, Will to Bouchon, and Skylar to Portland for some time with his family. The blurred days and hours of training and preparing had come to a screeching halt. It was a bittersweet moment. I knew life had to move on for each of us, but we had become a brotherhood, a disciplined unit, a family; it was hard to let it go. Despite everything we had accomplished, a wave of depression swept over me as I asked myself what I would do next.

After spending much-needed time with my wife and precious little ones, proud and thankful to have their papa back, I slowly began to realize that this journey wasn't at an end. In fact, it was at the very beginning. We had achieved what had seemed to be unachievable and had come so close to taking it all. We had a newfound confidence, potential, momentum. There was a great deal of work to be done—unfinished business—and I knew we had to seize the moment if we wanted to build a legacy for the United States at the Bocuse d'Or.

Those nine points that had separated us from the gold medal nagged at me. We could have won; many said we should have won. Certainly, for the first time there was no question that we had the potential to win the Bocuse d'Or. But as tempting as it might have been to compete again in 2017 and go for the gold, I had a broader vision that I knew couldn't be achieved by keeping my nose to the cutting board for the next two years. The United States needed to cement our rightful place on the culinary world stage as innovators, leaders—the best in our field. I wanted to study the models of the other winning countries, to find what made them so successful year after year, and then to build our own model. If we could capitalize on all that we had learned in the past two years, build an infrastructure around this knowledge, and attract the top talent in the country, we could establish a consistent, winning legacy.

The post-competition hangover slowly lifted and Gavin and I began to work with the Ment'or team to build what was necessary to discover, select, and train the next Team USA. Ment'or decided that I would assume the role of Head Coach for Team USA 2017, leaving only the big unanswered question: "Who would be the next candidate to compete for our country?" I was relieved and thankful when, in the spring of 2015, two talented chefs approached me with their interest in representing the United States at the Bocuse d'Or.

THE SEARCH

I met Brian Lockwood, chef de cuisine of NoMad, for the first time at a friend's restaurant on the Lower East Side in New York City. Brian was built like a runner, thin and fit, with a soft-spoken demeanor contrasted by a constant, focused gaze that revealed deep thought and determination. Greg had always spoken highly of his time working with Brian at Frasca in Boulder, Colorado, where Brian had worked after a two-year tenure at The French Laundry. It was evident that Brian didn't need any convincing about whether or not he should compete. He simply wanted to know how to get involved, what the next steps would be, and which of them he could start on immediately. He was all-in from the very start and I was excited at the prospect of having him in the running as a candidate for our country.

Mathew Peters and I had worked together for more than two years at The French Laundry before he returned to New York to fill the position of executive sous chef at Per Se. We knew each other well and I had immense respect for his work ethic, talent, and unique sense of style. Matt had just tied the knot and he and his wife, Lorin, whom he had met at The French Laundry, met me for a casual dinner at Michael Anthony's new Untitled restaurant at

the Whitney Museum of American Art in New York City to catch up and celebrate. Over the course of the evening's conversation it became more and more apparent that, much to my surprise, Matt was interested in competing for the Bocuse d'Or as well. Thinking about it afterward, it made perfect sense; Matt had been at several of my tastings and that experience, combined with our inspiring silver medal performance in Lyon, was all the convincing he needed.

Within the span of a month we had gone from an empty roster to having two talented and motivated candidates. I felt confident both had the potential to take the team to the next level.

While we continued to refine our approach to the US selection and the training structure for the candidates that would be involved, Skylar returned to work with me on a consulting project I had taken on with a young company called Hestan. I had joined them to help develop a guided cooking system that combined embedded thermocouple cookware, an induction burner, and an app that controlled the whole system via Bluetooth. It was a wild idea and a totally different venture for me but I was intrigued by the concept. It was also a perfect transition as I would be working with them only three days a week, giving me the time to focus on Bocuse d'Or and develop my restaurant concept. Skylar had come on to help me with recipe development and prototype testing and it was fun to work together in a lower stress environment. After a few months, I encouraged him to compete in the Young Chef & Commis competition that Ment'or had begun the previous year.

Skylar had been enjoying life outside the competition landscape, but he jumped back in full speed and began the search for a suitable commis to be his partner in the competition. Several different chefs in the Thomas Keller Restaurant Group had mentioned that there was a talented and self-motivated young cook who had just started working for the company. A meeting was arranged and Skylar and I soon found ourselves sitting across from Harrison Turone, a ruddy, athletic young man eager to take on whatever the world handed him. He was a great fit and over the next two months of training I observed everything one could hope for in a Bocuse d'Or commis: focus, slow to speak and quick to learn, thoughtful, eager and determined. Skylar took all of the training and systems we'd developed for the Bocuse d'Or and put them into play as they developed the food together. I coached them from a distance; I wanted this to be Skylar's moment to feel the pressure and build his own program. It was no surprise when they took first place in the Young Chef competition with a beautiful dish of striped bass, squash blossoms, brandade, and charred eggplant.

It was at about this time that I received a call from Matt saying he was having a hard time finding a suitable commis to apply with him for the Team USA Bocuse d'Or selection. The opportunity and timing couldn't have been more perfect. I told Matt about how well Harrison performed at the Young Chef competition, and that I thought he would be a perfect partner for him. Skylar had already given Harrison a crash course in our Bocuse d'Or training and Ad Lib, the popup Keller restaurant where Harrison was working, was just a few months away from closing. Within a few short weeks they figured out the logistics and Harrison was on his way to New York City to be Matt's commis for the US Selection.

I thought back to that historic dinner at Paul Bocuse's restaurant where Chef Keller gave a toast about the importance of one decision changing the lives of so many. In three months this young chef had gone from a line cook at Ad Lib, to Young Chef competitor, to Per Se commis, and Bocuse d'Or commis hopeful. His life's trajectory was forever altered because of Skylar's decision to commit and compete in the Young Chef competition. Almost without trying we were building the grassroots farm system we had hoped for, while developing the next generation of Bocuse d'Or competitors.

Stover and Harrison Turone compete in the 2015 Young Chef Competition in Los Angeles.

I N 2 0 0 7 we were basically the Jamaican bobsled team of the competition. I never really thought about whether we might win—it was just too crazy to imagine. It wasn't just about the funding or lack thereof, it was the logistics and everything else. I remember when I was competing I called Hartmut Handke, who competed in 2003, and asked where he had gotten his pots and pans and he said he brought them from his restaurant. Ten years ago I was cold-calling any company I could to get any product I could for free for the competition. We didn't have anything at all. I remember going to Office Depot in France when Richard Rosendale was competing and buying all the bookcases we needed, and then moving all our stuff from Daniel's parents' barn where we'd stored it all. It's amazing how far we've come, actually. To see how it's become this little army of chefs, everybody working together, and all the support that's come about. It all really started with the foundation being started. Thomas, Daniel, and Jérôme had the infrastructure in their businesses and frankly had more contacts to get us started down the right track. That's what it took to get people to take us seriously. Their perseverance and their tenacity on not giving up on the goal, that's what got us where we are. Every year we learned something important.

COMING FROM NOWHERE

GAVIN KAYSEN

B UILDING A WINNING TEAM for the Bocuse d'Or didn't take two years or even four years. It was a long, slow process and it was anything but straightforward. Still, it was always our dream to get there one day.

Even if sometimes we got set back a little bit, it was still evolution to us. Some years we didn't perform to top expectations, but it was great inside the team because we knew we'd learned something important along the way and we should apply it to the next team and competition.

We don't learn from just our mistakes. We learn from everything, really, because what we need is to understand this competition deeply. We needed to build this culture and this knowledge base. Certainly we learned a lot of practical things about how to manage it better. But we also learned just how many individuals are required to collaborate and make it happen—from the past competitors to the coaches and the many chefs who worked closely with Matt Peters and Harrison Turone, as well as the chefs who participated in the tastings or the chefs who promoted the competition itself.

Nothing moved very quickly. In the two years between each competition, we collect our thoughts, assess our knowledge, critique our performance, and use it all to plan for the next one. Each gap year we try to make sure we allocate enough support for the future candidate to be able to train properly, to really focus on the details that will matter at the end.

I don't have the statistics, but it's thousands of hours of work. There's lots of repetitive training. It's like the Olympics; you can't just go there, put on your swimsuit, and pretend you're going to win the gold. It's crazy. For the Bocuse d'Or, it's the same thing—for more than a year, training over and over again, just so you have a chance for the perfect performance when you need it.

A DECADE OF EFFORT

DANIEL BOULUD

CHAPTER TWO

TEAM CULTURE

"The day you think there is no improvements to be made

is a sad one for any player."

—LIONEL MESSI

A **S I CONTINUED TO WORK** and travel over the months leading up to the US Selection, I struggled with what Rasmus Kofoed (winner of bronze, silver, and eventually gold at the Bocuse d'Or) once described as his "Bocuse d'Or prison." I had come so close to winning the gold and, despite the decision to assume the role of coach instead of competitor, there was an ever-present competitive hunger and a drive to return and finish the job. In these moments I remembered what had originally motivated me to compete, the hope of winning respect and recognition, not for myself, but for America. The reminder that the mission had always been greater than myself gave me the key to free myself from that "prison" and find the clarity to not only focus on coaching but the determination to ensure that this was also the vision held by each of the future competitors.

It was with this mindset that I met with the four chefs who had made the final cut to compete against one another in the US Selection in late September 2015: Brian Lockwood (NoMad, NYC), Mathew Peters (Per Se, NYC), Angus McIntosh (The Broadmoor, CO) and Gerald Ford (Westchester Country Club, NY). I traveled to New York City, bringing the silver trophy along for inspiration, and we met as a group to ensure each of them was thoroughly prepared for the coming months of training. It was important that they began this journey with a sense of camaraderie and respect, and the knowledge that the rest of the Ment'or team and I were there to support and guide them throughout the process.

There were two clear goals to achieve with the US selection. First, the competition itself needed to be impressive in both the grandeur of the event and the quality of the candidates and their presentations. The world would be watching and we needed our candidates to impress. Second, we had spent the last two years building a systematic approach to training for the competition, and we wanted each of them to work within this system. Preparing for the US competition was the beginning of the long road to Lyon, and we wanted the eventual candidate to begin his training with a familiarity and confidence in the structure we had established. It was important that each of the candidates and their commis understood from the beginning that, despite the competitive nature of our assembly, ultimately we were all on the same journey to win gold for the United States.

After the initial overview of the rules for the competition, I took them through all of my training materials: brainstorming ideas, menus, recipes, timed run sheets, pack lists, equipment lists, platter presentations, etc. It was a lot of information to take in and they simply nodded as I essentially retraced my steps from the past two years. For the first time in our history, we had a formula that had been successful and the thought of building on this and strengthening our foundation was exciting. In previous years information had been passed down helter-skelter in Dropbox files, flash drives, and binders coming from various past competitors. Now, the candidates were receiving a clearly organized file outlining a method and approach that had been proven successful. Despite our success, however, there was much to learn and improve upon and this collaboration was the first step to doing so.

We walked through the technical file and answered questions before giving them the protein choice: Snake River Farms Kurobuta pork loin and Norwegian fjord trout. In just twelve short weeks, each of these chefs would be competing against each other and only one of them would walk away the winner. Each of the candidates was careful not to reveal their true emotions at the moment, but it was evident that they were all anxious to get started. That included me. For the past eight months we had been in a state of transition and for the first time we were back in the game!

GRASSROOTS

In October I had the privilege to travel to Oslo and be an honorary judge in the Norwegian national Bocuse d'Or selection. The Bocuse d'Or has become a big deal in Norway. For Norwegians it is the highest honor a chef can achieve and each selection is televised nationally. The day of their selection I gathered with the other judges in a room to discuss the rules and looked around the table at the group assembled. To say I was impressed would be a serious understatement. Rasmus Kofoed (Denmark: bronze, silver, gold) and Franck Putelat (France: silver) had also been invited as honorary judges along with all of the past Norwegian Bocuse d'Or winners. Thirteen trophies were represented at the table. But that was just the start. A few minutes later the Crown Prince of Norway himself came into the room to meet all of the judges. I expected him to simply shake hands and leave but he sat down with us and asked us to explain how the competition would take place today and how it would differ from Lyon. It was a really big deal in Norway.

Over the course of the next five hours I tasted an impressive array of creative and delicious dishes revealing world-class craftsmanship. Experiencing the competition through a judge's eyes for the first time drove home the importance of every tiny detail as we scrutinized every bite, every texture, and the temperature of each presentation. Between dishes at the judges table, we talked about the competitors and the state of the Bocuse d'Or in our respective countries. While I was impressed with the quality and clear talent of the candidates, what was most impressive was the culture of the Norwegian organization.

When Christopher Davidsen mounted the podium to claim his gold medal and be crowned the next Norwegian candidate, it was with an intensity and fervor second to none. "I've been dreaming of this since I was nine years old," he exclaimed. Ørjan Johannessen, who had taken gold for Norway in 2015, explained that most of the other five candidates who had competed against Davidsen would now come alongside and support him through his training over the next year. In this way they would offer Christopher incredibly talented support and continue their own training in anticipation of returning in two years to compete again for the honor of representing their country. There was an unrivaled sincerity, camaraderie, and respect for each other and it was evident that each of them cared more for their country than for their own individual success.

Talking to Ørjan afterward, the parallels between how the Norwegian team had been built and what we were trying to achieve became clear. Ørjan explained that it had been a slow process to arrive where they are today. Before Lars Erik Underthun had won his silver medal in 1991, the Bocuse d'Or was relatively unknown, just as it has been in the United States. From that point forward though, the Norwegians mounted a grassroots effort to form a stronger organization, resulting in Bent Stiansen taking home the gold in the next competition. The following decades had resulted in the steady build of what I had observed at the national selection a few days earlier.

After the national selection, my wife Rachel and I traveled with Ørjan and his wife to his picturesque home on the west coast of Norway in the small coastal town of Bekkjarvik where his father's restaurant is located. Rolling hills and forests gave way to a landscape of fishing villages, islands, and untouched, rocky coastline framed by the cold, clear waters of the Norwegian Sea. We spent the next few days exploring the islands, ocean, and culture of his hometown, trading Bocuse d'Or stories and eating some of the most beautiful and delicious seafood I have ever experienced: lobster, monkfish, langoustines, fjord trout, mackerel.

For the previous ten months I had been dreaming of building on our success and establishing a legacy in the United States. In the week prior I had seen the culmination of this vision and what it took to get there and I was eager to get home and share my ideas with the team at Ment'or. We needed this same grassroots approach to building a strong foundation,

beginning with the youngest chefs to ensure a solid foundation for future generations of competitors.

THE NEXT GENERATION

In November 2014, I began building two kitchens at our Hestan headquarters in Napa Valley. My consulting role with Hestan had quickly turned into a full-time position and we needed a new research and development space for the project. Looking at the space I realized that with minimal effort I could build a replica Bocuse d'Or kitchen as part of the show kitchen.

Meanwhile, the intensity of the competition training had ramped up for each of the candidates. I decided to travel to each of their locations to watch them do a full, timed training run and offer them my feedback. I booked a flight for a whirlwind trip to New York City, where I would observe Gerald, Brian, and Matt and the progress they had made. In two marathon days I observed each of them perform a full four-and-a-half-hour practice session with the current version of their fish plates and meat platter.

The first afternoon was spent with Gerald at the Westchester Country Club, where he was working as a sous chef. With time being short he got right to work and after powering through his practice run we sat down and I offered him my advice and direction. Because time was short, I had to focus on the most important points and challenge the areas that could be most easily improved. After congratulating him on a strong performance we headed back to the city as we had an early morning kickoff with Brian at the NoMad.

Brian was now guided by Greg Schesser, my former assistant. Brian had an impressive practice run and they were efficient and organized from the beginning of their 6:00 A.M. start downstairs in the NoMad kitchen. I was duly impressed. As impressive as their

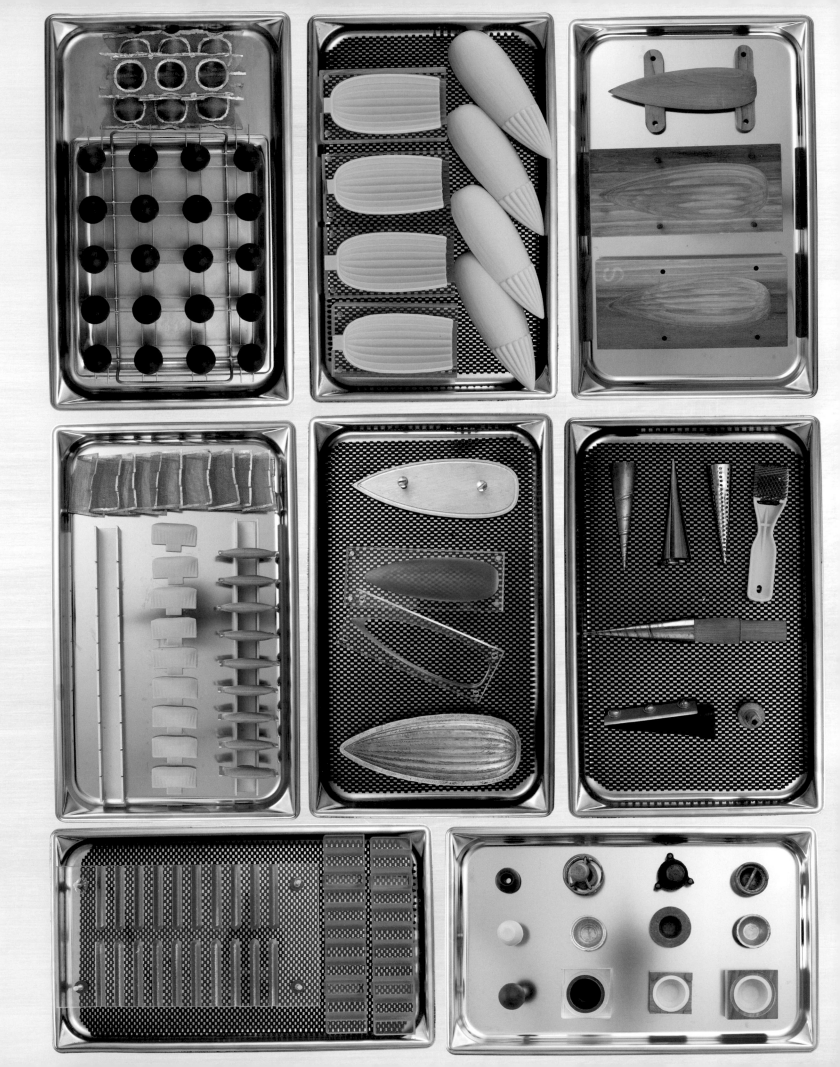

ESTABLISHING A CULTURE

ROBERT SULATYCKY

T'S A HUGE, LONG ENDEAVOR, getting to the podium of the Bocuse d'Or. It takes many years to put together not only the team of talented individuals who have developed experience with all the different aspects of the competition, but it's really also understanding how you take all of those talents and meld them into a team that gets onto the podium. That's the nut that has to be cracked. You need to keep the winning talent together for the next edition and then the next one. You need that expertise year-in and year-out to develop the opportunity to get onto the podium, to make that opportunity real. That's what I've seen growing with the American team over the last couple of competitions. We have a solid core. We've managed to get the right people in the right positions to build a culture where we openly share our experiences, expertise, and skills. And it all came together in Lyon. I guess you could say we've cracked that nut and we've figured out what it takes. But we're not going to rest on our laurels.

session was, I felt the food could evolve further both in presentation and in flavor, though the fish was a stunner with nori-wrapped trout surrounded by a ribbon of celery root purée and finished with caviar and crisped scales. We had a great discussion that was enhanced by some additional commentary by Rasmus Kofoed, the Danish champion who happened to be in the city.

I shook hands with Brian and his team and headed over to Per Se that same afternoon. Matt and Harrison were waiting for me and ready to start but had to wait until the pastry kitchen cleared out. I was excited to see what they would put together. All of the candidates had sent me pictures of their food for feedback and discussion, and while all of them were impressive, Matt's presentations had been refreshingly original. One garnish had the appearance of a mushroom but was actually an inventive use of braised pork garnished with watercress and apple that highlighted Matt's playful approach to cooking.

We kicked off their practice run around 6:00 P.M. and they began to power through their list with a very focused and promising first hour. Over the next few hours, however, it became evident that things weren't going as planned. They had been burning the candle at both ends, working full-time while also training for the competition. Equipment was missing, the "mushroom" garnish was not setting properly, and there was a need for improved organization and structure. At the final presentation of the food, the air was thick with frustration and disappointment.

It was after midnight when we sat down together. "This was our worst run ever," Matt stated matter-of-factly.

Thinking back to that fateful practice session Skylar and I had struggled through on our first trip to Lyon, I reassured him, "Sometimes that is the turning point."

I knew that time was short for Matt and Harrison, the competition was only three weeks away. I also knew they were talented and determined enough to turn things around. We went over what they needed to focus on if they were going to succeed.

"You guys need to take a step back from it all. Don't do any training runs for the next five days, just focus on getting organized, writing the lists, refining the food. And don't underestimate the importance of each and every tool, tray, and list," I told them.

They needed to simplify the approach to the food and do the things that made them successful every day in the kitchen at Per Se. More than anything they needed the time to practice and additional support to prepare, execute, and clean up from each training run. Up to that point, Matt was basically working full time at Per Se and trying to fit in training runs in the evenings and on his days off. If we were going to have an impressive competition, it was imperative each candidate have the time required to prepare.

A few weeks later I met with Angus at the Broadmoor in Colorado and offered him the same support and advice as the other candidates.

The stage was set for the selection competition. After seeing each of the candidates practice and knowing their strengths and weaknesses, I felt any of them could win the day. It is one thing to practice in your home kitchen and quite another to be out on the stage in front of friends, family, and the opposition . . . anything can happen on game day.

On December 17th, at the Venetian hotel in Las Vegas, the curtain went up on the culmination of four months of preparation—and it was everything I had hoped it would be. Each of the candidates put on an incredibly impressive display both through their performance in the kitchen and in the food they placed on the platters and plates. The chefs who had assembled to judge the competition were struck by the level of execution and talent on display.

The hundreds of supporters who had turned up to support their teams crowded the front of the room as the platters and plates were presented. As we tasted through each of the exquisite presentations it was evident that the scores were going to be close. The results were tallied and the points revealed that the scores weren't just close . . . they were beyond close. The difference between first and second was only three points out of a possible five hundred. Brian and Matt had both worked through technical difficulties in the kitchen that day and despite this they had kept their composure and cooked as though their lives depended on it. In the end, Matt and Harrison won the day and claimed the victory and the honor of representing the United States at the next Bocuse d'Or. It was a tough loss for Brian; he had performed nearly perfectly, and the point difference between the two teams was almost nonexistent. And, recalling how we lost the gold by only nine points out of two thousand, I knew exactly how that felt.

But the big question had been answered. We now had the next Team USA.

CHAPTER THREE

BUILDING THE TEAM

"The strength of the team is each individual member.

The strength of each member is the team."

—PHIL JACKSON

N OW THAT WE HAD DECIDED ON OUR TEAM, it was time to get busy assembling the coaching staff. One of my main goals was making sure that Matt always felt there was someone close by that he could lean on when he was going through the long, sometimes lonely training process. Two years earlier, when I was going through it, my closest coach had been more than two thousand miles away, which had made it difficult to communicate and collaborate. Whether working through the doldrums of developing the recipes or the intensity of training for the big event, I knew well the importance of feeling you weren't alone in the trenches. Certainly, I would be there in Napa working and training with Matt and Harrison, but I wanted the rest of the coaches to be close by as well.

I knew the first guy I wanted on board. Though he wasn't an official coach during my training, Robert Sulatycky had been one of the key voices in the buildup to the 2015 final. He had helped us to see things from a different perspective and shape our approach to training and organization. Robert had a long history with the Bocuse d'Or, having finished fourth for Canada in 1999. He had also served as the Canadian team coach for many years before becoming a Canadian judge for the finals. But his allegiances had shifted with a move south, consulting for the Four Seasons Hotel, and launching his own wine label in Napa Valley.

Robert was enthused to be part of the team again and we began discussing who could help support us as the core coaching staff. One of the names that resurfaced several times during our search for competitors for the next Team USA was Matthew Kirkley, who had most recently been chef at L2O in Chicago, the recently closed three-star Michelin project of Laurent Gras. Matt had expressed interest in competing himself, but when the time came to make the call he was unable to because he had just taken the position of executive chef at the adventurous COI in San Francisco, where he was taking over from founder Daniel Patterson. Though it hadn't worked out for Kirkley to be a candidate, I felt he would make a great addition to our coaching staff with his reputation as a talented and accomplished technical chef. Coincidentally, he and Robert Sulatycky had been friends for many years from their time working in Chicago and were thrilled to reunite coaching Team USA.

The first person I handed the trophy to after stepping off the podium in 2015 was Martin Kastner, our designer and secret weapon, who had dedicated countless hours to our success. When I asked Martin if he was up for another run at designing the platter and tools we would need for 2017, he had replied coyly, "It depends on who is selected." For Martin it wasn't just the challenge that interested him, it was the promise of collaboration and discovery that the journey would provide. Regardless of what he said, I could see he still had that fire in his eye and knew he wanted to finish what we had begun two years ago. Even though he hadn't said so explicitly, I could tell he was back before we had even started.

Additionally, we had newfound momentum with the recently formed Ment'or Foundation, operating under the guidance of Executive Director Young Yun. Young had patiently transformed the existing infrastructure into a stronger platform that would bring in increased support for Bocuse d'Or USA and the Young Chef competition. Alongside her was the highly motivated team of Jaimie Chew, Director of Events and Communication, and Tehani Levin, our new Team USA Manager.

At the end of January 2016 we held our first official meeting with the new team. I had waited almost a year for the moment when we could pick up where we had left off and begin again. The band was back together: Thomas Keller, Daniel Boulud, and Gavin Kaysen (who had been with the organization since 2008 and become vice president of Team USA) were all back to launch the next effort to mount the podium.

Two years earlier we had gathered on a snowy day in New York City to discuss what we could learn from other teams' successes and make it to the podium ourselves. This time, on a sunny day in Yountville, the discussion was not centered on the success of other teams but on continuing our own. And there was an unspoken belief that only one result would fulfill the dream we held—gold.

INFRASTRUCTURE

We had new coaches in place, a core group to advise the team, but I knew from experience that even more important would be the boots on the ground. No one could argue that my assistants Greg Schesser and Will Mouchet were not vital to our success. And so I was pleased when Chef Keller called and told me matter-of-factly, "I want you to take Will again. Bring him back as part of the team to help Matt."

As always, when Chef Keller asks for something, my reply was simple: "Yes, Chef." But I was surprised that he would commit Will to the team—after all, Will had just been promoted to sous chef at The French Laundry. I was even more surprised, however, by the reply when I asked when Will would be available to join the team. Without hesitation Chef Keller answered, "As soon as you need him. You let us know when you recommend him to join the team and we will make him available."

Things would be different this time around. Having Will on the team early in our training, five months earlier than I had been able to bring Will and Greg on board, would be an incredible asset. Not only was Will now more experienced, having spent the last year at The French Laundry, he also had been through the trenches with me and knew the ins and outs of our training approach as well as anyone.

Though I was happy with how the coaches and support team had come together, one looming question remained: "Where would we train?" The Bocuse House where Skylar and I had trained had been displaced by the massive remodel of The French Laundry kitchen, and despite initial hopes that the new facility would be finished by the time the team was ready to train, I had a gut feeling that—construction and Chef Keller's ambitions for a state-of-the-art kitchen being what they were—we might need an alternate plan.

Fortunately, the new kitchen I had designed in collaboration with Hestan Commercial was nearing completion. It was not only an exact replica of the Lyon competition kitchen, complete with the same oven and burners, it was equipped with a full commercial cooking suite and had plenty of space for us to expand into for storage and additional equipment. It was not without drawbacks. Hestan was a good forty-minute drive from Yountville, and its location in the hills east of Napa Valley meant deliveries would have to come to The French Laundry and then be brought up to the training kitchen. Despite the distance, it became clear there was no other reasonable option, and before we knew it, Team USA was training in the same building as our Hestan development team.

I couldn't have asked for a more perfect arrangement. Matt, Harrison, Will, and I would see each other every day. No longer would the communication of ideas and descriptions between competitors and coaches have to be done through emails and photos. I could simply walk over and see the progress of the dishes as they unfolded. And the rest of the coaches were never more than a short drive away. The new kitchen would allow Matt and Harrison to work with the same burners, oven, refrigerators, and table space that they would be given in France, an opportunity the Bocuse House had never afforded Skylar and me. With the infrastructure of the team and the kitchen in place, we had everything we could wish for. It was time for training to begin.

BEGINNING AGAIN

In March, we held our first coach's session in Chicago so the team could visit Martin's studio and see firsthand how he operated and what he was capable of. Dave Beran, one of the previous coaches, joined us in his kitchen at Next where he had offered to host our tasting. Our goal was to walk away from this session with a first look at the three garnishes for the meat platter and a clear sense of direction for the platter theme as a whole. With Dave, Robert, Brian, and Martin in attendance, Matt presented his initial thoughts on the direction he wanted to take with the theme and his food.

"The food I'm presenting today is inspired by spring in New York City with a specific focus on the Greenmarket," Matt began. "I've worked in the city for a long time and few things are anticipated there more than the debut of the market in the spring." The Greenmarket is the renowned farmer's market that takes over Manhattan's Union Square three times a week. The city's top chefs are often seen there selecting the best strawberries, onions, edible flowers, and other ingredients from the diverse landscape of produce.

It wouldn't be hard to develop this theme and connect with an international panel of judges. What chef hasn't been to a farmer's market in the middle of a major city?

In Lyon, twenty percent of our score would depend on how well we represented our country, a difficult task considering how Europeans assume our lack of culinary heritage. This theme would work well both to connect with the judges and to provide direction for Matt's food and the platter design.

After describing the thought process behind the food he had selected and the initial direction he had taken, Matt presented three garnish ideas for the meat platter. The first was a "morel" that he had ingeniously created by wrapping a *gaufrette*—a waffle-cut potato slice—around a piece of sausage. It was striking and presented an uncanny likeness to a morel. As we tasted the morel garnish, he continued to present a pea and ham custard and finally a carrot garnish, artfully wrapped with a delicate tuile.

As the session continued, I had a sense of déjà vu observing Matt ride the emotional roller coaster as the garnishes were dissected and the barrage of commentary began.

"This looks really beautiful but it doesn't taste better than a morel. I would expect to taste morel, so if it isn't a morel it should at least have a superior taste."

"The pea custard tastes really good, what form do you see this taking?"

"The carrot garnish is stunning but I don't taste carrot. What is the filling inside it?"

It's not easy putting on an "open house" when you are still just digging the foundation.

CRUCIAL DETAIL

The day after the session we went to Martin's studio and he walked us through the space and described his work there.

"Here at the studio we have three different types of projects," he began. "The first category encompasses projects we do for chefs and clients who want a specific service piece made and we collaborate and produce it for them. It makes up the majority of our business and covers a wide range of requests from a simple cork holder to a complex wine bottle sleeve.

"Secondly, we work on our own projects like the Porthole (a clever cocktail infuser that had received national attention). Right now we are working on coffee." He pointed to a table lined with different coffee presses and an old-style centrifuge. "It's a slow process and we work on these types of projects in between everything else we have going on."

"The third type of project we take on are projects like the Bocuse d'Or. These types of projects we take on as a process of discovery and learning and often," he paused and smiled, "we lose money in the process. But, they are often the most rewarding as well!"

He then led us on a tour through the space—through the woodcutting room, the kilns for china and glass work, ending at the display shelf where all his past work and prototypes were on view. It was clear that Matt and the team were experiencing the same sense of awe I had felt two years before when I had first met Martin and had his world opened up to me. Informed by the tasting the previous day and the team's richer understanding of Martin's process and abilities, we mapped out possibilities, ideas, timelines, and a list of initial goals for Martin and the team.

Though it was just the beginning for us, other countries were only a few months away from competing in the continental selections used to select the final twenty-four countries (the United States and Canada compete on an invitation basis). We knew they were already working at full tilt and we had no time to lose. With their heads full of new possibilities and a new task in hand, the team returned to Napa and hit the ground running in the new kitchen.

NEW IDEAS

Matt continued to train full-time while Will and Harrison split their time between working at The French Laundry and training. With the infrastructure in place and a strong sense of direction, the team quickly developed a routine as they picked up the pieces from the tasting in Chicago and continued refining the garnishes they had presented while also pursuing new ideas.

The carrot garnish continued to evolve as Matt gave the tuile a "new coat of paint," dipping it in lye to introduce a pretzel flavor and finishing it with a dusting of fresh fennel pollen. The resulting garnish offered a stunning experience through a delicate balance of flavors and textures. There was still some work to be done on the carrot filling, but this was a good development.

Whereas the carrot garnish just needed some refinement, the morel garnish, though beautiful, might

Crucial Detail | Team USA

SYNERGY

PLATTER | TOOLS | MOLDS

2015

CHICAGO | YOUNTVILLE | LYON

6 Circuits

6 Full-scale platter models

11 Platter model long-distance flights

23 Computer models of birds

25 Tools and molds created

36 Heating elements

43 CAD platter iterations

56 Batteries in the platter

3,200
Total Studio Hours

1,038 inches
Total length of electrical wire in the platter

2,900
Total Studio Hours

1,152 inches
Total length of electrical wire in the platter

PLATTER | TOOLS | MOLDS

2017

CHICAGO | NAPA | LYON

1 Pound of tin used to plate copper mold

4 Full-scale platter models

5 Circuits

6 Platter model long-distance flights

7 Hours to remake confiscated relay board

18 Pounds of copper melted to cast potato presses

20 Pounds of aluminum melted to cast chicken molds

28 Heating elements

34 Tools and molds created

48 CAD platter iterations

50 Batteries in the platter

61 Hours sanding and polishing brass platter components

460 Screws used

1,081 Holes drilled into platter

THEY SAY it takes a village to raise a child. As a father of three I can attest to the truth of that statement. Training to win the Bocuse d'Or is no different, and it takes a country to compete at the world's highest level. Behind every Team USA is a long list of supporters, family members, organizers, support staff, chefs, purveyors, and sponsors that are the foundation upon which each team stands.

Over the years our Bocuse d'Or family has grown, and we are incredibly fortunate to have the support and enthusiasm of key partners that fuel every day of training. One of our key partners during our 2016–17 training year was Hestan, providing not only the space to train at Hestan Vineyards, but a custom replica kitchen built for the team to train in. Through patient collaboration, Hestan Commercial worked alongside us to build each part of the kitchen to our specifications and provided additional support to keep the team running throughout the year.

Practicing daily in a kitchen equipped with the same burners, ovens, refrigeration, and table space used to compete at the Bocuse d'Or in France, we built the familiarity and muscle memory that would provide a strong sense of comfort and confidence amid the chaos of the final competition.

Throughout the year I would often take a step back to admire the incredible space we had to train in, and, if I am honest, fight away a few moments of jealousy as I coached the team. Having a replica kitchen as our training center was a huge step forward from previous years, when we had been limited to whatever spaces had been available to us.

We have never had a brighter future as we continue to work with Hestan Commercial and a new partner, The Culinary Institute of America, to build a permanent training kitchen in the Napa Valley. We are indebted to our sponsors, partners, supporters, and friends. Thank you for being the village that has raised us to these new heights.

COLLABORATION: HESTAN PHILIP TESSIER

Chef Mathew Peters and Tessier in the Bocuse d'Or USA kitchen at Hestan Vineyards in Napa, California.

I T WAS A GREAT PLEASURE for me to play a small role in such a tremendous endeavor. While there was a huge amount of time and energy committed to the cause by the entire Bocuse d'Or team, it was difficult to view it as hard work on my end because it was just too enjoyable. On my days off from COI, I would drive up to Napa to talk and taste food with a team of chefs whose company I genuinely enjoyed. Not a bad way to spend your free time. I approached the role foremost as a fan, both of the competition and of Team USA, with the intention of providing my thoughts and opinions when I believed they could be helpful. I hope that I was most helpful as a sounding board for Matt when he was developing his food and training runs.

As chefs, we exist in a world of instant gratification. We conceive a dish, execute and serve it, and get immediate feedback via our guests and our staff. Though we rarely pause to contemplate it, as we are accustomed to moving quickly on to the next task, this is what sustains us in our work. All chefs have a servant's heart—an eagerness to please others through our cooking.

But as a candidate for the Bocuse d'Or, you are removed from that daily basic joy. You exist in a vacuum. There is no guest, only you. You have a blank white sheet of paper to start from, and none of the crayons you are used to using are within reach, nor will most of them be available by the time the competition arrives.

Furthermore, you have been trained your entire career to focus on the negatives of your work in an effort to continually improve. It's never good enough. Ever. As the months go by in training for the competition, you will have to look at the same components of food that you have developed again and again. Are they good enough? Are they good enough to win against twenty-three other equally motivated chefs from around the globe in the most important culinary competition in the world?

These circumstances are at best highly disorienting, at worst utterly paralyzing. My hope is that I was able to function as a pressure release valve for Matt during his year for the extraordinary circumstances leading up to the big show. Yes, it is good enough. Yes, I think it is world class. Yes, I think you will stand above all others in January with your fabulous cooking and razor-sharp focus.

Turns out I was right. But like I said, I had the fun job.

THE SOUNDING BOARD

MATTHEW KIRKLEY

be misunderstood by the judges; we agreed we would have to go back to the drawing board. Matt began exploring some new ideas on how to keep the same flavors of potato, morel, and sausage, but with a different presentation.

The most rewarding times when preparing for the Bocuse d'Or are the moments of discovery, which often come in the most unexpected ways. One day while I was working with the Hestan team, Matt walked over. "Take a look at this," he said, handing me a golden brown, hollow shell. I knew Matt would never stop and show me anything unless he was super-excited about it so I was eager to see what he had made. "We took cooked, passed potato and fried it in the takoyaki machine. If you scoop out the center and re-fry it, you get this crisp, buttery shell." He had been using the takoyaki machine, a device used by the Japanese to make small round fritters, to develop a concept using waffle batter, when, out of curiosity, he had put some puréed potato in it to see how it would turn out. The result was an unexpected discovery.

"Wow," I said, after breaking off a piece and tasting it. "This tastes really good, like a super-crunchy potato chip fried in butter. This has real potential if we can refine the form."

Matt smiled knowingly. "I'm going to work on it some more and then we can talk to Martin and see what his thoughts are on how we can make some tools that will make it more efficient to produce."

The next discovery was Harrison's. I was walking through the kitchen one afternoon when he reached over and handed me a vibrantly green, thin crisp. "What is this?" I asked as I turned it over in my hand. One of the things I like about Harrison is that he rarely showed emotion, always playing the part of the focused, self-disciplined commis. But I could tell from the gleam in his eye that he was proud of himself. "I pulled the membrane from the inside of a pea pod, compressed it in glucose solution and then dried it slowly."

"Is there food coloring in this?"

"Chef," he replied, "Do you think I would use food coloring in my food?"

I smiled. He played the part of commis well but his spirit and sense of humor always came through. "This is really beautiful," I continued. "Nice job, chef. Let's turn this into something amazing!"

The creative process had begun again and it was rewarding to see the initial results. The road ahead was a blank canvas waiting to be painted, and though the paints were still being mixed, it was exciting to think about the masterpiece it could all become.

Early version of the potato garnish.

CHAPTER FOUR

A NEW PERSPECTIVE

"Every strike brings me closer to the next home run."

—BABE RUTH

WITH THE MEMBERS of the team and coaching staff set, the training kitchen built, and the initial food concepts settled, it was time to turn up the heat, building momentum toward the big event. Each week brought a new set of goals. One of the pivotal moments would be the European qualification stage of the competition, the Bocuse d'Or Europe, where we would get a chance to see many of the teams we'd be competing against as they vied for the chance to take part in the main event. Because Matt and Harrison had never seen the Bocuse d'Or, this preliminary competition would be crucial to their understanding of what they would face in Lyon. This could be a defining moment for them—their first chance to feel the full volume, pace, and intensity of the Bocuse d'Or.

Unlike the Bocuse d'Or final, which always takes place in Lyon, the European selection moves to a different country each cycle and this year we booked our flights to Budapest to see the competition unfold. I had been selected to be a judge for the Best Commis prize, and while I was honored to have the responsibility, I was more keen to gain unlimited access to the competition floor, where I could closely watch the top competitors in action. Brian Lockwood and Martin Kastner would join us on the trip and we were all eager to absorb the energy and emotion that comes from being in the center of it all.

Two years earlier, in 2014, I had come away from the European finals in Stockholm intimidated by what I would be facing, as four of the candidates had returned for their second or third Bocuse d'Or. It had been a field of veterans and I recalled how daunted I had been at their organization and polished technique. This year, however, there was only one returning competitor, Tomas Szell from Hungary, and there was a noticeable difference as we watched the teams go through their paces. Perhaps it was because I had been through this before and was more familiar with the competition, but only a few teams impressed, most notably Norway and Hungary. The host team had a notable advantage in that they were being coached by none other than Rasmus Kofoed, the three-time medalist from Denmark, and his fingerprints were evident everywhere in their kitchen. The tart shells, mosaic-wrapped meat, and shaved gelée sheets were just a few examples of the techniques he had used to win the Bocuse d'Or in 2011.

Observing the twenty different countries from this vantage point, it was evident which had a strong team culture and which didn't. Three of the six chefs I had seen compete in the Norwegian selection were there as assistants for Team Norway. Albin Edberg, the commis for Sweden in 2015, stood across from the new commis and coached him through the first few hours of the competition.

Despite being smaller than the finals in Lyon, the noise and intensity coming from the crowd at the European selection was second to none. The stadium was packed as the Hungarian supporters had come in droves, their dedication rewarded as Team Hungary won the Bocuse d'Or Europe for the first time ever, receiving their first trophy in the history of the competition. Predictably, Norway took second and Sweden third, with France a distant fourth. The British team failed to even qualify, finishing in seventeenth place—a cautionary tale pointing to the importance of team culture and commitment in competition.

With the European finals at our backs, we headed to Lyon for a few days to introduce the team to the city and to inventory the equipment we still had in storage there. We retraced our steps from 2015 and walked through the markets of Lyon, enjoying the iconic bistro fare along the way. Olivier Couvin, one of the three chefs at Paul Bocuse, spotted us taking a photo in the courtyard of the restaurant and scolded me, informing me that I was a friend of the restaurant and should always say hello when we were there. He then proceeded to give us the VIP tour through the kitchen, dining room, and spectacular wine cellar before taking a photo for us and sending us on our way. It was humbling to be treated with such hospitality and respect at this storied establishment.

That night we hiked up to the Basilique de Notre Dame de Fourvière and stared out over the streets of Lyon and the flickering lights of the city. Eventually we would return to compete but a long road of train-ing lay between that day and this. The anticipation and eagerness the team had gained from this trip was exactly what I had hoped for and would give us the frame of mind necessary for the training ahead.

AN UNFAMILIAR PATH

The summer months flew by with multiple fundrais-ing events and tastings, along with the daily grind of development back in Napa Valley. These were the months I had come to label the "doldrums," as we still lacked any solid information on what the assigned proteins would be. To counter the uncertainty, we continued to move ahead on what we did know, developing the potato, pea, and carrot elements that had become our three core garnishes.

The potato was becoming especially impressive with Matt working on a "potato glass" dome to cover the garnish. It was a technique we had used at The French Laundry—blanched potatoes puréed until smooth, spread thin, dehydrated, and then fried, cre-ating a potato crisp so clear you can see through it. The challenge came when trying to shape the potato as it dried so we could form it into a precise shape. It would take Matt and Martin the next six months before we could consistently shape and fry the glass in an efficient way that would fit in the timed train-ing runs. The result, however, was worth it as the garnish was a showstopper, making everyone ask, "How did they do that?" The carrot garnish remained largely the same with subtle changes to the flavor of the filling and the finishing touches. But the pea had transformed dramatically. Matt had further refined Harrison's initial idea and now they were drying the entire shell of the snow pea and filling it with crisped potato and truffled pea purée. The challenge was keeping the shell from becoming soggy as it sat after being assembled. It still needed some work to solve that problem and to bring out the pea flavor, but it was heading rapidly in the right direction.

The meat, however, was a different story, as we wouldn't know until September what it would be—pork, beef, lamb, or possibly a repeat of poultry. Essentially, we were driving blind down a dark road wondering if we were heading in the right direction. This drove Matt crazy and I could see he was spinning his wheels, trying to find a way forward. Every week he would ask, "When are they going to release the protein?" "Is there any way to figure out what it is going to be?" To address the lack of information, we analyzed the proteins that had been used in the past twelve years of the Bocuse d'Or and decided the next logical selection would be lamb. Since we had to start somewhere, Matt began working with different cuts of lamb, using the grill to enhance the flavor. It was a gamble, much like the one we had placed on duck being the protein two years ago. Would we guess right again?

Though the road we were traveling was familiar in many ways, I was experiencing it all in a very unfamiliar way. Despite my being alongside the team every week, I missed being in the daily trenches and even enduring the pressure that only the candidate can feel. There is something deeply addictive about the Bocuse d'Or. With the pressure comes an incredible focus and a desire to succeed that pushes you beyond your normal limits to a place of determination unrivaled by anything else I have experienced.

Despite the occasions when those doubts crept in, I was confident in my decision, especially when I looked back on what our organization had achieved in the last year: a solid US competition with promising prospects for 2019, a successful Young Chef competition that yielded three new assistants joining later in the year, a replica training kitchen, an evolving training infrastructure, and a solid team for 2017. We were moving forward and my most important role was finding how I could best assist, inspire, and guide Matt and Harrison, and ultimately the United States, to success.

Keller observes the garnish assembly.

FINDING OUR WAY MATHEW PETERS

REALLY STRUGGLED with developing the food I wanted, especially early on, before they gave us the guidelines on the protein and the theme of the plated dish. We're told we can create and do whatever we want, but as chefs we're so used to working in a restaurant where we're developing food around a specific ingredient or a specific theme. Without those, I felt kind of lost.

Our first concept was a little disconnected. They were pieces that we had created but they just didn't marry well with each other. We tried to make them work for a long time, but they never came together the way we wanted. So we squashed it all, took it back to the drawing board, and thought about what we really wanted to do. The trick is to somehow wiggle your way through all of that, but at the same time stay true to yourself and still somehow take in all the information you're being given and make some sense of it.

When I finally got to that point, probably sometime in the midsummer, that's when things started to click. There were still a lot of dead ends—for a long time we played around with the idea of using a broth or a consommé, but I never fell in love with it. Failures are not particularly exciting—that's an understatement—but you keep pushing and you keep driving and eventually they can turn into something you're excited about. You keep developing ideas and even if those don't work, they lead to other ideas, and finally you have something you're happy with. It's like Phil always said: put the time in and eventually something sticks.

It would take some time before we would find our footing as coach and candidate. Matt was riding the success-failure roller coaster as he developed new ideas for dishes. In addition, we held monthly tastings where, no matter what state of readiness each element might be in, it had to be presented to the team. Matt had always been quiet, focused, and stoic, and it often took time to draw him out. I had decided to take a soft approach to coaching in the beginning, giving him time to develop a solid foundation preparing food he was excited about and that he "owned." From that point I could guide him through the process of refinement while ensuring we didn't slip the unrelenting taskmasters of time and schedule. I knew I would eventually have to push harder to get us organized for training runs, but for now I wanted to be more of a support and a voice of affirmation.

I was thankful for the rapport we had developed when the news of the meat theme finally broke on the first of September: instead of working with a single set protein, each team would prepare a version of the classic Lyonnaise dish *poulet de Bresse aux écrevisses* (Bresse chicken with shellfish), one that would represent both the essence of the classic dish and the influence of the competing country. We hadn't seen this coming. I'd gambled on lamb, but unlike 2015, what seemed to be the logical answer wasn't the correct answer. We had our work cut out for us and we had to work together quickly if we were to stay on schedule.

DEFINING A DIRECTION

The release of the meat theme meant an immediate emergency war room meeting. There were many implications to the new theme and we had to quickly weigh each of them and prioritize our path forward. The good news was that the tech file had been released three weeks earlier than expected and each of the garnishes we had developed would still work well.

The downside was that all the techniques developed with lamb over the last few months had to be thrown over the fence—we were back at ground zero on the protein. It also meant that we had a lot less freedom with the flavors and presentation of the meat platter as we were now working with a very classic dish that was well known both in flavor and specificity as well as design and presentation.

What we were feeling was akin to parents who desperately await the birth of their child but then, faced with the realities of new parenthood, wonder why they were in such a rush. The relief in knowing, at last, what direction to head toward was quickly tempered by heightened stress and pressure. None of these hurdles were difficult to overcome but time was against us; our next board tasting was less than three weeks away, and full-training runs would need to begin immediately after. Matt and I outlined our immediate goals and scheduled an emergency trip to Chicago to work through the task list with Martin and define the platter design together.

Matt and I landed in Chicago ready to tackle the long list of open questions, leaving Will and Harrison behind to continue working on refining the current garnishes. But of course, there was a catch. Scrolling through my texts as we landed, there was discouraging news from Martin: his whole computer system at the studio was down. He was trying to fix it, but wasn't sure how soon he'd have it back up. This wasn't good. Without Martin's design software we wouldn't be able to model or lay out anything. Oddly enough, I wasn't panicked. Martin and I had worked through a number of equipment and technical failures in the past and I knew we'd somehow get through this one as well. It turned out to be serendipitous as Martin met us at the air-conditioned Airbnb and we decided not to head back out into the sweltering heat and humidity that had hit us when we stepped off the plane. Though Martin always claimed there was no creativity in comfort, I was okay being slightly less creative and not having to sweat it out in his non-air-conditioned studio.

After dismantling his laptop to replace the compromised hardware, Martin rebooted the software and we were back online. We worked late into the evening on various platter designs, pausing only for some fried chicken and frozen Dark and Stormies. Martin's assistant Graham joined us with some good news: he had managed to get the studio back up and running! We headed over after dinner to set up the 3D printer to print out a cutter concept Martin had developed for the carrot garnish. He had rigged the KitchenAid mixer with an attachment shaped like an oversized pencil sharpener that would facilitate shaving carrots into identical shapes and sizes. If we could develop the tools, we could shave it into the conical form we needed in a matter of seconds. After setting the printer to run through its six-hour cycle, we called it a night and planned the next day's tasks: define platter direction, develop cloche and underliner concepts, review tools for pea crisp and the potato garnish, and map out the critical path for both the board tasting and the goals for the coming months.

Martin would argue we were more creative the next day. As the mercury passed 90 degrees and the relative humidity seemed to top 120 percent, we were certainly less comfortable. Fueled by our own perspiration we worked through the various tools and then laid out the groundwork for the platter, which we decided needed to showcase the classic nature of the meat theme and at the same time honor the thirty-year anniversary of the Bocuse d'Or itself. Inspired by the historic *pièces montées* of the Carême days, Martin laid out a unique form that paid homage to these classic presentations without being trapped in the past.

Though we would leave with as many questions as we had arrived with, there was a sense that we had a direction we could begin to work toward. Over the next few weeks the energy and tempo of the team escalated significantly as the intensity and pressure mounted in the face of looming deadlines. The days of simply working on new ideas and refining them were behind us. Any slipping of schedule now would mean that we wouldn't have the time to properly develop the food, tools, and platter, affecting our training schedule and the time we needed to develop confidence and consistency.

OPEN HOUSE

As we walked into the familiar kitchens of Per Se to prepare for the big board tasting in mid-September, I could sense an uneasiness in Matt. I knew exactly how he felt. He was about to present his food to some of the best chefs in the country, but everything was still in a state of transition and continued evolution. Martin had brought several new tools, the first prototype of the platter; Matt was still developing the protein, sauce, and several of the garnishes. Yet we had to "open our restaurant" four months before it was ready, and for some of the toughest critics imaginable.

I reminded Matt that the key takeaways from these tastings would be the refinement of our direction and the gleaning of key points in regard to the flavor profile of the dishes as well as the overall design. We laid out the platter (a wooden prototype wrapped in silver vinyl wrap) as best we could and presented it to the board. We didn't have the centerpiece of the platter and we had tried to arrange the chicken and lobster vertically in the center. It hadn't worked very well and the frustration was visible on Matt's face. There was a long pause and then Chef Keller broke the silence: "What do you think, Matt?"

Matt looked up and with a forced smile simply stated, "It needs a lot of work. This is our first time putting everything together and it's pretty clear we have a long way to go."

It was clear that the protein was far from any real state of presentation, but Chef Keller focused on the positives, "I like the direction the platter is headed in and the garnishes look really good today."

Martin walked the group through the thought process of the platter and where we were headed, highlighting the idea of "contemporary classicism," which received nods of approval from the room. We plated the food for everyone to taste and took notes as the comments came in. The key topic of discussion was the interpretation of the meat theme. We had taken a more liberal approach with the dish, finishing the chicken on a grill, but the consensus was that we needed to be as true to the classic dish as possible.

"This is the thirty-year anniversary of the competition," Chef Boulud reminded us. "We should focus everything on the classic nature of the assigned dish, the anniversary, and the history of Monsieur Paul himself."

"The grilled flavor," he continued, "doesn't belong and fights with the rest of the dish, especially the sauce. The potato is beautiful and the flavor of the carrot and the pea with it are exceptional. We need to heighten the flavor of the sauce as well, it is a little over-reduced and flat. Add more lobster roe in the end and work on getting a cleaner, more lobster-forward flavor in the base of the sauce."

This was the feedback we needed—a clear direction that would help focus our future work and a challenge we would meet head-on in the coming weeks. Packing up to board the flight home I thought about what lay ahead for the team and wondered how they would handle the escalating stress of the coming months as we entered the next phase of training. We were officially out of the doldrums and into the trenches.

Assembling the plated dish for the Per Se board tasting.

CHAPTER FIVE

TRANSITION

"It isn't the mountain ahead to climb that wears you out;

it's the pebble in your shoe."

—MUHAMMAD ALI

THOUGH WE WERE OFFICIALLY a month behind schedule compared to where Skylar and I had been two years before, it wasn't cause for open panic . . . yet. Because Skylar and I had never competed together, we had pushed hard to start our timed training runs by mid-September, but Matt and Harrison had already gained valuable experience working together through the US competition. In addition, they were familiar with how the team would approach the upcoming practice runs, having trained for the US competition following the same structure and system we had developed in 2015.

It was clear, however, that we had no more time to lose. A lot of open-ended questions remained—especially in regards to the chicken centerpiece of the meat platter and what form it would take. Matt had worked on a few ideas with layering the morel sausage, brining the breast and wrapping it in the skin but it lacked a specific form, and we were at a point where we needed to commit. I knew how long it would take once we began the conversation with Martin to turn concepts into mold prototypes and then prototypes into final pieces, all of this while beginning timed runs. We decided to work off the concept we had used two years earlier with the guinea hen and build molds in a similar way but with a completely different form. A month had passed since the meat theme was announced and the luxury of time to work on new ideas was quickly expiring.

POSITIVES

Despite the challenges in front of us, there were several key moments that lifted the team's spirits and increased our momentum. First, the live random drawing on Facebook that would decide the kitchen assignments and team schedules for the final had just taken place and it was the complete opposite of 2015, with Day One seeing all the Scandinavian countries, along with France, Japan, and Hungary, drawn together. Of the teams that had finished in the top seven two years earlier, only the United States was drawn on Day Two: Box 5, 8:40 A.M. start time.

This was better than we could have hoped for. Not only would it allow us to compete without the presence of our strongest competitors and the deafening noise of their large cheering sections, but also in the history of the Bocuse d'Or, no country competing on Day One had ever won the competition. Though there were no guarantees, this draw set us up to be in pole position when we competed at the final.

In addition, two fresh recruits joined us full time, offering much-needed support and momentum. Vincenzo Loseto, who had won the Young Chef competition, and Chance Schwab, Matt's assistant for the US competition, injected the team with fresh energy and enthusiasm. By working more directly with Harrison and helping with all the logistical needs, prep, and the never-ending stream of dirty dishes the team produced, their support allowed Will to focus almost exclusively on working with Matt.

Bringing Vinny and Chance on board couldn't have come any sooner, as our training trip to Lyon was only a few weeks away. The challenge of taking hundreds of individual steps and compiling them into a seamless, organized training regimen was no small task and we had precious little time to achieve this.

LYON

There was a great sense of anticipation as we landed in Lyon and made our way to the house we had found for the team's lodging, located strategically between our training kitchen and the city of Lyon. I thought back to our fateful training trip two years prior and couldn't help but wonder how this week would unfold. Would it be the successful trip we hoped for or would we find ourselves retreating back home hoping to regain our footing?

We had tempered our expectations for the week's practice run and placed our emphasis on the importance of walking through every step we would take in January. The chicken centerpiece was still coming together and there were a lot of tools yet unfinished that made a realistic full practice run nearly impossible. It would have been foolish to expect a seamless 5-and-a-half-hour run this early on, and the last thing we wanted to do was put unnecessary pressure on ourselves.

From left to right: Tessier, Peters, Chance Schwab, Vincenzo Loseto, Mouchet, and Turone in Lyon, France.

The week was mapped out with the first day and a half allowing us to settle in, see a few sights in Lyon, and get the equipment staged in the kitchen. We would pause on Tuesday for the highlight of the week: lunch at L'Auberge du Pont de Collonges where we could finally taste the *poulet aux écrevisses* that our dish was based on. Not only would this be a key opportunity to taste the classic dish prepared by those who knew it best, but also a moment of inspiration for the team as they dined at the fabled restaurant for the first time. The rest of the week would be building the run, organizing the kitchen, the run itself, and then packing up and reorganizing before heading home on Saturday.

I was thankful to have an opportunity to dig in with the team and spend uninterrupted time in the kitchen with them without the distraction of other responsibilities. We celebrated our first night in Lyon at l'Est, one of Paul Bocuse's traditional bistros, with escargots, turbot meunière, *côte de boeuf*, and *baba au rhum*. It was a warm welcome to this historical city and despite our tiredness we left energized and ready for the week ahead.

We began the week without missing a beat: the training kitchen at C-Gastronomie was as perfectly arranged as we remembered it, and all the equipment from storage was in place. Staying at a house instead of a hotel the way we had done in the past would prove to be one of the best changes for the team. Not only was the house perfect, with enough space for everyone to gather in the evening, it also featured a warm open-fire hearth in the kitchen where we could prepare our own meals, offering us both a flexible schedule and the diet we wanted through the week.

DETOUR

Tuesday began with a sense of excitement for the lunch at L'Auberge. Despite a growing familiarity with the legendary establishment over the past two years, I experienced a renewed sense of awe and rev-erence each time I entered the doors of this gastronomic temple, and I was especially excited to share it with the team for the first time.

We were soon ushered into the kitchen for the traditional photo behind the pass with Olivier Couvin and Gilles Reinhardt, two of the three Meilleur Ouvriers de France who run the restaurant. Standing there I couldn't help but dream that we would soon return with a golden statue on the pass in front of us. It almost seemed like too much to hope for.

Once we had taken our seats at the table and toasted the health of Monsieur Paul with a glass of Kir Royale, we began discussing our anticipation of his famed Truffle Soup V.G.E., which he created in 1975 for then French President, Valéry Giscard d'Estaing. Tehani Levin, the team manager who oversaw all of our logistical support and planning, was especially excited to finally try the soup after having heard so much about it.

As a cold rain fell outside, our lunch began in perfect contrast with a small canapé of warm pumpkin soup and star anise cream. Unfortunately, that was as far as I got. Throughout the morning I had dismissed an uneasy feeling in my stomach, blinded perhaps by my anticipation of the meal, and attributed it to the late dinner the night before and the bumpy cab rides through Lyon that morning. But that soon proved to be a mistake as I was hit with a sudden wave of nausea. Setting my gaze on Matt and Harrison I announced, "I don't feel so good," and blacked out.

We wouldn't realize it till later, but I had suffered an extreme case of food poisoning. Within minutes the day had shifted from experiencing the classic *poulet aux écrevisses* at L'Auberge to riding in the back of an ambulance on the way to the hospital. Tehani was gracious enough to accompany me, though it meant sacrificing a taste of the famed truffle soup she had been looking so forward to. I promised her that we would return in January and that I would make sure she wouldn't miss it then.

HAVING HELPED THE TEAMS from the last two Bocuse d'Or competitions, I'd say the biggest difference is the carryover effect from the farm team system we've developed—the way Phil and others from 2015 laid the groundwork and established the processes the 2017 team needed to be successful. Without Phil's knowledge of the competition and him having documented everything we did, we would have been starting over from scratch with Matt's team. That's really the heart of the American Bocuse d'Or program now—the commitment of the previous year's candidate to document what they did and what they learned for the current candidate.

The competition is about cooking, of course, but that relies on sound organization—how you approach your day-to-day training, specifically by creating lists for every single process you go through. You need to know how to transport things from the practice kitchen to the competition kitchen and then document it all so that nothing is missing. When you show up, you need to know that every single thing you're going to need is going to be there.

This is where the American Bocuse d'Or foundation comes in. The food is going to shine at the end of the day, and winning the competition is always about having the best food and the best flavor. But there are so many factors that make creating that food possible.

BUILDING A BENCH

WILL MOUCHET

After a day in the hospital we tracked the source of the food poisoning to a café in the old town where I had decided to enjoy the steak tartare the day before, a poor decision the chefs at L'Auberge would later chide me for.

BACK ON TRACK

At C-Gastronomie on Wednesday evening we reviewed their setup for the run that we would begin on Thursday morning. Matt practiced working with the new mold for the chicken while I walked through Harrison's list and discussed how he had organized his station, food, and equipment. We wrapped things up around 10:30 P.M. and headed back to the house where the rest of the team were making dinner.

Will and Chance had roasted two chickens over the fire and had laid them out with a beautiful spread of green beans, crisped potatoes with raclette cheese, and a salad of endive and mixed greens. It was a welcome sight for the team and I was glad to ease back

into the world of eating with a meal we had cooked for ourselves!

I called my wife, Rachel, to reassure her that I was doing fine and was on the road to recovery. "I promise I'll take it easy," I said. "I'll be good . . . you know me." "Yeah, that's what I'm afraid of," she replied before again admonishing me to not overdo it. I said goodnight and thought of the day that lay ahead of us. It was the biggest day of the week and I was eager to see how it would unfold.

THE TEST

All year I had sought the best way to be an effective coach for the team, trying to find the delicate balance between letting them discover their own path and stepping in to offer guidance, direction, and advice. I was glad to finally be in the throes of training runs where coaching would become more tangible and direct and less abstract. I had given them space to lay out the run as a team, based on the structure we had established.

This would be only their third practice and technically their first timed run from beginning to end.

We arrived at the kitchen at 7:30 in the morning and everyone went to work setting everything in place. I reminded the team that though we obviously needed to maintain a high level of intensity throughout the practice, it was less important to be on time and more important to work through the whole process. We kicked off a little before noon and the team set to work on their first projects with Harrison breaking down lobsters and Matt going after the Bresse chickens.

The first hour hummed by with both of them on task and on time. This was a promising start. Over the next half-hour, however, Matt seemed to begin working ad lib, moving around from task to task instead of following his regimented list. This was never a good sign; it indicated that things weren't taking the expected time or the list wasn't accurately laid out. Meanwhile, Harrison was struggling to get the carrots done in time—it was surprising that there were still so many steps involved to shape them, despite how long we had been working on this garnish and the help Martin's tools offered.

As the run progressed, Will and I discussed the key areas we had to focus on as we moved forward. The main takeaway for both of us was that the team needed to mentally approach each practice as though it was the final, pushing through the challenges that these early training runs presented.

At 7:30 P.M., after a long and laborious run, the team began service for the plated dish. The combination of fish and meat on the platter theme and the vague wording in the technical file all pointed to a vegetable-focused plated dish and this was the direction we had decided to take. Matt had put together a beautiful plate with a clever artichoke and almond garnish, a brioche-wrapped egg, and green almonds from back home. They presented the dish and we stopped the clock so we could taste through the dish (a practice we would continue especially during the early stages of the training runs) and briefly discuss the main points before restarting the engines to finish the meat platter.

We treated the service of the meat platter a bit more casually, assembling the garnishes one by one and looking at how each of them would come together. The platter was looking better each time it came together and though there was much to work on, it was reassuring to see progress from the previous month. As we tasted the food, Matt expressed his thoughts on what he wanted to change over the coming weeks. It was now close to 9 P.M. and they had been going at it for over nine hours.

I looked over my long list of notes and fought a sense of anxiety as I pondered how this rough run could eventually progress into a seamless and efficient dance between the two of them. I reassured myself that we had time to get it right, recalling Matt and Harrison's ill-fated run before the US competition a year earlier and how they had been able to turn things around in less than three weeks and go on to win.

CRITIQUE

We had agreed that we would clean up and head back to the house for dinner before meeting to review all of our notes. It was 11:30 P.M. by the time we finally sat down to eat dinner together. We were all too tired and hungry to complain about the quality of pizza which Tehani and our photographer David Escalante had apparently found at a pizza vending machine, an invention that should be outlawed.

After dinner, we opened a bottle of Champagne our hosts had generously left us and toasted the team's completion of their first full run. Sufficiently cheered, we sat down to review our notes, going around the room as each team member shared their thoughts on how the run had progressed.

"We have got to tighten up how we are organizing ourselves and make our lists more accurate," Matt began. "Also, our communication is pretty poor right now. Harry and I are both focused on our own tasks and aren't talking enough because we have our heads down and are in our own worlds."

"I think we simply underestimate the importance of every little detail," Will added. "Every piece of equipment, whether parchment paper, a deli container, or a paper towel needs to be counted and in place. We have bigger challenges. We don't want to struggle with the simple things."

Everyone continued to add their thoughts on how the practice had gone and the key elements we needed to work on. After everyone had shared their comments, it was my turn. I knew how Matt felt at this moment—exhausted from the week's work, a long full run and his mind filled with dozens of changes he already wanted to make to the food and their preparations. I remembered having that feeling throughout my training back in 2015, and though it was tempting to sugarcoat my feedback, I knew it wasn't what they needed.

One of the most unique aspects of the Bocuse d'Or is the constant and unsparing critique of the team as it is pushed on every level. Every aspect of the food, execution, technique, organization, and even composure is scrutinized by teammates and coaches to make it as perfect as possible. Training for this competition places you in a constant state of vulnerability and it's a challenge keeping everything in perspective. I remember how uncomfortable it had felt, but over time I had learned to crave the feedback and critique. I knew I would rather hear it from the trusted chefs around me than to find out at the final that we had missed the mark.

I plowed through my four pages of notes, covering the run from beginning to end, spending a little more time on the crucial focus points that needed special attention when we returned home. It was a grueling list, and a few parts sparked conversation among the team as we covered everything from the importance of clean wipe towels, cutting carrots, setting timers, approaching service, and the food itself.

I knew Matt already understood for himself most of what I had to say, but I also knew the value of hearing it from someone else. In one of my final runs, when Robert had told me our fish was "refrigerator cold," I made sure it was hot from that point forward. Sometimes you need to hear it from a different perspective and, as hard as it is, remember that everyone is there to help make you better.

"Overall, we've achieved our goals on this trip," I said as I closed my notebook. "Our goal was to come here and go through each and every step we are going to take in January. We have a great place to stay as a team, the equipment we need, a replica kitchen to work in, and we did a full run-through of the food. I think we should all be content with how things have gone and where we are. When we get back, we focus on the details, finalize the open-ended questions, and solidify the foundation of the whole program."

"In a month we'll know what the plated dish theme is," I continued. "We have to make sure our foundation is solid when that information comes through at the end of November. There is a lot of work to do but we have strong talent in this room and the experience of success behind us. Now let's get to bed!"

It was 2 A.M. by the time we wrapped things up. Chance and Vinny were so exhausted they were struggling to keep their eyes open throughout the conversation and received occasional prods from Matt and Will. It had been a long day, a long week in fact, and everyone needed to get some rest.

It didn't take long before all the lights were out.

HEADED HOME

Despite the late night, everyone was energized the next morning. We had everything packed up in a matter of hours with the boxes ready to ship home and the truck loaded up with the equipment marked for storage. The team had really come together this week and it affirmed the decision we had made to build more support for the team this year. Though the days had been long, they had been efficient and we had been able to move through everything without a struggle and with less for Matt to have to worry about.

On our last night in Lyon we gathered at Café des Fédérations, one of the oldest bistros in Lyon, for our final, and most authentic bistro experience. With the week of work behind us, we blended in with the locals out on a Friday night, our table filling with *salade Lyonnaise*, wild boar pâté, lentil salad, *rosette de Lyon*, and baguettes. Harrison practiced his French with our host who made us feel at home and toasted our success with a small glass of Chartreuse as the night came to a close.

It was the perfect way to end our week. We were ready to head home.

In action in the Lyon training kitchen.

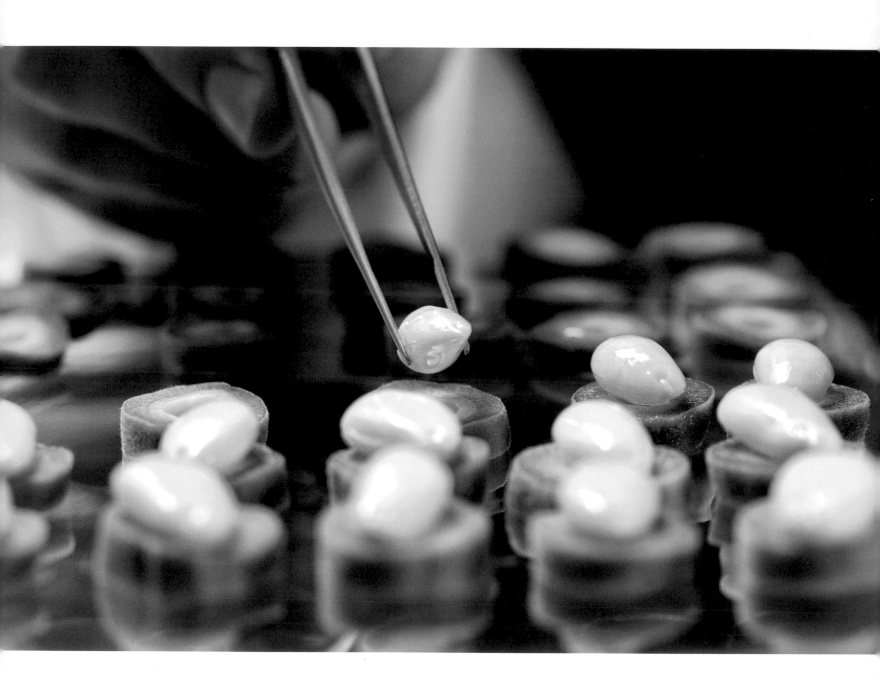

CHAPTER SIX

THE TRENCHES

"Whatever you do in life, surround yourself with smart people

who will argue with you."

—JOHN WOODEN

T HERE WAS A NOTICEABLE SHIFT in intensity as we returned from Lyon and the team faced the challenge of two training runs per week. D-Day was less than three months away; we needed to have the run timing down and the meat platter fully dialed in before the release of the plated theme at the end of November. I knew what lay ahead for the team the moment the theme was announced, and if we didn't have everything else locked in by then we would really struggle through December.

Overall, the team was showing great energy, camaraderie, and teamwork; it seemed we were finally hitting our stride. Though there were still a few areas of concern. Harrison, while focused and disciplined as usual, was showing signs of stress when things didn't go just right during training runs. In one particular run, when he found himself ten minutes behind at the first-hour mark, he slammed down his knife and exclaimed, "Why can't I do this? Why am I always too slow?"

Alarmed by his sudden outburst, I walked over to calmly reassure him. "Harrison, this is our timeline, our schedule. We are in control of our own destiny here. The whole reason we are doing this is to get this right and to understand the time we need for each task. Let's go, Chef, we're going to be fine. Push through it."

He returned to his work, somewhat mollified, but still visibly agitated. Over the coming weeks I would record him on my phone so he could see his own face, mannerisms, and responses, especially when things were challenging. No matter what happened, we had to look like we were in control, even if the wheels were starting to come off. Robert had put it the best: "When you are in the kitchen that day you have to be like a duck in water, calm as can be above the surface, but below your feet are moving furiously to get you where you're going."

The other area of growing concern was the schedule, which seemed against us now more than ever. Matt had spent a lot of time going back and forth with Martin on each of the tools, especially for the potato bases. Every change meant at least another week before we would see the modified piece and then an additional week after it was approved to make the tools in quantity. There was still so much left to resolve—each of the elements of the platter, what form the cloches would take, the underliners for the plates, and finalizing the chicken molds. We were virtually out of time to spend on other projects. The schedule was slipping each week and thoughts of those stressful days leading up to the 2015 final began to creep into my mind. I did not want to relive those days again . . . though they seemed inevitable.

REFINEMENT

On the upside, the chicken had begun to progress well and Martin had developed a new mold with a scalloped surface that tied well into our classic theme. One of the challenges we had faced was that the form of the chicken was lost when we went to color the skin, so he had built four individual cast aluminum "pans" with the same form. It was a unique approach that allowed the chicken to retain the scalloped appearance throughout the process and reduced the amount of time needed to sear the skin.

We had incorporated the braised wings, neck, and offal into the base of the chicken and it brought a roasted flavor to the chicken that, coupled with the seared skin and morel mushroom glaze, was delicious and well balanced. One of the challenges left to resolve was that the form tapered sharply at the end and we needed each piece to be the same size when portioned.

Though the food was innovative and beautiful, it seemed we still lacked the element of surprise the guinea hen on our 2015 platter had provided at the carving table—the moment when the food on the platter transformed into something unexpected on the plate. If we could find a way to treat the tapered end differently than the rest of the chicken, we might find that transformative moment. Because the skin wrapped around the whole piece, we could feasibly layer out the interior of the mold any way we wanted.

"What if the main section is the chicken with the morel sausage and the braised meat and then the tip, where it begins to taper, is lobster?" I asked. "This would allow us to represent both aspects of the dish at the same time and offer an element of surprise at the plating table. We could slice that section lengthwise to make all the portions the same at the end."

I could see Matt weighing this concept in his mind and visualizing how it might come together. "That could work," he replied slowly, "We could put the claw of the lobster in the tip and keep the tail as a separate piece like we've been doing. I'll work on something today and see what we come up with."

Between training runs Matt continued to work on the chicken and on finalizing how each of the garnishes would be finished. We had refined the crispy pea shell and it was now filled with a fried potato crumble, truffled pea purée, and "peas" made from pea purée. The potato and carrot garnish were largely unchanged, though we were still toying with how to finish garnishing them.

The garnish that needed the most work was the newest one, a foie gras mousse and corn custard that would sit toward the center of the platter. We were still adjusting the foie gras recipe and had begun looking at shifting from the poured corn "custard" to a traditional, steamed one. A reduction of homemade celery vinegar, celery leaves, and black truffle brought a delicate balance of acidity and sweetness to the rich flavors of the corn and foie gras.

APPLYING THE PRESSURE

Though we were making progress and each of the components were taking shape, I knew that our momentum on the chicken platter would be stalled once the plated dish theme was announced at the end of November and we needed to begin focusing on it.

Since September, I had been applying steady pressure as we sought to make up time on the schedule and transition into timed training runs. The support team we had worked hard to develop at the beginning of the year would be most crucial in the coming months as we dug deeper into the trenches and the competition grew ever closer. My presence with the team every week, Will at my side, and Robert at nearly every training run, enabled us to offer unprecedented support to Matt and Harrison, not to mention the boots on the ground that Vinny and Chance provided. It affirmed the decisions we had made in forming the team and together we sought for the balance between encouraging them as they progressed and challenging them as they pushed forward.

It was a new vantage point for me, standing across the table as a coach, instead of driving things forward inside the kitchen as a competitor. All year my primary goal had been to keep Matt focused on the food, developing and refining the flavors and techniques applied to each element.

During each training run Vinny would sit across from Harrison, clocking every task and making notes to review while Will and I did the same for Matt. The result was a step-by-step, minute-by-minute graph of every task. Once this was built, we could then shift each task around as needed based on future changes. After every training run, we would gather to review our challenges and progress. Matt and Harrison would lead off first, followed by Robert, Will, and the rest of the team as they laid out their additional insights.

I would usually close the sessions, always beginning by focusing on the progress made from the previous run. Then I would dive into the details and simply lay things out as they were at that moment. "Every training run must be a commitment to the tasks and times on the run sheet. This is game day and we have to mentally treat it as such. We went from a run last Saturday being only ten minutes late to today's scattered service period for both veg and meat. Much of this could be avoided if we ease into the new ideas instead of throwing them into full runs when they are only partially developed . . ."

"An inaccurate run list is our worse enemy. Allotting seven minutes to a task that takes nine minutes, or even having no written time at all, is a setup for certain failure. If we want to build confidence, we need to be successful in each run from this point forward and place extra emphasis on our organization."

At first I had struggled to find the right voice but with a strong foundation of respect and a common focus, I knew I could be hard on Matt and Harrison in a way that they would respond well to. None of us wanted to look back and think we could have given or done more somewhere along the way. We knew our ability to collaborate would be the key to success.

One thing I never had to do was push Matt or Harrison to work harder or be more dedicated. They consistently gave 110 percent and made it easy for us to focus on and improve their weakest points, elevating the level of their performance and the quality of the food overall.

A month after our bumpy training run in France, Thanksgiving was upon us and we were all ready for a break from the daily grind. There was also a strong sense of anticipation as we expected the plated dish theme to be released at any moment. We hung up our hats and enjoyed a day of rest and good food while trying not to think about the floodgates that were about to open.

THE UNEXPECTED

So far we'd been concentrating most of our energies on the meat platter, because that was the known quantity—we had gotten the technical files specifying all the ingredients and themes back in September. But we were still waiting on the plated theme. The late-November release of this second theme was an

POTATO

- Continue to work on making glass more clear
- Refine Potato Press
- Finalize Sausage & Garnish on top

CARROT

- Ricotta seasoned w/ Carrot tops and Freeze dried Fennel Pollen
- Pretzel tuile
- Roasted Bottom
- Clarified carrot juice to glaze carrot.

WHEN THEY TOLD US that the plated dish theme was going to be vegan, a lot of people were freaking out. But honestly, I was kind of excited about it. It was definitely a challenge, but I have some experience dealing with vegan dishes because I had the opportunity to work on vegetable tasting menus at Per Se and The French Laundry.

I was excited about the idea, but I wasn't excited about the list of vegetables they gave us to work with. Thankfully, we had the option of using two vegetables we could bring from our own country, so we decided to use those as our focal point. That's how we ended up with asparagus as the centerpiece of the platter, but that didn't really come about until the middle of December, the week before we had to turn all the recipes in.

Until then we just kept going back and forth. I was very indecisive and nothing ever really stuck. We weren't getting the umami factor that everyone was preaching to us about delivering. We had a rough patch figuring out what that was going to be. But once we did, that brought us new life. It gave us new excitement.

Everything else came forward after that. We changed almost the entire plate two weeks into December. We just kind of made it happen at that point, but it was down to the wire for sure.

THE VEGAN CHALLENGE
MATHEW PETERS

intentional challenge that forced the teams to adapt and adjust quickly. There was no time to learn new skills at this point in the game.

Rumor had it that it was going to be vegetable centered, so we had been playing around with ideas that fit that theme. But when we finally received the technical files for the plated theme, there was a surprise: "The plated dish theme will be 100 percent vegetal." I reread the line to myself, wondering what exactly this meant. Our hunch that it would be a vegetable-focused dish was confirmed, but as I kept reading I came across the shocking words, "no eggs, dairy or animal products may be used." In other words, purely vegan—a first for the competition.

This was certainly an unexpected turn and we immediately began to analyze everything we had worked on up to this point and how it would have to change. The almond purée, artichoke garnish, red wine sauce, and egg component would all have to change. These weren't insurmountable tasks but it meant we would have to take a significant step back.

It was the last day of November and, anticipating the release of the plated theme, we had allotted ourselves five days to work on the new theme. This would be the last open stretch before we pushed into two to three runs per week. It was imperative that we make quick and definitive progress so we could dive back into our training without multiple changes.

I wasn't concerned about Matt's ability to tackle the vegan aspect of the dish as his experience at Per Se and The French Laundry, where a lot of emphasis is placed on the vegetable tasting menu, would certainly serve him well. He even had a sense of

excitement and curiosity as to what a Bocuse d'Or vegan dish could look like.

The other interesting twist was that chefs were told which market ingredients they could choose from beforehand and they could bring two ingredients from their home country. This was a welcome change from two years prior when everything was a mystery and we were kept guessing until the last minute. At least this time we could plan everything ahead and lock things in before the final weeks were upon us.

We met to discuss the details of the tech file and reviewed the appendix they had sent that listed the vegetables that would be in the market. It was a surprisingly small selection and a lot of things we were hoping to use were missing from the market list. We would really have to be creative and careful about what we brought with us to make this dish something special.

Matt laid out a plan with the team and the next day the kitchen looked like a farmer's market as each of the team members took on a group of vegetables, applying different techniques to each one. It was exciting to see what would come of their work over the next few days—and what the possibilities were for this dish.

As November turned to December there was no question that we were deep in the trenches. Thankfully, the team's spirits were high and the team culture we had fought hard for was firmly in place. The next two months would be the hardest, much like the last few miles of a marathon are said to be half the race, and the challenges the team was sure to face would be the final test of our teamwork, tenacity, and resolve.

CHAPTER SEVEN

THE LAST MILE

"Climb the mountain . . . so you can see the world,

not so the world can see you."

—DAVID MCCULLOUGH JR.

W E ONLY HAD ONE MONTH to develop, refine, and perfect the vegan dish before the menu was due to the Bocuse d'Or committee at the end of December. It wasn't a lot of time and I was thankful for the efforts we had made over the past months to finalize the meat platter. There were still bits and pieces to work out, but on the whole we could shift our attention completely to the vegan dish, which was imperative given our time constraints. We had our last tasting with Chef Keller scheduled for December 12—less than two weeks away—and our goal was to present a semi-final version of the dish to him at that time.

We turned our attention to the elements we could carry over from the vegetable dish we had been working on, and within a few days we thought we had a strong starting point. The artichoke-almond garnish, almond purée, and green almonds made a foundation for the new components that Matt and the team had begun to develop. Satsuma orange segments were dipped in onion soubise and sprinkled with quinoa, and a clever beet garnish—formed with sheets of shaved beets—was shaped into a cone and filled with almond purée. Cabbage had become one of the focal points with Matt looking to grill and glaze the hearts to achieve a "meaty" flavor. The leaves he had transformed into a translucent crisp that, when sprinkled with gold dust, looked like stained glass.

THE STRUGGLE

But a week later, Matt was still trying to find the right approach to the cabbage and had yet to arrive at the balance of flavor he was after. The challenge was that we still needed to progress with training but we couldn't incorporate the technique if the method and timing weren't established. I had learned the hard way that trying to throw a partially thought-out garnish into the five-hour marathon was a sure recipe for failure.

All year long I had half-jokingly told Matt and Harrison that one thing I had discovered in 2015 was that it is easy to make anything look beautiful when you are doing one portion and serving it cold. Take that same approach during a training run and multiply it times fourteen with the need to serve it hot and you are in a totally different place. It was my way of reminding them that if we failed to develop the techniques enough we would suffer the consequences during our training runs.

This was never more true than right now and I began to see Matt experience the frustration I remembered all too well from my time as a competitor. Between each run there is this small window of time when you have to be creative and original and develop the best dish of your life, and then the next day you have to execute it perfectly in the middle of a detailed and highly choreographed service. I began to see this take its toll on Matt and for the first time I watched him struggle to find his creative stride.

After the tasting, Chef Keller confirmed our own thoughts that the vegan plate was not ready—the cabbage component and sauce were missing the mark.

"The smokiness I'm looking for from the grill doesn't really come through. I'd want to get more of a charred flavor. What is the sauce? It tastes a bit over-reduced and the sweet and sour aspect of it overpowers the dish."

"The almond and artichoke garnish continues to be very good and I like the beet garnish though it could use a bit more acid to balance the almond purée."

And so the next day we went back to the drawing board, knowing the cabbage needed to change but having no clear direction—despite the next practice run being only a day away. I had begun questioning whether cabbage was the right vegetable at all, and was frustrated by the dark, wintry appearance of the dish, which lacked Matt's characteristic whimsy and artistry.

At the end of the week, as I watched Matt work through the training run that Saturday, it seemed as though he was almost angry at the food. The excitement he had for the vegan dish at the beginning of the month was completely gone, replaced by a sense of detachment and duty. Something needed to change, and quickly.

Peters assembles the prototype meat platter during a training run.

BREAKTHROUGHS

We sat down after the run as usual but instead of the customary detailed analysis of how they'd performed, Robert and I decided to address the main issue.

"This isn't your food, Matt," Robert began. "I look at your Instagram account and I see beautiful, amazing dishes; incredible stuff. If you had a clean slate right now and you had to cook for the most important person you can think of, what would that dish become?"

I continued, "We've lost the excitement and enthusiasm when this dish was first announced and there is a sense of defeat, even a sense of anger at the challenge in front of us. I think the best thing we can do is take a step back, wipe the slate clean as Robert said and find new inspiration. You guys have been working nonstop since this dish was announced. Take tomorrow off, don't think about it, go somewhere, find inspiration and come back on Monday with a fresh perspective.

"I recommend we cancel the practice run on Tuesday to give us enough time to address the changes we need to make without the pressure of doing a run the next day. We need to catch our breath and I think we can afford to push the run back a day."

Everyone was in agreement and after discussing some of the details of the run and of the meat dish, we packed up and headed out. I was hopeful for what Monday might bring as we needed to turn this around quickly. We had, in a sense, lost a week, and at this stage in the game that felt like a month. We couldn't afford to lose another day.

When Monday rolled around, the smile was back on Matt's face. He seemed motivated and energized, ready to see what the day had to offer and what we could discover. But by the time evening approached, the dark clouds returned. Aside from a few possible techniques for some of the smaller garnishes, he hadn't made the progress he was hoping for. This wasn't good. It was already December 19; Christmas was around the corner and recipes were due in twelve days. We had to find a way through this.

I sat down across from Matt as he worked in the kitchen and opened my laptop. We confessed to each other that neither of us were still convinced that bringing along artichokes and almonds as our two optional ingredients was the right choice. The green almonds were special but the artichoke only provided a smaller garnish and nothing else. We needed more.

"Matt, if we can bring any two ingredients we want, are we really sure artichokes and almonds are the best ones?" We began scrolling through the list of produce from FreshPoint, one of our purveyors from Southern California. The first few pages were mostly the usual suspects. Then came a picture of bright green, jumbo asparagus. "We always look forward to asparagus in spring," I said. "It offers the color we're looking for and we can use it a hundred different ways. It could also become the centerpiece instead of the cabbage we've been challenged with."

Matt nodded slowly and then began to dive into conversation excitedly. "We could collar them or wrap them in something and then do something with the stems."

Will immediately jumped on it and within the hour we were moving in a different direction—cabbage and artichokes were out, asparagus was in. We had the breath of fresh air we had been looking for and change was on the way. We were back in the hunt, and not a moment too soon.

TENSION

Matt and the team worked diligently over the next week and the results were brilliant. The asparagus was blanched and then wrapped in potato and a thin sheet of sliced mushrooms before being portioned into two pieces. The red wine sauce was back and Meyer lemon was introduced, bringing a delicate brightness to the dish. The cabbage refused to go away completely as the translucent chip showed promise and Matt was continuing to work on refining the form. After just three days, the dish was ready enough to go into the next run and allow the team to take their first stab with the asparagus and new garnishes.

Christmas came and everyone took a few well-deserved days off and I was thankful that we at last had a strong and clear direction. The weeks following Christmas were a blur of activity with training runs, finalizing the vegan recipes, a photo shoot for our menu books (these were given to the judges before they tasted the food), and wrapping up the tools and platter decisions. Fortunately, our team was bolstered by the addition of Mimi Chen and Danny Garcia, both commis winners from the Young Chef & Commis Competition. Once again the timing couldn't have been more perfect as they dove right in and quickly became part of the team, bringing their new energy and enthusiasm with them.

Our last big push would be powering through five full training runs in ten days. Aside from a few details, everything was locked in. Now was the time to perfect their timing and execution in the kitchen. It would be challenging going from run to run with barely a breath in between, but they would gain momentum and confidence as they built on each run with fewer and fewer changes each time. These runs would be crucial to ensuring that we were confident when we left for France on January 15.

The first few runs weren't perfect but by the third time around things were going smoothly and Matt and Harrison had their best run to date, nailing the timing all the way through service. Just a few weeks earlier we were completely changing the vegan dish and now it was locked in and we were on time. They had worked hard to get to this point and had come so far so quickly.

With momentum and positive energy coursing through the team, we certainly were ill prepared for the events that followed that very night. We had just finished our post-run meeting. Will and I were finalizing details from our notes while the rest of the team finished cleaning up the kitchen. Suddenly Harrison yelled out from behind me, "Aaaah, I cut my hand. I cut my tendon!" It was a bloodcurdling scream and I spun around to see what happened.

He and Chance had been joking around when a friendly shove had caused Harrison to grab the sink to steady himself, in the process somehow cutting his hand on the exposed stainless steel underneath. Every worst-case scenario went through my head—losing Harrison to injury would be a massive setback.

After finally managing to calm Harrison down, I forced him to show me his hand. I held my breath as he reluctantly removed the towel, expecting to see a deep cut and an exposed tendon. I looked at the cut and then looked back at Harrison. "You'll be fine Harrison, you didn't cut a tendon. That's two stitches, three tops."

Though it wasn't as bad as feared, it was still something Harrison would have to deal with during the coming runs and he seemed inconsolably upset about it. Matt agreed to take him to the hospital and I hoped that after it was stitched up he would be back on track.

There was a noticeable tension in the air Monday morning as the team was making final preparations before the day's run. Harrison was nowhere to be seen and Matt expressed concern as Harrison had arrived late the day before and had been unusually quiet and reserved. This wasn't a good sign, but it wasn't surprising. Though he would never admit to it, Harrison had internalized all the stress and pressure and it was simmering inside him. I recalled what Skylar and I had gone through together two years prior and I expected the pressure to get to Harrison at some point.

MATT MADE a bold choice in his selection of ingredients for the meat platter garnish, but one that might not be immediately obvious. Because really, how daring can peas, carrots, and potatoes be?

As chefs, we are always searching to create superlative tastes for our guests. There are two ways to get that "WOW" moment in cooking—a new combination of ingredients or cooking familiar ingredients superbly. The former is an easier route to take as you don't have to live up to people's established taste memories.

But early on in our training, Matt homed in on peas, carrots, and potatoes for his meat platter. At best, I thought this was a ballsy approach. At worst, I thought it was downright suicidal. *You're going to serve these utterly basic ingredients to a judging panel of twenty-four accomplished chefs from around the world? Peas, carrots, and potatoes? They have decades more experience cooking those very same ingredients than you! You're going to serve Joël Robuchon mashed potatoes?!*

If you're going to win on peas, carrots, and potatoes with judges like that, they had better be the best peas, carrots, and potatoes they've ever had. That's the real challenge: How do you exceed expectations with very common ingredients? It's difficult, but through his innate talent, and through endless hours of practice and refinement, Matt was able to capture that "WOW" moment to impress the judges—with nothing more than pantry staples.

PEAS, CARROTS, AND POTATOES

MATTHEW KIRKLEY

But with less than a week left before we departed for France, this would be bad timing.

Harrison arrived just before the run kicked off and quietly shook in with the team before taking his position in the kitchen. I checked in with him to see how his hand was and reminded him to make sure he wore a glove over his rather large bandage. The last thing we wanted was for it to get infected. He didn't seem too happy about it but we needed his hand to heal completely before the final.

I had several meetings that morning so I was going to have to check in and out with the team until a few hours later, when I could join them for the remainder of the run. The tension had steadily increased all morning and I had an uneasy feeling about how this run would go with Matt visibly off center and Harrison withdrawn and frustrated. They kicked off the run and the first thirty minutes progressed without incident—maybe they would make it through okay after all.

I was moments away from walking into a meeting across the room when suddenly I heard shouts behind me.

"I've got this, I'll do it all! Just stand over there!" It was Harrison, his face flushed in anger, as he yelled at the commis who had come in to help that day and play the part of the student we would be given at the final. Harrison had found this commis especially difficult to work with and he couldn't take it anymore.

"Harrison, stop!" Matt said sternly as he turned and took in what was going on behind him.

"I've got this chef!" Harrison shouted back as he continued to vigorously chop the shallots that were on the commis' cutting board. There was no way he could do both his job and that of the second commis.

"Stop, stop, everyone stop!" Matt repeated. "Harrison, get some air."

Harrison stormed out of the front door and began walking down the vineyard road. I looked back at the kitchen, thought about the meeting I was supposed to be headed to, and then without hesitation darted out the door after Harrison.

"Harrison, wait up," I called. "Let's take a walk."

"Chef, I'm fine. I just need to do this, I'll be okay. I know what I need to do," he tried to assure me.

I looked at him squarely in the eye. "No, you're not. I'm glad that you know what you need to do but right now what you need and what the team needs doesn't seem to line up, and that's a problem. I know you are frustrated with your hand but there are some bigger underlying issues here and we need to work through this. Walk with me."

We headed down the road toward the vineyard reservoir and the one kilometer path surrounding it.

"Talk to me, what's going on? I'll walk around this lake until the sun goes down if that's what it takes to get us back to solid footing. I'm here for you. We are all here for you."

It was clear he didn't want to share anything beyond our training and the competition but I could sense this wasn't just about the team. I wasn't going to force him to share anything he didn't want to, but one thing was clear in my mind—we weren't going back to the kitchen until I was confident he was back on the right path.

As we hit our third lap around the lake, it was becoming quite clear to me that for Harrison, winning

gold had become everything. It was so important to him that anything less would be unacceptable—an utter failure. The pressure had built to such an intensity that he would react to anything that threatened this goal with anger and frustration. I listened to him talk and it became clear what he needed to hear.

"Harrison," I began. "What happens if you don't win gold? Are you going to jump off a cliff? Drive your car off a bridge? Let's get some perspective. This is just a cooking competition, this isn't life, man."

He looked at me as if that was the last thing he expected to hear. How could these words be coming from me, the coach, of all people?

"We all want the gold," I continued. "That's why we are all here, to finish the job and be on top of that podium with an American flag waving over our heads. None of us wants anything less. But life is bigger than this moment and winning this competition. So much is out of our control, all we can do is give it everything we've got, enjoy the journey, and leave the results in God's hands. You've got to let go of what you can't control and focus on what you can."

Harrison nodded and I could see the words sink in. As we continued walking, his countenance began to change, and slowly a smile returned to his face. I could almost see the pressure, tension, and stress leave his body. We had been walking for quite a while when we finally turned to head back after our fifth lap around the reservoir. Time would tell but I had a sense that Harrison was back in the game.

We walked back into the kitchen and Harrison apologized to the team for his behavior and they went back to resetting the run from the beginning. After a brief lunch, the clock was reset and the team began again. Five and half hours later they had put in their best performance to date. Sometimes the quickest way forward is to take a step back.

PACKING UP

Two days later we had our final run and we invited friends to join in the crowd noise and bring additional pressure. Despite the blaring music, cowbells, and banging of pots and pans, the team put in a solid performance and fed off the energy in the room.

It was a rewarding feeling to see these two talented chefs working together with the choreography we had worked so hard to achieve. Almost more important, however, was the fact that they seemed to be having fun again. We finished the run on the highest note possible with a well-timed run and near-perfect food. We had arrived and at just the right time.

Though the next several days were busy with packing up and shipping everything out, for the first time in four months there wasn't a training run scheduled. The team would have a solid ten days before their last practice run in Lyon and we were all thankful for the break after the marathon series of runs we had just finished.

On Saturday, the day before we would leave, I spent some time with my wife and three kids and enjoyed a day off from it all. Everything was shipped out and there was no work to do until we landed in France a few days later. As I finished dinner the phone rang—it was Harrison. I took a deep breath before slowly answering it. I didn't know what news awaited me.

"Hi Chef, you got a minute?" Harrison asked.

"Sure, what's up?" I asked hesitantly.

"I just wanted to call and say thank you for everything you've done for me over the last year and a half. I wouldn't have this opportunity right now if it wasn't for you opening the door for me with Skylar and then with Matt. I want to thank you for believing in me all the way through."

This was completely unexpected and it took me a second to respond. "Harrison, you've worked hard for this and overcome every challenge along the way. You're here because you are talented, you have trained well, and you stuck with it. I appreciate you calling to say thank you, it means a lot."

We talked for a few minutes about the journey together to get to this point and as we prepared to hang up Harrison interjected, "Chef, one more thing."

"Yeah, what is it?"

"We are going to win gold in Lyon."

I smiled to myself. "Yes, we are, Harrison. Yes, we are."

A vegan garnish: braised shallot and almond custard.

CHAPTER EIGHT

TOGETHERNESS

"Talent wins games, but teamwork and intelligence wins championships."

—MICHAEL JORDAN

O NCE WE WERE ON THE GROUND in Lyon, we established the main house as our base, set up the kitchen, and sourced the products we needed, retracing the same steps we had taken during our practice trip back in October. It was gratifying to see how far we had come compared to 2015, when we had landed with a team of five, traveled in rented cars, lodged at hotel rooms on the far side of Lyon, established a kitchen without being able to test it, and waited helplessly as all our food and equipment got stuck in customs. This year it was an entirely different experience from the moment we landed. Our team of ten traveled in four sponsored luxury vehicles with our official logo on the side, all our equipment was shipped directly to us, and we stayed in three houses in close proximity to a kitchen we already knew well. More important, we had a history of success behind us and with that came confidence. Everyone was determined to make this trip count.

We planned our practice run for Friday with the goal of having everything organized by Thursday morning, which would give us time to work with Martin on the platter when he arrived. We had yet to see the final platter, as its three-dimensional design, with twenty-eight individual heating elements, had proved to be a challenge to construct. Even though Martin, his brother, Lukas, and his assistant, Graham, were working nonstop, there was still much more that needed to be done in order to complete it. We were cutting it close.

CRUCIAL DETAILS

When the Crucial Detail team arrived on Thursday afternoon, the main house was instantly transformed from our end-of-the-workday retreat into a satellite studio for Martin and his crew. It was also immediately evident that we were "in the weeds" and there was a great deal yet to finish in the five days remaining before the competition.

After pausing briefly for a satisfying dinner of Robert's braised pork and stew, Martin took charge of the team. All of the tables were cleared off and Graham began a class in the dining room on how to fold the vellum cloches that would envelope both the vegan and meat plates when we presented them.

Learning from the costly lesson of our fish plate in 2015, Martin had developed a rule-friendly cloche that, when folded origami-like, had a beautiful, fractal pattern that rested over the edge of the plate, fitting exactly onto an underliner folded in the same way. The magic of it was that the cloche had no visible way to open it, but Martin had attached a small metal disc under the cloche that would enable the servers to lift it with a small magnet held in their hand. When he showed Matt and I how it worked, we looked at each other and smiled. It was beautiful, exactly the X factor we needed for our presentation of the dishes.

There were multiple steps to the process—tracing the pattern, cutting the paper, using a tool to press the pattern through, and then painstakingly folding each individual crease. If you were good, you could fold a quality cloche in an hour, not including tracing, cutting, and pressing the pattern. We needed sixty pieces—thirty tops and thirty bottoms—which would require more than a hundred hours of work.

Tehani, Mimi, Danny, Vinny, and Chance began the task of processing the cloches, chatting and playing music, trying not to focus on the daunting number that needed to be completed.

Meanwhile, Martin and Lukas had turned the large kitchen table into a workshop, with vice grips, hacksaws, glue, clamps, and various tools scattered around the centerpiece they were working to assemble. We began talking through all of the processes that were left to finish and it became clear that we should push our final practice run back until Saturday if we wanted to use the platter in its finished state.

Because of the additional time we had spent on tools and molds, we still had unresolved questions about how the chickens and lobsters would be displayed on the platter. We would have to work through this over the coming days to ensure the final approach was tested and proven.

While we were discussing Martin's proposed solutions, the first cloches began to come off the assembly

Team meeting in the main house kitchen, Chaponost, France.

line. Martin examined a few of them, turning them over in his hands. It was immediately evident that he was not pleased. The cloche team was not performing to Martin's standard and he was not happy about it.

After flipping a cloche over several times and closely examining the creases and folds, he walked quickly into the dining room. "These are not coming out right," said the normally mild-mannered designer. "Look at these creases, they are pressed too hard and you are marking the paper. These creases aren't on the right lines and it's throwing the whole piece off. Turn the music off, stop talking in here and focus."

Then he turned to Graham. "You need to go back over each of the steps again and supervise this more closely."

The room was quiet for the rest of the evening and the quality of the cloches slowly improved. I don't think anyone had found it amusing at the time, but we would later joke about the night when Martin had "gone chef" on everyone. Though our tools and ingredients may differ, the kitchen and the design studio are very similar disciplines and everyone quickly learned they require the same attention to detail, focus, and tenacity to deliver high-level results.

In order to keep progress moving on all fronts, the day before our final practice we divided up the team. Matt and his group finalized the equipment and food in the kitchen, Mimi and Tehani became the full-time cloche team, Lukas and Graham worked on finishing the platter, and Martin and I went shopping for additional tools and materials he needed.

FINAL CHALLENGES

The next morning, as Matt and Harrison went through their one-hour setup, I tried to get a pulse on where they were mentally. They hadn't done a run for a week and a half and they were also away from the comfort and familiarity of the kitchen back home. This would be the last chance to reinforce our con-

fidence before the final, and we all hoped to have a strong finish to our training.

We started the clock and just thirty minutes into the run it was apparent our hopes were in jeopardy. Harrison's commis, Nais, a young French apprentice we had arranged to help us, had cut her finger in the first five minutes and that had slowed Harrison considerably. Meanwhile, Matt had lost time butchering the Bresse chickens because the skin is much thicker than the chickens we had used back home (we had been unable to get Bresse chickens for practice in the United States because they are illegal to import), and cleaning them had taken longer. We were already ten minutes behind at the first-hour mark.

Nais was visibly rattled by her finger cut, so I leaned over to Harrison and said, "Your commis is super nervous. You need to calm her down, encourage her and tell her we are back on track and she is doing a great job. Make her part of the team." He nodded and his ensuing pep talk brought a smile to her face and a noticeable calming to her movements.

While Harrison and Nais seemed to regain their footing, Matt struggled to recover after falling behind. Whether it was the new environment, a lack of sleep, the pressure of this final run, or a combination of all three, it was evident he wasn't at his best.

"He hasn't been getting enough rest," Robert said as he leaned over to look at the clock in front of me. "You can see it in his response to everything that goes wrong. He's tired and it is having an effect today. We need to talk to him about this."

I had made the same observation and also began to question whether our training had been too easy in our replica kitchen. They had never done a full run in a different kitchen and this change of space and equipment seemed to hurt more than I had expected.

They worked hard to make the timing for the vegan service, barely making the cut-off, but several things had to be pushed back for the meat platter service. Despite their best efforts, the platter was several minutes late when the clock stopped and though no one said it aloud, everyone had the same thought—this wasn't the run we were hoping for.

TENSION

The next day, Sunday, was quiet. No one was eager to discuss the events of the previous day and it was clear everyone was tired from the nonstop pace of the week. We sat down after a late breakfast and began talking through the run from the previous day.

"Matt, I know you don't want to hear it from any of us and I know you already know what you need to change, but the one thing you have to prioritize is rest," Robert began. "I've watched you do over a dozen runs and it is clear to all of us that your lack of sleep coupled with the added stress of this week had a significant effect yesterday."

I offered my own thoughts but, sensing that adding more would only exacerbate Matt's own frustrations, I switched to the tangible problems in front of us.

"The key thing right now is to resolve how the lobsters are going to sit on the platter," I said. "The chicken glaze and final attachment we can figure out more quickly but the lobsters are still an open question and this is a big concern. Tomorrow everything begins with our first official meetings and the market selection, so we have to push for a solution today."

Despite my inclination to dive in and solve the problems myself, the best thing I could do was let Matt lay out how he wanted to plan the next few days. At this point, we either had it or we didn't and Matt and Harrison needed to own the final approach. Will and I reviewed the final changes and adjustments, walking through the run sheet step by step to make sure the equipment and food were adjusted accordingly.

That night was our team send-off dinner, the same dinner that had inspired me in 2013 when I watched Richard Rosendale compete. We arrived at Le Comptoir de l'Est, one of Paul Bocuse's bistros, to a festive and almost boisterous atmosphere, a sharp contrast to the tension we had all been feeling since Saturday.

Peters and Keller shop the official market.

I smiled as a generous portion of *poulet aux écrevisses* was placed on the table—I would have a chance to taste this dish in Lyon after all. While we ate I couldn't help but take in the celebratory atmosphere around me and compare it to our quiet and reserved send-off dinner two years prior. This new sense of expectation and excitement was a welcome boost to our spirits and for a brief moment we enjoyed a reprieve from the stress we were all facing.

EXPECTATIONS

The next morning, after making final decisions with Martin on the centerpiece, we arrived at the official hotel where the teams were gathering to register and board the bus to the expo. The lobby slowly began to fill and we greeted the other teams, including the Norwegian contingent I had become friends with from my visit the previous year.

But something was different. We caught the glances, stares, and occasional nods from the other teams, and I realized that this year everyone was watching us as we waited. Two years ago it had been Tommy Myllymäki and the Swedish team that had drawn all the attention—including my own—because he had been the clear favorite to win.

Though I knew our chances to win this year were strong, never before had I considered us to be the favorites. But as the day progressed, many of the team presidents, coaches, and even candidates congratulated me on our 2015 performance, expressing high expectations for what we would do next.

After receiving our official jackets, we were ready to go into the market and "shop" for the ingredients we would use for the vegan dish. Knowing in advance which products would be available at that time of year, we had been able to make our shopping list short and concise. We had thirty minutes to make our selections, and after sending the market assistant back several times to search for the perfect mushrooms, we double-checked the lists, then sealed our box until the day of the competition. Everything had gone according to plan and there were no surprises. This first hurdle had been cleared effortlessly.

After the second wave of teams chose their market ingredients, we paraded back across the food show floor and regrouped in the meeting room adjacent to the main competition hall. One of the committee members went through the load-in process for the teams and after answering a few questions said, "OK, all Day Two teams can leave now. Make sure you are here by 4 P.M. tomorrow afternoon for the official photo."

It was 7:30 P.M. and we were finished. I turned to Matt and Harrison and joked, "Aren't you glad you don't have to load into your kitchen tonight? Last year we didn't leave here until 10:30. You'd better make it count!"

I felt for the teams that had to set up their kitchens that night and return early the following morning to compete. It was a huge advantage for us to compete on Day Two and I was thankful as we left the expo and headed to dinner. We still had a whole day to regroup and organize, finalize the platter, and then load in our kitchen tomorrow night.

After dinner I returned to the house to find the Crucial Detail team still hard at work. Over the weekend, when Graham's bag had finally arrived, a day late, we discovered TSA had confiscated all of the electronics that were needed to power the heating elements in the platter. Without these the heating elements would be useless and the corn custard and carrot garnishes would have no way to stay warm while the platter was presented.

With the stores closed on Sundays, Martin had been forced to wait until Monday morning to run to different electronics stores all over Lyon to find the missing parts. I hadn't realized the extent of the setback until I walked in to see Martin, noticeably exhausted from weeks of nonstop work, poring over

MENT'OR

PHILIP TESSIER

T
HE BOCUSE D'OR isn't much different than the World Cup. Both contests have the usual powerhouses, the favorites. They also have dark horses: the same countries year after year with the occasional surprise coming close to the mark but not quite hitting it.

The United States had never been any of those. We were the faithful contender, always there, always with potential but never breaking through to the top five. Until now.

Today Bocuse d'Or USA is firmly built on nearly a decade of steady learning, hard work, and persistence; the fruit of the Ment'or foundation and the vision of Chefs Keller, Boulud, and Bocuse. Because of their leadership, we've recognized what it takes to win—total commitment, diverse resources, and layers of support.

We have arrived in a different era, an era in which American chefs no longer have to support themselves, raise their own funds, or find time to train between shifts. No longer do we start over year after year, picking up the pieces from the previous candidate. Additionally, we have the Young Chef & Commis competitions, a grant program connecting young chefs to opportunity, and new initiatives that continue to bring us forward.

My opportunity to compete in the Bocuse d'Or while being mentored by some of the best chefs in America was a once in a lifetime opportunity and the pinnacle of what Ment'or stands for—inspiring culinary excellence in young chefs across the country. Without the inspiration, mentorship, and constant support of these legendary chefs, none of this would have been possible. Thank you for the opportunities you have made possible for each of us.

Now, because of this new foundation, the winds have changed at the Bocuse d'Or. There is a new powerhouse. A new favorite. And history has been changed forever.

THE MENT'OR TEAM
2015-2017

THOMAS KELLER, *President*

JÉRÔME BOCUSE, *Vice President*

DANIEL BOULUD, *Chairman*

YOUNG YUN, *Executive Director*

GAVIN KAYSEN, *Vice President, Team USA*

JAIMIE CHEW, *Director of Events and Communications*

MONICA BHAMBHANI, *Team Manager (2015)*

TEHANI LEVIN, *Team Manager (2017)*

PHILIP TESSIER, *Head Coach*

a blank power board that he had just begun to solder together. Hunched over under the bright glow of the desk lamp, he was soldering the board from scratch, section by section, like it was 1985.

"It looks like you are going to be up late tonight," I said. "Are you really going to do that by hand?"

Martin looked up with a tired smile and stated the obvious, "We don't have a choice. We have to get it done."

I used to be surprised at the number of disciplines Martin was proficient in. Now it was just normal. Across the room Graham and Lukas were polishing the platter and finishing the last heating element connections for the new electronics. We were incredibly fortunate to have such a dedicated and talented team that would go to such extraordinary lengths for us. There was little anyone could do to help so I said thank you to each of them and then wished them a good night, knowing they would most likely be still awake and working in the morning.

POLE POSITION

We entered the competition hall early Tuesday morning to the sound of beating drums, cowbells, and air horns already in full swing. Most of the Day One teams had already begun cooking and were working at top speed through their first projects, with kitchen judges and committee members hovering around their boxes. For the first few hours I observed the strongest teams and watched them while I continued to work the floor to glean information about how service was being approached, the order of the judges, and any other bits of information that would help us when it was our at bat.

Throughout the morning I was approached and congratulated by chefs from the revered group who make up the Bocuse d'Or official committee. This was the first time we had met since I had stepped off the podium two years ago and, as we conversed in French, it became apparent that America had earned a great deal of respect in their eyes. I thanked them for their kind words and assured them that we were back to impress once again.

As the morning wore on, the floor was cleared to make way for the judge's tables. Sweden was in Box 1 and soon their vegan dish was paraded across the floor with dramatic fanfare and a roar from their fans. For the next two hours, as the crowd grew louder, I watched as each plate and platter was presented, straining to see if any of the presentations were as good or better than ours.

I still had yet to see any presentations that I felt were better than ours, but the final kitchens of the day were Norway and Hungary. These had been the two to watch and I waited with anticipation as the time for their presentations neared.

Norway delivered on the high expectations with a vegan dish that was clean, elegant, and traditional. It was certainly the best presentation of the day. Then came Hungary's. It was beautiful, too. With a glass cloche covering a circle of delicate garnishes surrounding a ring of sauce neatly contained in the center, this was definitely the most technical presentation. If the flavor matched the appearance, it would probably be the best.

I waited as Norway's and Hungary's meat platters were presented and was surprised to see that they were very traditional. I had expected that with our avant-garde presentation two years earlier, more of the platters would be "out of the box" and push the boundaries more than they had in the past.

As Day One came to a close, I couldn't help but think: We have a real shot at this. No one had been clearly impressive and I hadn't seen anything that reminded me of France's Versailles platter back in 2013, which had been so dramatic the normally raucous crowd had gone silent. The door was wide open; all we had to do was walk through it.

RELAIS DE PUISSANCE

MARTIN KASTNER | CRUCIAL DETAIL

ARRIVED ON THURSDAY. All that was left to finish the centerpiece was to assemble the centerpiece, wire the electronics, hook up the heating elements, attach magnet mounts for the chicken hubcaps, and finish the lobster hooks. This in four and a half days with plenty of hands on board to pitch in. We should be able to get it all done and actually get some sleep before the competition. Easy breezy.

Let's divvy up the work. Lukas will work on the centerpiece, I will work on the electronics, Graham will work on the heating elements. Most of the crucial electronics we'd need were transported in Graham's checked bag.

Ehmm . . . what's that? The bag never got delivered. But it should be here soon. OK, no worries.

The team's house was amazing. Large windows glowing into the night, lovely view of the city glittering below, big hearth with a crackling fire. Robert was stirring a big pot of lentils on the open fire, filling the house with a fantastic scent. Cozy with a capital C. Maybe too cozy? Too warm, too comfortable, too nice after the insane intensity of the past few weeks in Chicago. We need more friction. This doesn't feel right.

Late on Friday, Graham's bag arrives. I get to the house after working on lobster hooks and the centerpiece. Alright, let's hook up the electronics before tomorrow's final test run.

"We don't have the electronics."

What do you mean we don't have the electronics?

"TSA took them out of my bag."

All of them?

"All of them."

But NiMH batteries are not prohibited and all the components of the relay board were individually bagged so they would not look dangerous!

"I know. TSA left a note in the bag, that's all."

It's Friday night! We're in France. The platter has to be delivered on Tuesday. Specialty electronics shops won't be open on the weekend. We don't have time to order it from anywhere.

I found a shop that sold a relay board that I could modify for our purposes. Merci, Google! According to the website it's in stock. Great. Not open on the weekend. Of course.

Over the next two and a half days we finished various elements of the platter. Monday afternoon we headed to the store. The crew dropped me off on a busy street in front of what turned out to be a small hobby shop. It reminded me so much of the hobby shops we grew up with in the Czech Republic, a narrow shop on the main street, packed to the ceiling with bits and pieces of electricity-powered imagination fodder.

Not in stock here? Wait five days? This needs to be finished tonight! Do you have something similar here? Anything? My rusty French was not making this any easier. The clerk replied, "We have an eight-channel relay kit. Much bigger. Wait for the other one, it's cheaper." No, I'll take this one. And four meters of two-conductor wire, please.

I ripped off the plastic shrink wrap and opened the box. He said it was a kit. The box said it was a kit. I don't know what I was expecting. It was a kit. I was looking at a printed circuit and over a hundred loose components on the side. Diodes, resistors, capacitors, transistors, relays, jump wires, connectors. Oh great . . . I haven't soldered a kit since I was twelve in the '80s . . . I open the instructions. Assembly Tip No. 1: "Make sure the skill level matches your experience, to avoid disappointments."

Perfect. I knew it had been too cozy, too comfortable, too nice so far. It finally started to feel about right.

A section of the 2017 platter.

CHAPTER NINE

THE FINAL BATTLE

"It always seems impossible until it's done."

—NELSON MANDELA

THE VAN WAS QUIET as we made our way to the exposition hall through the early morning darkness. The only sound was the voice of Arnold Schwarzenegger coming through the stereo: "You've got to have a vision. Know where you are going," he said in his familiar accent. Harrison had played this motivational talk before every run for the last three months and we all knew every line by heart. It was perfect for the moment, both motivating and humorous as we recited our favorite bits in our own Arnold accents.

We arrived at the expo, unloaded the few items that we hadn't loaded in the night before and went to wait in the meeting room until it was our turn to start. I was thankful for the full American breakfast of bacon and eggs we had enjoyed back at the house, a stark contrast to the day-old sandwich I had hurriedly eaten in the back of the SUV two years before. After all the challenges of the past week, I felt we had recovered well and Matt and Harrison were healthy, rested, and ready.

Ten minutes before our start time, we headed to the staging area and met Yo-Che, the young Taiwanese culinary student the competition had assigned to be our second commis. "You can call me Yoo," he said with a smile. "I think we'll be able to remember that name," Harrison joked as we welcomed him to the team, trying to make him feel as comfortable as we could in the few short minutes before we began. Moments later a committee member called, "U-S-A." We were up.

OUT OF THE GATE

As soon as we entered our kitchen, competition mode set in and Matt and Harrison quickly went about their prep lists while I selected the proteins, organized the market vegetables, and set up the coach's counter with menus, run lists, and the two iPads running over fifty timers I would keep track of throughout the competition.

Our goal was to set up the kitchen in the first thirty minutes. That way we'd be ready when the kitchen judges came in to check through our equipment and food to make sure we were following the rules. Matt set up quickly and began cleaning the greens and blossoms from the market basket, but Harrison was struggling to get started. Yoo seemed to have good skills in the kitchen but the language barrier was a clear challenge and Harrison had to physically show him every step he needed him to do.

The judges came through and, after thorough examination, signed off on our kitchen. I breathed a sigh of relief as they departed without incident, recalling the ordeal I had been through when they had rejected our foie gras two years prior. The official timekeeper approached our box and called out, "Three minutes until you start." Matt checked in on Harrison and took over a few small projects to help him get organized. They both seemed confident and rested.

I looked at Matt and Harrison. "This is it, it's our show now. Let's make this our best run ever." We gave each other a fist bump and the clock started. Calls of "Let's go Harry!," "U-S-A!," and others came from behind me as the support team cheered them on. The timekeeper counted down: "Five, four, three, two, one . . . *bonne chance!*"

All week we had preached the importance of getting a strong start and putting "time in the bank" as Robert called it. If we could finish the first hour ahead, I was fully confident we would have no trouble putting in a gold medal run. Despite Harrison's challenges setting up, he seemed like he was getting back on track, and once Yoo was at the cutting board it appeared he would be okay.

Matt began racing through his first projects. The practice with the Bresse chickens he had put in over the past few days paid off as he quickly began to gain time. If Matt had a few extra minutes at the end and Harrison needed a push, he could get him back on track.

Harrison pulled his pretzel tuiles out of the oven and began to unmold them with Yoo working furiously next to him. I set a few timers for Matt as I watched the first sauces on the stove. But when I looked at Harrison's table, my heart sank. Half of the cones on which the tuiles were baked had cracked pieces of pastry

stuck to them. What was going on? He had never had trouble unmolding these during practice.

Quickly, Harrison cleaned off the metal cones, sprayed them again and pulled out the extra dough he had cut in case this happened. He began to wrap new tuiles, only to find the pre-made dough had already begun to dry out. Before I knew it, he was back to the very beginning of the project, re-rolling dough and starting over completely. This was not good.

At the end of the first hour, Harrison was twenty minutes behind, with Yoo still struggling to understand what he needed. The only reassuring factor was Matt was ten minutes ahead and calmly pushing through each of his tasks. I leaned over to him and said, "Harrison is in trouble, he's lost half his tuiles and is remaking them. We're going to have to take some things from his list and help him out. Get the soubise going for him and when you're ready, we can take on the lobster claws up here as well."

"No problem," Matt nodded as he added morels to the chicken jus. Over the next hour we slowly began to regain the time, and by the end of the third hour Harrison was only four minutes behind. I was thoroughly impressed with the poise he had shown despite everything that had gone wrong. The look in his eye showed his determination to succeed—nothing was going to go down on his watch. This mental toughness was a dramatic departure from the meltdown just two weeks prior.

All morning long the crowd of committee members and judges surrounding us had swelled as they expectantly observed the team. They wanted to be impressed today and were eager to see if we could deliver. All around me chefs were taking pictures and videos of the tools and molds as Matt went through the various steps. The commentary and questions came nonstop as they thumbed through the photos of the food in our menu books.

Two years ago no one had even cast a glance our way until they began to see our food come together in the kitchen. After twenty-eight years of missing the podium, we hadn't even been on the radar. Here we were, just two years later and it seemed the clear expectation was that America would contend for the gold.

"This is it," I thought to myself as I watched Matt and Harrison going through their moves. "This is the gold medal run." But we still had an hour and a half before vegan service and though we were nearly on time now, anything could happen. And it did.

A STICKY SITUATION

Matt was in the middle of the most crucial part of the run, where timing was everything and each task had to happen exactly as planned. But Harrison's mushrooms had gone into the oven to steam ten minutes later than usual and that had created a domino effect, pushing back the lobsters and potato shells Matt needed the oven for next.

We shifted the list around to accommodate the change and Matt was working back and forth between finishing the red wine sauce and the asparagus glaze as the lobsters finished steaming. His next task was to bake the potato shells. This was normally a simple step: invert the metal press holding the partially dehydrated potato shell into small metal cups containing clarified butter. Once in the butter, the potato shells were baked until crisp. Then they were unmolded before being finished a second time in the oven. But it was crucial that they go into the oven immediately after being placed in the butter. We had painfully discovered that if they sat before baking, the potato cups would soften and stick like glue to the metal press.

I called out to Harrison the next projects he needed Yoo to complete and turned back to see that Matt had already placed the potatoes into the butter.

INSPIRING EXCELLENCE

YOUNG YUN

THE YEAR 2013 feels like it was just yesterday. I sat surrounded by Chefs Boulud, Keller, and Bocuse, our lawyer Joel Buchman, Treasurer Marcel Doron, and then Director of Competitions, Monica Bhambhani. The highlight of the discussion: "expanding our mission" and "rebranding."

Our mission has always focused on building a strong pipeline of talent in the United States to compete in the Bocuse d'Or. We wanted to expand beyond Team USA and develop programs to inspire and educate more young chefs in America. But first we needed a new name. After several brainstorming sessions, a lightbulb went off: What do our Chef Founders and Culinary Council ultimately represent? The answer was "mentorship." Mentors play a critical role in the kitchen, which will continue for generations to come.

In 2014, Ment'or was born and it was time to compose our team. A former colleague, Tehani Levin, jumped in to oversee our grant and Young Chef Programs. Next Julia Russell, Sean Weissbart, and chef Gavin Kaysen joined the Board, and with the addition of Jaimie Chew, who would lead Communications and Events, our vision was coming alive.

As Ment'or, we have touched the lives of more than one hundred young chefs around the country and awarded almost one million dollars in educational opportunities. Many have fulfilled their dream to work in some of the most renowned kitchens in the United States and around the world. Others had the opportunity to experience what it means to train for the Bocuse d'Or and now truly understand the sacrifice, dedication, and commitment required for Team USA to make it onto the podium.

We continue to grow but will always remember what brought us together. We are a community . . . we are proud of our culinary history . . . we are all Team USA. Hearing "United States" announced at the 2015 and 2017 Bocuse d'Or Competitions is forever memorialized in our hearts and minds. We hope this continues to inspire the next generation of great American chefs and we look forward to sharing our journey with you.

I immediately glanced at the oven, but it was still a few minutes away from switching over completely from steam to dry. I hoped the wait wouldn't be too long. As soon as the oven was ready, Matt put the potatoes in and I started the ten-minute timer for the first bake.

He returned to the stove and finished the lobster sauce and crisped quinoa, the last few tasks before rolling the asparagus. The timer went off for the potato shells. Matt pulled them from the oven and pulled the first one to un-mold. He pushed at the edges with his tweezers to release it from the metal press. Nothing. He turned it in his hand to loosen it from the other side. Still nothing.

He looked across at me and stated matter of factly, "They're stuck." We looked at each other, each hoping the other would have an answer to how we could fix this. We had never been able to get them off once they had stuck.

"Maybe we can soften the potato somehow so it will release," I offered. He nodded in agreement and after removing the butter, started pouring water into the molds. As he filled them I realized that this would only make the shells soggy and they would tear when we tried to push them off.

"Matt, what if we tried them in butter first," I said. "Maybe they will soften enough with just the butter."

He agreed and poured the water out, replacing it with fresh clarified butter. We replaced the potatoes in the butter and went back to the list. There was no time to lose waiting around to see if this would work. At this point, Matt had many other things to worry about. We set a timer and he moved into assembling the asparagus and mushroom garnish.

Ten minutes later he went back to the molds to test our theory. Nothing. They were just as stuck as they had been when we had first pulled them out. Only now we had cracked a few in our effort to get them off.

Matt looked up and asked, "What should we do?" We racked our brains for a way to get these things off. Time was ticking and Matt still had a long list of tasks to complete.

Suddenly a thought crossed my mind. "Let's put them in the steamer." This would be gentler than soaking them in water. It just might work. Within a few minutes the potato shells were in the steamer. We were losing precious time, not to mention that we still had to un-mold, refry, and trim the shells before vegan service, which was looming in front of us. But the worst thought was the big "what if?" What if they didn't come off the presses? We would be missing one of our central garnishes.

I set a five-minute timer for the potatoes and then shot off a text to my friend Nate, my parents and my wife, "Pray these potatoes come off . . . they are sticking!" Matt returned to the asparagus project— our cut-off to start service only twenty minutes away.

Matt periodically checked the shells. I set the timer first for ten more minutes, then fifteen minutes, then twenty. Finally, he was able to pop one of the shells off the molds. Carefully he removed three or four more before we had to set them aside and reset to serve the vegan plate. The reassurance that we would be able to salvage the potato shells was balanced by the realization of how much time we had lost. We had counted on Matt helping to get Harrison back on track before service, but now they were both ten minutes behind on the garnishes for the meat platter.

Setting that reality aside for the moment, we turned our focus to the vegan course. With the eighteen steps it took to plate the dish, we could not afford to start service a moment late. Fortunately, we had carefully planned where each finished element of the dish was placed and we were able to quickly transition into service despite the challenges both Matt and Harrison were facing.

Service for the vegan dish went incredibly smoothly and the plates were nearly perfect. As they neared completion, I searched desperately for the head server. I had carefully explained to him the complex layering of the cloches, carrying of the magnets, and lifting of the lids. But he was nowhere to be found.

I had flashbacks to two years earlier when several of the servers had poured my mushroom consommé all over my trout dish instead of into the small glasses we had provided. It had been a costly mistake that had certainly affected our final score. I was determined nothing was going to fail this time, and after a momentary scramble at the pass to get the committee and servers to understand the process, the vegan plates were finished.

LASER FOCUS

The next thirty-five minutes were a total blur. Matt and Harrison worked at top speed but with incredible precision. All of those practice runs clearly paid off. Despite the challenges we had faced, they exuded a calm sense of confidence and focus.

We had planned for me to guide the second commis through the foie gras garnish. Harrison brought everything up to the front where I could instruct him.

"Okay, Yoo," I said. "Put one truffle down in the center. No, the center. Yes, there, just like that. Now repeat that with the rest. Grab the black-eyed peas, three per. With a spoon, lay them on the side. No, a spoon, not the tweezers. Quickly but carefully. Yes, yes, now go." I instructed him as best I could without being able to physically touch anything.

By this time, Harrison was nearly finished with the carrot garnishes and Matt was working to finish the lobster and chicken, which had to go on the platter first.

Matt finished the lobsters and went to hook them on the platter at the base of the centerpiece. He set

the first two on and immediately they came loose. He switched to two different ones and they didn't stay either. The heating of the shells in the oven had caused them to firm up and curl, and now they weren't fitting on together.

Had we been on time, we would have had a few minutes to trim and adjust the shells. But the harsh reality was that we couldn't lose a single second. He set them on the center of the platter as close to the centerpiece as he could and went back to grab the chickens.

Harrison set Yoo to finishing the carrot garnish with the greens and began bringing the foie gras and pea garnishes to the platter. Matt set the chickens in place and then turned his attention to the potatoes. With all the activity in front of me, I couldn't tell if they were all coming off but I hoped desperately that they were.

Harrison was nearly finished with the pea garnishes and about to place the carrots on the platter when one of the pea garnishes fell over and scattered crumbs all over. He reacted immediately by scooping up the crumbs with a bowl scraper and wiping the platter with a polishing cloth. Fortunately there were no smudge marks when he was finished. While he plated the carrots, Yoo began to bring finished potato bases to the platter one at a time as Matt placed the truffle slices on them at breakneck pace.

The timekeeper had already come to our box and I called out to Matt and Harrison, "Ninety seconds guys. Ninety seconds!" The noise was deafening and we could hear the encouraging cheers of the more than three hundred American supporters who had been cheering us on all day.

"Thirty seconds!" I yelled across as Matt raced to finish the last two potatoes and Harrison laid the glass domes on top of each one. We were short only one potato shell and Matt had fried one of the

Final assembly of the pea crisp.

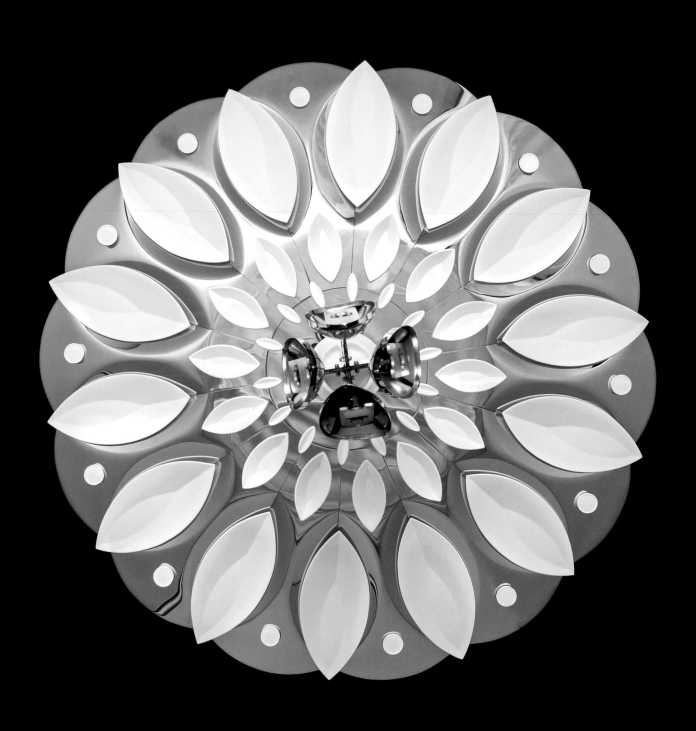

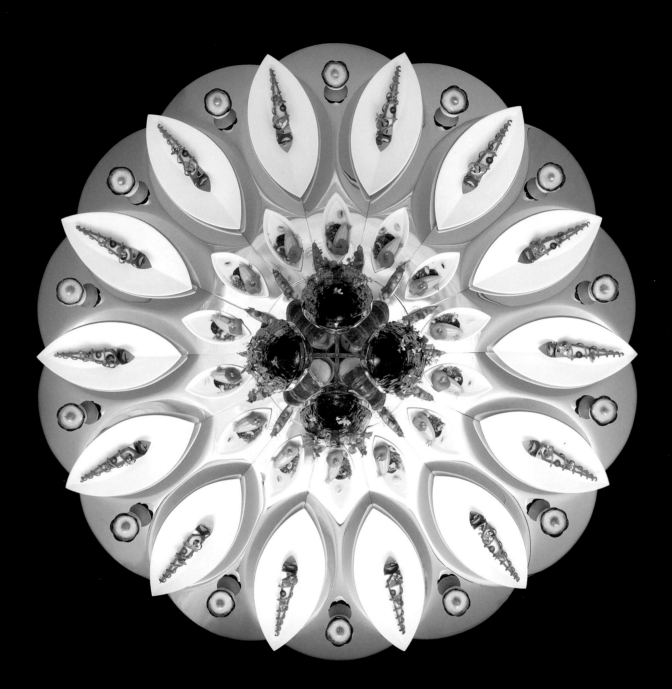

A culinary kaleidoscope: Team USA's 2017 meat platter.

Above: *Poulet de Bresse* and American lobsters, the centerpiece. | Opposite: Team USA's 2017 meat plate.

Above: The vellum cloche reveal. | Opposite: Team USA's 2017 vegan plate.

A FTER ALL THE PRACTICE, the actual competition was in a way kind of anticlimactic. I even slept well the night before. At that point we knew exactly what we were going to do. There had been some last-minute changes, but nothing major. And I was exhausted from the week—the travel, the practice, the time change. I went to bed early and got a good six or seven hours without any issue and woke up excited to go.

I remember watching the woman who was giving us the countdown to begin. All of the fans were already surrounding us with loud cheers of encouragement. Right before she began the final countdown there was one last fist bump between the team to let each other know we were ready to go.

To see the crowd of people around us, the lights and the actual competition finally starting, it was everything I thought it would be. But once the clock starts ticking and you start cooking, everything else is blocked out and you're just doing your thing. I never looked up. It was just easier to look down, concentrate on the food, look at the kitchen behind you. Because of our countless practices, it just felt like we were at home; it felt like just any other day. We simply executed what we knew. That's where all that practice and training paid off.

IN THE ZONE

MATHEW PETERS

potato glasses to serve as a base for the last one. Harrison quickly placed the last dome and with only ten seconds to go, the platter was lifted across the counter and it walked.

Though the platter was out the battle wasn't over yet. They still had the task of breaking down the platter onto individual plates for the judges at the carving table positioned at the end of the judging tables. With the timing between platters being only ten minutes, it would be a race to dismantle, portion, and plate the fourteen plates needed in the eight minutes we had trained for.

We knew we had pushed the boundaries of time for the platter to walk and that meant time at the carving table would already be cut short when they arrived. Matt and Harrison quickly cleaned down the counters, reset their aprons, grabbed the equipment they needed, and headed to the table where the

platter would be placed. They walked across the judging floor and disappeared into a sea of toques across the room. I could only stand there and wait (the rules stated the coach wasn't allowed at the plating table), trying to process what had just happened and how things would be perceived by the judges.

Harrison returned first, visibly frustrated, "Chef, you have no idea what just happened over there. They only gave us four minutes. I want to kill myself right now."

When Matt returned, it was clear Harrison had not exaggerated. He looked defeated, shaking his head as he went about cleaning. I noticed the tip of the chicken with the lobster mousse still sitting on the cutting board, evidence of the lack of time they'd had at the table. There was a somber mood as Will and the crew appeared at the back of the kitchen to assist in returning everything to the truck.

Peters places the *Poulet de Bresse* on the meat platter under the watchful eye of the kitchen jury.

We had just trained for over a year to execute extraordinary, perfect food, but despite all that hard work there had been significant stumbles at the end. As we regrouped out in the staging area, I reassured Matt and Harrison. "Only we know exactly how things were supposed to go. From the judge's perspective, they saw extraordinary technique and a breathtaking platter. I don't know where we will place, but we still have a strong chance."

Despite our challenges, I was sure we were on the podium—the vegan dish had been flawless and I was positive we had scored the highest for it. I also knew the meat dish, despite our challenges, *tasted* amazing, and if the judges couldn't see the flaws, which were all we could see, we still had a chance at gold.

SUSPENSE

Over the next few hours as we waited for the awards ceremony, the team slowly rebounded and began recovering their equilibrium. The results were out of our hands now and all we could do was hope and wait to hear the final verdict. I was determined to enjoy the moment, and tried to get Harrison back to a positive place.

"Harrison, no matter what the results are, just think—here you are at the age of only twenty-one, and you're considering the possibility of mounting the podium at the Bocuse d'Or. That was an unachievable dream four years ago, now it's almost a reality."

I could see it sink in and within a few minutes he seemed once again at ease with himself. Chef Keller added to the moment, "We stand on the backs of everyone who's come before us. Gavin, Tim, James, Richard, and Phil all paved the way for us to get here." We nodded in unison and knew that all the support, resources, and knowledge we had throughout the training year were only possible because of the dedication and efforts of a long line of chefs and allies.

We entered the competition floor with Harrison leading the procession, waving the flag with passion and vigor. Skylar would have been proud. Standing close together, we waited as the presentations of past Bocuse d'Or winners, sponsor recognitions, and various awards dragged on for what seemed an eternity. Finally, we arrived at the awards for best meat platter and best vegan dish, known to be the consolation prizes for fifth and fourth places—these were not awards we wanted to win. This was it, the countdown to the final verdict.

My heartbeat quickened and I listened intently, unable to see the announcer, as the awards were called—France for best vegan dish, Hungary for best meat platter. I breathed a sigh of relief. At a minimum, we should be on the podium. A shuffle of more announcers and sponsors again delayed the announcement of the bronze, but there was a telltale hint who was about to take it. The announcer asked for the Icelandic supporters to do their traditional Viking "thunder clap" to count down to the reveal. It was riveting to watch the entire stadium follow their lead and clap to their beat until the final moment when Iceland was announced as winning bronze.

Silver and gold were all that remained, and in my mind there were only two countries that still had a chance—Norway and us, the same as two years before. First the silver. My heart raced. "Please don't call us, please don't call us!" I stood still, staring at the floor listening intently until at last the announcer paused before emphatically announcing, "Norway!"

"Yes!" I let out a cry as I turned to Matt. "This is happening. This is going to happen!"

As Norway mounted the podium and claimed the silver trophy, there was no question in my mind that this was our moment . . . or it would be a long way to fall. Still, nothing was certain until the words were spoken. Chef Keller, Matt, Harrison, and I put our

Chef Joël Robuchon (second from left) prepares to take a photo of Team USA's meat platter.

arms together as we waited through the endless procession of sponsors and thank yous before the announcement of the winner was made.

Standing there as the world waited, my thoughts filled with everything that had transpired to get us here—the blood, sweat, and tears of 2015, when we broke through to the podium for the first time; the slow building of the foundation for training the new team; and the long road and hours of work Matt and Harrison had put in to get to this moment. I felt myself choke up as the reality began to set in that we, Team USA, were on the cusp of winning the Bocuse d'Or.

Chef Keller had his hand on my shoulder and, sensing the emotion coursing through my body, began to massage it with a fatherly touch to calm me down. I was thankful for the delay in the announcement as I certainly would have broken down in tears had the award been called at that moment. I gathered my thoughts and felt a wave of pride and joy that we were about to be rewarded. It didn't even occur to me that we might not be the winners.

At long last the microphone was passed to Jérôme Bocuse to make the final announcement. He toyed with the envelope for a moment, looked out at the crowd and then in an emphatic voice called out, "UNITED STATES!!!"

The ensuing moments were a blur of emotion as we raced to the stage, embraced one another and made the last step of our long journey to the top of the podium. It was a beautiful step and one that I took slowly to cherish the moment. Joël Robuchon handed the golden trophy to us and together we lifted it over our heads to a roar of support and chants of "U-S-A" from our hundreds of supporters. As our national anthem rang out across the stadium, my heart filled with an incredible sense of pride as our golden dream had become a reality.

CELEBRATION

Our physical and emotional exhaustion was quickly replaced with a euphoria and adrenaline that would carry us through the night as our contingent of Americans gathered to celebrate this extraordinary achievement together. As night began to turn to morning, magnums of Dom Perignon were passed to and fro as we serenaded one another with "The Star Spangled Banner" at the top of our lungs.

In the midst of the celebration there was a moment when I looked across the room and saw Chef Keller standing there with tears streaming down his face as he held the trophy in his hand. I will never forget it. The reality had finally sunk in that his promise nine years earlier to his hero, Monsieur Paul, had at long last been fulfilled. As he gathered himself, with Chef Boulud's arm around his shoulder, a smile returned to his face, deep with gratitude and a new sense of freedom. He had been released from his own Bocuse d'Or prison.

After a few short hours of sleep, we braved the cold and made our way to Paul Bocuse's restaurant where the winners gathered for our final celebration together. Though I had experienced the winners' breakfast and engraving ceremony two years before, the moment was no less magical as I watched Matt's name, next to the letters U-S-A, being laid into the walkway in front of Paul Bocuse's restaurant.

Together we had made history and with each turn of the screw tightening the plaque to the walkway, the finality of it became more real. The impossible had been achieved and we, the United States of America, were now the new standard bearers at the Bocuse d'Or.

Top: Turone waves the flag for Team USA. | Bottom: Tessier, Peters, and Keller celebrate the gold-medal win.

Team USA | June 2015–January 2017

THE JOURNEY TIMELINE

JAN	FEB	MAR	APR	MAY	JUN	JUL	AUG	SEP	OCT	NOV	DEC
					Mathew Peters asks Philip Tessier to meet and discuss Bocuse d'Or application		Skylar Stover and Harrison Turone compete in Young Chef & Commis Competition	Four US candidates selected; Tessier travels to NYC to meet and begin training	Visit to Norway's national selection	Tessier visits all four US candidates to advise teams	US selection in Las Vegas; Peters and Turone selected

2015

JAN	FEB	MAR	APR	MAY	JUN	JUL	AUG	SEP	OCT	NOV	DEC
First team meeting in Yountville, CA with new team and coaches		First team session in Chicago; Peters and Turone move to Napa Valley	Will Mouchet joins the team	European finals in Budapest; visit Lyon to survey equipment and city	Young Chef competition; new winners join team later in the year		Mouchet and Turone start full-time training	Meat announced: poulet aux écrevisses; Impromptu visit to Martin Kastner's studio; Ment'or Board tasting in NYC	Vinny Loseto and Chance Schwab join the team; Lyon practice trip	Vegan theme announced	Last Ment'or Board tasting; Mimi Chen and Danny Garcia join the team

2016

13	15	19	24	25	25	26
Team USA supplies shipped to France	Depart for Lyon, France via New York City	Platter electronics confiscated by TSA	Final preparations	D–DAY!	GOLD!	
JAN	JAN	JAN	JAN	JAN	JAN	JAN

2017

Forever engraved in front of Paul Bocuse restaurant

(**19**) Months   (**1**) Team

Robuchon presents the gold trophy to Team USA.

Opposite: Team USA celebrates with Bocuse in his historic kitchen. From left to right: Keller, Tessier, Bocuse, Peters, and Turone.
Above: Team USA 2017, from left to right: Danny Garcia, Loseto, Schwab, Tessier, Mouchet, Peters, Turone, Keller, Mimi Chen, Martin Kastner, Lukas Kastner, Graham Burns, and Kaysen.

CHAPTER TEN

EPILOGUE

"Success is the sum of a lot of small things done correctly."

—FERNAND POINT

TWENTY YEARS AGO, when I peeled my first potato in a restaurant kitchen, the culinary land-scape in our country was in the midst of a revolution. I watched in admiration as names like Thomas Keller, Alice Waters, and many others became synonymous with a new, modern style of American cuisine. These chefs not only stepped beyond the foundation of classical cuisine, they built relationships with farmers, fishmongers, and purveyors, relying on the bounty of American ingredients to inspire their kitchens.

Over the past two decades, this fertile soil, tilled by these culinary pioneers, has been the foundation of a transformative growth of food and cooking in our country. The days of iceberg lettuce and hard tomatoes has long since been replaced by farmer's markets, slow-food movements, culinary festivals, and a long list of food entertainments. Chefs across America have built on this foundation and today a growing list of American restaurants boast three Michelin stars and rank among the best in the world.

Now, we have won the Bocuse d'Or.

We have, at long last, arrived at the top of the world stage and shown that the revolution of American cuisine isn't over; rather, it is beginning a new chapter. As the pursuit of culinary excellence continues across our great nation, it is exciting to see a growing spirit of collaboration forming as organizations like Ment'or connect young chefs to opportunity.

This is the essence of being a chef. Exploring, discovering, and pushing the boundaries of what is possible. And then, most crucially, inspiring those who work in our kitchens, giving them the tools they need to pursue their own dreams. It is not only a privilege to guide and train the generation following us, it is our responsibility to ensure its diversity and growth.

In 2016, inspired by her mentor, Daniel Boulud, eighteen-year-old Mimi Chen won the first Young Chef & Commis competition; and with it came the chance to work alongside the Bocuse d'Or team as they pursued gold. Fighting back tears of gratitude for the opportunity she had been given, she accepted her prize to join the team during training. This talented young chef became an integral part of the group and played a key role in our historic victory.

In the same way, Skylar Stover, Harrison Turone, Will Mouchet, Gregory Schesser, Chance Schwab, Vincenzo Loseto, and Danny Garcia were young chefs working their way through our kitchens, hoping to be discovered, trained, mentored, and empowered to succeed. Each of these young chefs won the chance through competitive cooking to step out of their kitchens and were rewarded with incredible opportunities. They were unaware of the path that awaited them and were thrust into a journey that would exceed their wildest dreams as they worked alongside America's best chefs in pursuit of glory.

The question we, the new generation of American chefs, have in front of us every day is: Who are the young chefs peeling potatoes in our kitchens? Who is going to continue our legacy? How do we identify them? How do we connect them to opportunity? If our goal is to make the next generation successful, and success is defined as preparation meeting opportunity, then we need to look beyond ourselves, beyond the borders of our own schools and restaurants,

and collaborate to provide the openings these young chefs need to succeed.

We are the new standard bearers at the Bocuse d'Or, and we have a unique platform to inspire those who come after us and build on the spirit of collaboration that made this possible. This is just the beginning and, as our extraordinary journey illustrates, it takes a nation to achieve success. Whether you are a food enthusiast, a young cook, an accomplished chef, or simply a patriotic American, there is a role to play in supporting Team USA and establishing our future legacy.

As Ment'or continues to grow, offering grant programs, young chefs' competitions, and new initiatives to unite America's best chefs, we have an unprecedented chance to inspire the generations coming after us. Together we can dream big, overcome the greatest odds, create opportunity, and continue the work that Thomas Keller, Alice Waters, and many others began so many years ago.

There has never been a more exciting time to be a chef in America.

Tessier and Peters on the Winners' Walk with the golden Bocuse d'Or trophy.

PERSEVERANCE

HARRISON TURONE

I REMEMBER THE MOMENT the reality of it all first hit me: we were in Lyon and we saw the platter being pulled out of its box for the first time. All the work we had put into the preparation, all the talk and the mockups. And then there's this big beautiful shiny platter Martin has been working on. Whoa! It's real! All we had to do was pull it together and compete.

Sure, there were stressful moments. Competing at such a high level, perfection is what you're striving for. There were definitely boiling points but in the end we always came back together as a team to do what we had to do. You train for two years, every day for two years, twelve- to eighteen-hour days, six days a week, for two years straight. You dream about being at a certain point. When it doesn't exactly go how you want, naturally you feel frustrated. You know you could have done better.

Even though we had our hiccups, we fought through them. I ended up breaking some of my tuiles. I was one short at the end. But at that point you have no choice but to put your head down, keep pushing forward, and get the job done.

In the end, I knew that we'd be on the podium but I didn't know exactly where. They called bronze and I was like, "Okay, where are we at?" Then they called silver and at that point I knew that we'd won the gold. When they actually announced it, I don't know if I can describe the feeling. It was my "Braveheart" moment right there. I was working for that moment for two years. I knew I could have done a lot better and I knew things hadn't gone the way I wanted them to but then at that moment, all I could think was, "Holy crap, we actually did this! We pushed through all of our obstacles and we're here on the podium and we won gold."

BOCUSE D'OR

THOMAS KELLER

SOMEONE ASKED ME one night what were the most significant things to happen in my professional life. Certainly, being the first American chef to win three Michelin stars. Receiving the French Légion d'Honneur. And winning the Bocuse d'Or. I have been blessed beyond belief in my career, but those are the three things that matter most, professionally.

In some ways, the Bocuse d'Or is the most important of all because it's not about just one person or one restaurant, it's about our country. Over the last forty years, the increase in the influence of American restaurants has been extraordinary. This was about recognizing that. It was about elevating the standards of our profession. It's not about me but about elevating the respect that the world has for our profession and what we do in the United States.

This was the last missing piece in that puzzle that has cemented our position on the world stage from a culinary point of view. There's nobody now who can argue that America isn't achieving on the same level as France or any other country. Our farmers, fishermen, foragers, gardeners, service staff, wine professionals, and chefs are some of the best in the world and this win just confirms that.

Up until the Bocuse d'Or, everything had been about my restaurants and my profession. This was about a national effort. It wasn't just Matt and Harrison and Phil and me. It expanded far beyond that—there were seventeen people who worked on that team for the last two years. And the win wasn't just for them. This was for everyone in America, whether they know it or not. It was magical, emotional, exhilarating, humbling, all those things.

Someone else said to me, "This is great for your legacy." No, this is about building a dynasty. And we'll continue to do just that, and put even better teams together. We've reached our goal. We've fulfilled our dream. Now we want to do it again.

RECIPES

THE JOURNEY
IN RECIPES

ONE OF THE SHORTCOMINGS of the Bocuse d'Or is that after the dishes are paraded in front of the audience, only the judges get to taste the food. All of the cheering fans are left to wonder, "Did it taste as good as it looked?"

It would be unfair to tell a story laden with the imagery of delicious food and not open the doors to access the food itself. The recipes in this section continue to tell the story of our Bocuse d'Or journey as we travel through the competition recipes themselves, the streets of Lyon, and into the kitchens of each of those who contributed their talents to this incredible adventure.

I invite you to experience the road to Lyon as we did, through the sounds, smells, and tastes of the kitchen. Enjoy the journey and bon appétit!

THOUGH WE COULD FILL a whole book with the recipes used to develop the final dishes from the 2015 and 2017 Bocuse d'Or competitions, the ones selected here are of the final garnishes Matt, Harrison, Skylar, and I developed. This collection of recipes has been left in their original format, just as we used them at the competition.

Though there is a high level of technical skill and detail in each recipe, and most require specialized molds or tools that Martin Kastner made for us, they also reveal the basic cooking methods that we made just a little more soigné.

Read through them, be inspired, and if you feel ambitious, attempt a recipe or two!

PHILIP TESSIER AND SKYLAR STOVER

INGREDIENTS

TROUT FOR THE PRESSÉ
16 brown trout fillets
   (700 to 750 grams total weight),
   skin removed
50 grams kosher salt
50 grams granulated sugar
Activa GS

TROUT MOUSSE
50 grams scallops
5 grams potato starch
4 grams kosher salt
1.6 grams polyphosphate
1 gram granulated sugar
30 grams egg whites

90 grams heavy cream
65 grams crème fraîche
2 drops Baume des Anges dill seed extract
1 preserved Meyer lemon rind, finely chopped
10 grams chopped dill or fennel fronds

SPECIALIZED EQUIPMENT
• 2 one-eighth tray silicone mousse molds
  by Crucial Detail

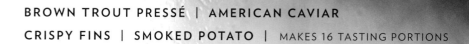

BROWN TROUT PRESSÉ | AMERICAN CAVIAR
CRISPY FINS | SMOKED POTATO | MAKES 16 TASTING PORTIONS

TROUT PRESSÉ

LEEK SOUBISE

15 grams unsalted butter

75 grams leek, white portion only

3 grams kosher salt

1 medium garlic clove, peeled

1 thyme sprig

½ bay leaf

66 grams dry white wine

200 grams heavy cream

SMOKED POMMES PURÉE

75 grams fingerling potatoes, peeled

1.5 grams kosher salt

20 grams unsalted butter,
   at room temperature

SPECIALIZED EQUIPMENT

• Immersion circulator with
   water bath

• 1 smoking gun

ONION MARMALADE

8 grams bacon fat

120 grams finely minced white onion

Kosher salt

30 grams glucose

30 grams champagne vinegar

EGG WHITE PEARLS

1 liter canola oil

60 grams egg white, blended and strained

5 grams Pickled Mustard Seeds
   (see Base Recipes, page 304)

Kosher salt

> > >

TROUT SKIN CIGARS AND CRISPY SKINS

200 grams water

4 grams kosher salt, plus additional
   for seasoning

10 pieces trout skin

10 trout tail fins

10 trout dorsal fins

50 grams egg whites

30 grams cornstarch

2 sheets feuille de brick

750 ml canola oil, for frying

Silver-gold luster mix

SPECIALIZED EQUIPMENT

• Sixteen ¾ x 6-inch metal tubes

ASSEMBLED TROUT PRESSÉ

One 9-inch loaf brioche, crust removed from
   the ends, as well as from one side

30 grams cornstarch

50 grams egg whites

Activa GS

FINISHING

30 grams clarified butter

Silver-gold luster mix

160 grams American Sterling caviar

16 pea shoots

50 grams smoked trout roe

16 begonia blossoms

SPECIALIZED EQUIPMENT

• 16 glass cloches

FOR THE PRESSÉ

1. Split the trout fillets just below the pin bones. The belly portions will be used for the pressé. The top fillets with the bones will be used for the mousse. (You will need 150 grams for the mousse. It is not necessary to remove any pin bones.)
2. Combine the salt and sugar for the cure in a small bowl. Spread half of the cure in an even layer on a parchment-lined sheet pan.
3. Lay the belly portions down evenly on the cure. Season the fish evenly with the remaining cure. Let sit at room temperature for 15 minutes.
4. Rinse the trout under cold running water. Spread on a lint-free towel and dry thoroughly.
5. Line up the cured belly portions on a one-eighth tray in an even layer, trimming the edges to fit the tray. This should be about 550 grams.
6. Lay a piece of plastic wrap large enough for the cured bellies on the work surface and dust lightly with Activa.
7. Lay all of the belly portions on the wrap with the Activa and dust the top with Activa.
8. In a sprayed, Cryovacked one-eighth tray, layer the trout fillets, overlapping each one halfway. (See Note)

9. Wrap tightly in plastic wrap.
10. Using a sausage pricker, prick a few holes around the edges.
11. Set another sprayed Cryovacked one-eighth tray on top and wrap tightly in plastic wrap.
12. Slide the whole pressé in another bag and Cryovac to remove excess air and to press the pressé evenly.
13. Transfer to the freezer for 1 hour until partially frozen.

NOTE: *For this application we put one-eighth trays in a bag and Cryovac them. This proves much easier than lining the trays with plastic wrap for ease of removal.*

FOR THE TROUT MOUSSE

1. Put 150 grams of the reserved trout fillets and the scallops into a chilled Robot Coupe bowl. Process on high for 1 minute.
2. Add the potato starch, salt, polyphosphate, and sugar, and process until evenly incorporated.
3. Add the egg whites and process until combined.
4. With the Robot Coupe running, stream in the cream until smooth.
5. Pass the mousse through a fine-mesh tamis and remove to a medium bowl.

6. Beat in the crème fraîche until emulsified.
7. Stir in the dill seed extract, Meyer lemon, and chopped dill.
8. Spread the mousse into the two custom silicone molds.
9. Freeze until completely set.

FOR THE LEEK SOUBISE

1. Melt the butter in a medium sauté pan over medium heat, add the leeks, salt, garlic, thyme, and bay leaf and cook until starting to soften, adjusting the heat so the leeks take on no color.
2. Pour in the wine and continue to cook until the wine has cooked off.
3. Add the cream and cook on low heat until the leeks are completely tender, but still take on no color, about 20 minutes.
4. Transfer to a high-powered blender, preferably a Vita-Prep and blend until smooth.
5. Pass through a fine-mesh strainer into a small bowl and set aside.

FOR THE SMOKED POMMES PURÉE

1. Set up an immersion circulator in a water bath and set to 194°F (90°C). (The circulator will be used for the purée, the marmalade, and the pearls.)
2. Put the potatoes and salt in a Cryovac bag and seal.
3. Cook sous vide in the water bath for 40 minutes.
4. Meanwhile, put the butter in a small storage container with a lid. Using a smoking gun, smoke the butter and seal the lid, trapping the smoke inside. Refrigerate until ready to use.
5. Remove the potatoes from the bag, pass through a fine-mesh tamis, and put in a small saucepan.
6. Add 50 grams of the leek soubise and beat with a small spatula until smooth.
7. Add the smoked butter a little at a time, beating until smooth between each addition.
8. Set aside.

FOR THE ONION MARMALADE

1. Combine the bacon fat, onion, and a pinch of salt in a Cryovac bag and seal.
2. Cook sous vide in the water bath still set to 194°F (90°C) for 20 minutes.
3. Transfer to a small saucepan. Add the glucose and champagne vinegar, set over medium heat, and cook until just dry.
4. Set aside.

FOR THE EGG WHITE PEARLS

1. Fill a large Cryovac bag with the canola oil and tape the bag to the side of the water bath at 194°F (90°C). Allow the oil to come to temperature, about 30 minutes.
2. Put the strained egg whites into a medium squeeze bottle with a fine tip.
3. Carefully, open the top of the heated bag of oil and, in a steady stream, spray the egg whites into the hot oil and allow the whites to form small droplets and settle at the bottom of the bag. Let sit for 2 to 3 minutes.
4. Using a small whisk, break the egg whites up into pearls.
5. Slowly pour the oil through a small strainer into a large bowl.
6. Let the pearls drain in the strainer.
7. Mix the egg whites with the pickled mustard seeds in a small bowl and season with salt.
8. Set aside.

TO COOK THE TROUT SKIN AND FINS

1. Whisk the water and 4 grams of salt together until the salt has dissolved.
2. Divide the brine between two 12-ounce Mason jars.
3. Add the trout skins to one and the tail and dorsal fins to the other. Seal with the lids.
4. Place a towel in the bottom of a pressure cooker and add 1 inch of water.
5. Put the two jars in the pressure cooker and secure the lid.

>>>

⑥ Bring the pressure cooker to 15 psi over high heat and then, immediately turn off and remove from the heat.

⑦ Let cool until the pressure has fully dissipated, about 10 minutes. Take off the lid and remove the jar of skins.

⑧ Return the pressure cooker to the burner and continue to cook the fins at 15 psi for 45 minutes more.

⑨ Remove from the heat and let cool completely.

⑩ Remove the jar of cooked fins.

FOR THE ASSEMBLY OF THE PRESSÉ

① Set an immersion circulator in a water bath and set to 130°F (55°C).

② Unmold 1 of the molds of frozen mousse and put on a sprayed, Cryovacked one-eighth tray. Dust with a light layer of Activa.

③ Unmold the trout pressé and lay it over the mousse. Dust with a light layer of Activa.

④ Unwrap the other mousse and set on top. Wrap the now fully layered pressé thoroughly with plastic wrap and poke a few small holes around the edges with a sausage pricker.

⑤ Set another sprayed Cryovacked one-eighth tray on top and wrap tightly in plastic wrap.

⑥ Slide the whole pressé into another bag and Cryovac on full vac to remove excess air and to press together evenly.

⑦ Cook sous vide in the water bath for 25 minutes.

⑧ Immediately, immerse the pressé in a large ice bath and let cool completely.

⑨ Slice the brioche to four ⅛-inch-thick pieces, measuring 8 x 2.5 inches and two pieces measuring 8 x 1.5 inches. Lay two of the wider pieces and one of the narrower pieces side by side in the bottom of a Cryovacked one-eighth tray.

⑩ Make a slurry mixing the cornstarch with the egg whites.

⑪ Unmold the trout pressé, brush the bottom with the slurry, and lay, slurry-side down on the brioche.

⑫ Brush the top with the slurry and place the remaining three pieces of brioche on top.

⑬ Wrap the tray tightly with plastic wrap. Set another sprayed Cryovacked one-eighth tray on top and wrap again. Cryovac on full vacuum to press the brioche into place.

⑭ Unmold the pressé and slice lengthwise down the center.

⑮ Slice into 2½ x 1-inch wide pressé portions. Trim the remaining edge. Set aside.

FOR THE TROUT SKIN CIGARS

① Spray the metal tubes with nonstick cooking spray.

② Combine the egg whites and cornstarch in the high-powered blender, and blend until smooth. Set aside.

③ Using a ruler and a chef's knife, cut the feuille de brick into sixteen ¾ x 2-inch strips. Set aside.

④ Drain the trout skins, and very gently lay them on a cutting board. Carefully spread each one flat on the board.

⑤ Cut the skins into sixteen perfect, 1 x 2½-inch rectangles.

⑥ Brush each piece of feuille de brik with the cornstarch mixture and lay on each piece of skin, brushed side down to adhere.

⑦ Roll around the sprayed metal tubes, taking care that the skin overlaps on itself to seal it tightly.

⑧ Set on the rack of a dehydrator and dehydrate at 155°F (68°C) for 30 minutes.

⑨ Meanwhile, preheat a deep-fat fryer to 350°F (176°C). (You will need the fryer at this temperature for the fins as well.)

⑩ Line a half sheet pan with a cooling rack.

⑪ Weave a piece of kitchen twine through the center of each tube.

⑫ Using the twine to hold the tubes, fry until fully cooked and the bubbling has subsided, about 90 seconds.

⑬ Transfer to the rack and while still hot, carefully remove the tubes. Season with salt.

⑭ Dip the tip of a pastry brush into the silver-gold luster mix and blow the dust over the cigars.

⑮ Set aside.

FOR THE TROUT FINS

① Remove the pressure-cooked fins and gently dry on a towel lined tray.

② Lay the fins on a quarter-sheet sized silicone baking mat and cover with another. Set a quarter sheet pan on top and press down firmly and evenly to press the fins.

③ Remove the quarter sheet pan and the top baking mat.

④ Carefully transfer the fins, still on the baking mat to the rack of the dehydrator and dehydrate at 155°F (68°C) for 30 minutes.

⑤ Remove and trim the base of the fins and any uneven edges.

⑥ Line a half sheet pan with a cooling rack.

⑦ Fry the fins in the deep-fat fryer at 350°F (176°C) until they are crisp and the bubbling has subsided, 30 to 45 seconds.

⑧ Transfer to the towel-lined pan and season with salt.

⑨ Dip the tip of a pastry brush into the silver-gold luster mix and blow the dust over the fins.

TO ASSEMBLE THE CIGARS

① Arrange sixteen trout skin cigars on a parchment-lined half sheet pan.

② Put the pommes purée into a piping bag fitted with a #808 piping tip.

③ Put the onion marmalade into a disposable piping bag and cut off the end.

④ Pipe each cigar half-full with the pommes purée.

⑤ Pipe in the onion marmalade until each cigar is two-thirds full.

⑥ Using a small spoon, fill the top with trout roe, smoothing the top with the back of the spoon.

TO FINISH THE PAVÉ AND ASSEMBLE THE PLATE

① Preheat the oven to 175°F (80°C).

② Set a cooling rack on a half sheet pan.

③ Brush both brioche sides of each pavé with clarified butter and brown in a nonstick pan over medium heat until golden brown and transfer to the rack.

④ Bake until heated through, 3 to 4 minutes.

⑤ Dust the top with silver-gold luster.

⑥ Spoon a quenelle of caviar on top of each portion of trout.

⑦ Place a crispy fin on top of the caviar.

⑧ Lay a pea shoot over the pavé.

⑨ Spoon a small amount of the egg white pearl mixture in the center of each cigar and place a single begonia petal on top.

⑩ Place each under a glass cloche.

⑪ Smoke the glass cloche and serve immediately, removing the glass in front of the guest.

CORN NESTS

CORN SILK | **POPPED SORGHUM** | **EGG** | MAKES 16 NESTS

INGREDIENTS

CORN SILK

150 grams glucose syrup

150 grams water

10 ears corn, silk removed and
reserved (harvested from
young, very fresh corn)

1 liter grapeseed oil, for frying

SORGHUM

15 grams sorghum

10 grams clarified butter

1 gram kosher salt

0.15 grams pimentón

EGG

20 grams dried corn powder,
ground and passed through
a fine-mesh strainer

0.26 grams kappa carrageenan

0.26 grams iota carrageenan

0.2 grams agar agar

0.2 grams low acyl gellan

66 grams whole milk

66 grams water

6.5 grams unsalted butter

1 gram kosher salt

SPECIALIZED EQUIPMENT

• One 16-cavity quenelle
mold by Crucial Detail

FINISHING

Gold luster

>>>

FOR THE CORN SILK

1. Combine the glucose and water in a medium sauce-pan and bring to a boil.
2. Add the corn silk and submerge it in the syrup.
3. Transfer the corn silk and syrup to an 8-ounce Mason jar and seal with the lid.
4. Place a towel in the bottom of a pressure cooker and add 1 inch of water.
5. Put the jar in the pressure cooker and secure the lid.
6. Bring the pressure cooker to 15 psi and cook for 1 hour.
7. Remove and let cool to room temperature.
8. Drain the corn silk through a small fine-mesh strainer and discard the syrup.
9. Rinse the corn silk in warm water, shaking off any excess water, and dry thoroughly between lint-free towels.
10. Divide the silk into 5-gram portions, putting each in a tea ball strainer. (There will be extra silk.) Put the tea ball strainers on a small tray. Line another small tray with paper towels.
11. Heat the grapeseed oil in a medium saucepan to 400°F (205°C).
12. Add the corn-silk-filled tea balls and fry until all of the water evaporates and the oil stops bubbling.
13. Transfer to the towel-lined tray, and cool until the tea balls can be handled.
14. Remove the nests from the tea balls and put on a clean small tray.
15. Put the nests on the rack of a dehydrator set to 200°F (95°C) until ready to serve.

FOR THE SORGHUM

1. Combine the sorghum and clarified butter in a medium saucepan with a lid.
2. Set over medium-high heat, cover, shake the pan, and wait for the kernels to pop.
3. Drain the sorghum on a towel-lined tray. Combine the salt and pimentón and season the popped sorghum. Reserve the remaining pimentón salt for the nests.

FOR THE EGG

1. Put the halves of the mold together and secure the sides with rubber bands or tape. Refrigerate the molds.
2. Combine all of the powders in a small bowl.
3. Whisk the milk and water in a small saucepan and set over high heat. Whisk in the combined powders, bringing the mixture to a boil. Lower to a simmer for 15 seconds and remove from the heat.
4. Whisk in the butter and the salt and quickly transfer to a squeeze bottle.
5. Fill the cold quenelle molds and refrigerate until set.
6. Open the molds, trim the bottoms of the quenelles (the eggs), if needed, and transfer to a tray.
7. Warm the eggs gently in a warming box or oven at 165°F (75°C).

TO SERVE

1. Sprinkle the nests with pimentón salt. Brush the nests with the gold luster and put on a platter.
2. Build the nests by placing one warm egg on each nest. Using tweezers, place 2 pieces of popped sorghum on each.
3. Serve immediately.

SWEET PEA "GARDEN"

BLACK TRUMPET MUSHROOM
PANADE | PEA PURÉE | SNAP PEAS
LEAVES AND BLOSSOMS

MAKES 16 GARDENS

INGREDIENTS

BLACK TRUMPET PURÉE

30 grams dried black trumpets, rehydrated

15 grams clarified butter

1.6 grams kosher salt

1 thyme sprig

1 garlic clove

116 grams mushroom essence

26 grams heavy cream

BLACK TRUMPET PANADE

1 large egg

2.6 grams squid ink powder

40 grams brioche, finely ground

4 turns black pepper

Wondra, for dusting

25 grams finely ground black trumpet powder

SPECIALIZED EQUIPMENT

• 3 silicone panade molds by Crucial Detail

• Combi oven, for steaming

>>>

PEA SKEWERS AND PEA PURÉE

320 shucked snap peas,
   sorted for size (for skewers)

49 grams snap peas, shucked
   (for purée)

90 grams Leek Soubise (see page 205)

80 grams spinach, washed, dried,
   and stems removed

45 grams whole milk

2.4 grams agar agar (1%)

4 grams gelatin (1.6%), bloomed

SPECIALIZED EQUIPMENT

• 3 silicone pea garden molds by
   Crucial Detail

• 32 metal pins by Crucial Detail

MEYER LEMON GEL

0.75 gram kosher salt

30 grams granulated sugar

30 grams water

0.75 gram agar agar

2.5 grams gelatin, bloomed

2 Meyer lemons, zested with a rasp grater

40 grams Meyer lemon juice

GARDEN HERBS AND BLOSSOMS

48 pea tendrils

48 broccolini florets

32 micro red mustard frills

32 micro mizuna

32 oxalis blooms,
   just blooming

16 white star flower

16 bachelor buttons, blue

Freshly ground black pepper

Kosher salt

Lemon oil

NOTE:

*The herbs and blossoms are best
stored and transported in a
tackle box.*

FOR THE BLACK TRUMPET PURÉE

1. Put the rehydrated black trumpets in the clarified butter over high heat. Season with the salt and add the thyme and garlic and sauté until crisp and fragrant.
2. Stir in the mushroom essence and cream. Cook to reduce by half.
3. Remove and discard the thyme and garlic.
4. Transfer the reduced mushrooms and the liquid to a high-powered blender, preferably a Vita-Prep and purée until smooth.
5. Strain and weigh out 110 grams of the purée for the panade.

FOR THE PANADE

1. Spray the custom silicone panade molds.
2. Clean out the blender jug and put the reserved 110 grams of black trumpet purée, the eggs, squid ink powder, and pepper in the jug and purée until smooth. Add the ground brioche and purée until smooth.
3. Pour the mixture into the prepared molds. Carefully smooth the top with a pastry scraper.
4. Set the molds on a parchment-lined half sheet pan. Holding another half sheet pan on top, invert onto that sheet pan. Wrap tightly in plastic wrap.

5. Steam in a combi oven set at 190°F (88°C) for 25 minutes.
6. Unwrap and let cool completely in the molds in the refrigerator.
7. Remove the panades from the molds and lay on a parchment-lined sheet pan, bottom-side up.
8. Dust the panades with Wondra flour.
9. Spray a nonstick pan or griddle with nonstick cooking spray.
10. Sear the floured side of the panades until golden brown and crisp, about 45 seconds.
11. Remove to a rack-lined sheet pan.
12. Dust the tops with the black trumpet powder.

FOR THE PEA PURÉE AND PEAS

1. Spray the custom silicone pea garden molds.
2. Arrange the 320 peas on the small wires, placing 10 per wire, being careful to arrange them all in the same direction.
3. Bring a medium pot of salted water to a boil. Fill a medium bowl with ice water.
4. Blanch the pea skewers until just tender, about 90 seconds. Immediately transfer to the ice water until cold.
5. Drain on a dry towel.

⑥ Blanch the 49 grams of shucked peas for the purée until tender. Add the spinach to the peas and blanch for 1 minute more. Strain, and while still hot, squeeze out the excess water, put in the blender with the leek soubise, and purée until smooth.

⑦ Put the milk in a small saucepan and slowly whisk in the agar agar over medium-high heat. Bring to a simmer, whisking constantly for 1 minute. Add the gelatin and remove from the heat. Add to the blender and blend until incorporated with the pea-leek mixture.

⑧ Strain through a fine-mesh strainer and spread in the sprayed garden molds. Work quickly so the purée doesn't set too fast. And, be sure to spread well to avoid air bubbles. Smooth the tops with a pastry scraper.

⑨ Refrigerate until cold.

FOR THE LEMON GEL

① Combine the salt, sugar, and water in a small saucepan. Slowly whisk in the agar agar.

② Bring to a simmer over medium heat and simmer for 1 minute, whisking occasionally.

③ Add the gelatin and gently whisk in to incorporate.

④ Add the lemon zest and juice, remove from the heat, and let steep for 5 minutes.

⑤ Strain through a fine-mesh strainer into a small bain marie, pressing the zest to release its flavor.

⑥ Reserve in a warm place until ready to use.

TO ASSEMBLE

① Place a layer of pea purée on top of each black trumpet base.

② Working with one pea skewer at a time, dip into the lemon gel, gently tapping off any excess gel.

③ Lay the skewer on the groove of the pea purée and gently remove the wire, holding the peas in place.

④ Repeat with the remaining pea skewers.

⑤ Arrange the herbs and blossoms: 3 pea tendrils, 3 broccolini, 2 mustard frills, 2 mizuna leaves, 2 oxalis blooms, 1 star flower, and 1 bachelor button.

⑥ Just before serving, season with black pepper, kosher salt, and a few drops of lemon oil.

BEEHIVES

INGREDIENTS

FOIE GRAS BOUDIN |
TEA & HONEY GLAZE |
PISTACHIO PAIN DES GÊNES

MAKES 16 BEEHIVES

GUINEA FOIE SAUCE

20 grams Pastrami Brined and
   Cold Smoked Foie Gras
   (see Base Recipes, page 304)
100 grams guinea hen livers, cooked
   (86 grams cooked weight)
2 grams Curing Mix
   (2%, see Base Recipes, page 304)
12 grams clarified butter
15 grams thinly sliced shallots
1 garlic clove, smashed
1 thyme sprig
1.5 grams green peppercorns,
   rinsed and smashed
8 grams Madeira, plus additional
   for finishing
40 grams Guinea Hen Jus
   (see Base Recipes, page 305)
30 grams crème fraîche
0.7 grams Ultra-tex (1%)
0.5 grams black pepper mignonette

SPECIALIZED EQUIPMENT
• Four sets sauce insert molds with
   tops and wires by Crucial Detail

FOIE BOUDIN

130 grams ground guinea hen,
   brined and cold smoked
6.2 grams potato starch
6 grams Curing Mix
   (see Base Recipes, page 304)
3 grams lecithin
2 grams polyphosphate
0.4 grams Pastrami Spice
   (see Base Recipes, page 304)
1 large egg

200 grams Pastrami Brined and
   Cold Smoked Foie Gras (see
   Base Recipes, page 304),
   partially frozen
Activa GS

SPECIALIZED EQUIPMENT
• One 4 x 4-inch metal hive mold
   by Crucial Detail
• Combi oven, for steaming

PISTACHIO PAIN DE GÊNES

19 grams pistachio flour
3 grams all-purpose flour
3 grams cornstarch
1 pinch Meyer lemon zest,
   grated with a rasp grater
0.25 grams fennel buds
19 grams unsalted butter,
   at room temerature
6 grams granulated sugar
30 grams eggs

SPECIALIZED EQUIPMENT
• One 1 x 15-inch silicone
   pain de Gênes mold by
   Crucial Detail

RED ONION CHIPS

5 red pearl onions
40 grams water
10 grams glucose
1 drop red food coloring
1.5 grams Ultra-tex

WHIPPED HONEY

70 grams star thistle honey
20 grams lemon juice

15 grams water
1.25 grams Versawhip

SPECIALIZED EQUIPMENT
• One 1 x 15-inch silicone honey
   mold by Crucial Detail

TEA GLAZE

10 grams star thistle honey
80 grams topaz wine
50 grams dried apricots
16.5 grams honey vinegar
100 grams verjus
0.5 gram turmeric
0.5 grams gelatin (0.25%)
0.8 grams agar agar (0.4%)
0.6 grams gellan, la (0.3%)
0.8 grams guar gum (0.4%)
0.3 grams calcium (0.15%)
1.5 grams osmanthus
0.5 grams Earl Grey tea
0.8 grams kosher salt

SPECIALIZED EQUIPMENT
• 16 silicone glaze molds with
   bands by Crucial Detail

GARNISH

5 grams tempered butter
50 grams pistachios,
   grated with a rasp grater
20 grams Pickled Mustard Seeds
   (see Base Recipes, page 304),
   red and yellow
16 bronze fennel plouches
32 mustard blossoms
16 pieces fennel blossoms,
   fresh or freeze dried

>>>

FOR THE FOIE SAUCE

1. Pass the pastrami cured foie gras through a fine-mesh tamis and set to the side.
2. Freeze the custom sauce insert molds.
3. Sprinkle the livers with the curing mix and lightly toss to coat.
4. Heat the clarified butter in a small saucepan over high heat. Add the livers and cook to caramelize on the first side. Transfer to a small tray lined with paper towels and refrigerate until cold. (The livers will be used for the boudin.)
5. Quickly add shallots, garlic, thyme, and green peppercorns and cook until the shallots are translucent.
6. Pour in the Madeira to deglaze.
7. Whisk in the guinea stock and crème fraîche, followed by the passed pastrami cured foie gras. Continue to whisk until emulsified.
8. Add the Ultra-tex for consistency.
9. Strain the mixture into a small storage container and stir in the black pepper mignonette.
10. Season with additional Madeira to taste.
11. Transfer 50 grams to a squeeze bottle and fill the frozen sauce insert molds. Insert the tops and wires into the molds and put in the freezer. (There will be extra sauce.)

FOR THE BOUDIN

1. Spray the metal hive molds with nonstick spray and wipe off any excess.
2. Put the halves of the molds together and secure the sides with rubber bands or tape.
3. Put the ground guinea and 43 grams of the reserved livers from the foie sauce in a Robot Coupe and spin until smooth.
4. Add the potato starch, curing mix, lecithin, polyphosphate, and pastrami spice, and mix until evenly distributed.
5. Add the egg and mix again until smooth.
6. With the Robot Coupe running, slowly add the cold smoked foie gras keeping the mixture as cold as possible. (We dispense liquid nitrogen to keep it cold.)
7. Using a bowl scraper, pass the mixture through a fine-mesh tamis set over parchment paper.
8. Transfer the mixture into a piping bag and pipe into the cavities of the mold.
9. Unmold the frozen sauce "plugs" and insert one in each mold. Remove the pins and smooth the tops.
10. Place the molds on a quarter-sheet pan and wrap tightly in plastic wrap.
11. Steam in a combi oven at 147°F (64°C) for 15 minutes.
12. Unmold.

FOR THE PAIN DE GÊNES

1. Spray the custom silicone mold with nonstick cooking spray wiping off any excess.
2. Combine the pistachio and all-purpose flours, cornstarch, lemon zest, and fennel buds in a small bowl.
3. With a mixer or by hand, cream the butter and sugar until fluffy.
4. Add half of the eggs to the butter-sugar mixure and mix until combined.
5. Add the combined dry ingredients until incorporated.
6. Add the remaining eggs until just combined.
7. Spread in the cavities of the mold and even the top with a small offset spatula. Press a piece of plastic wrap on top and wrap the mold and tray tightly with more plastic wrap.
8. Steam in the combi oven at 190°F (88°C) for 20 minutes.
9. Unmold while still warm.
10. Let cool to room temperature.
11. Invert onto a sheet of parchment paper and gently unmold being careful not to break.

FOR THE RED ONION CHIPS

1. Slice the onions 2 mm thick on a mandoline.
2. Discard any uneven or incomplete rounds. Put the full round slices in a bowl.
3. In a separate bowl, combine the water and glucose. Add the food coloring and then slowly whisk in the Ultra-tex.
4. Pour the red liquid over the onions.
5. Put in a bag and Cryovac.
6. Strain the onion slices and lightly dry.
7. Line a quarter sheet pan with silicone baking mats and arrange the onion slices on them.
8. Put on the tray of a dehydrator set to 175°F (80°C) for 20 minutes to gently cook the onions.
9. Remove the top baking mat and dehydrate until completely crisp, about 4 hours.

FOR THE WHIPPED HONEY

1. Put all of the ingredients into the bowl of a stand mixer and whip on high until very thick.
2. Transfer the mixture to a piping bag with a small, straight tip.

FOR THE TEA GLAZE

1. Combine the honey, 60 grams of the topaz wine, honey vinegar, verjus, apricots, turmeric, and 66 grams of water in a small saucepan and bring to a simmer. Reduce to 100 grams and strain into a new pan.
2. Meanwhile, bloom the gelatin in enough ice water to cover.
3. Add 80 grams of water, the remaining 20 grams of topaz wine, and the bloomed gelatin into the strained mixture in the clean saucepan. Whisk in the agar agar and gellan, return to the heat, and bring to a simmer for 30 seconds.
4. Whisk in the remaining ingredients and let steep over low heat for 2 minutes.
5. Strain through a fine-mesh strainer and then, working quickly, pour a small amount of glaze

into 1 silicone mold at a time. It is best not to overfill the mold; about one-third is best.
6. Dust the beehives with Activa GS and place in the molds.
7. Let cool for 30 minutes. Trim the tops of the mold with a flat razor blade. Turn over and unmold onto a board or tray.
8. Reheat as desired in the combi oven at full steam set to 160°(72°C) for 6 to 7 minutes.

TO ASSEMBLE AND SERVE

1. Brush the pistachio bases with tempered butter and dust with the ground pistachio, tapping off any excess.
2. Using a brush, scatter the mustard seeds evenly over the beehives.
3. Place one beehive into the center ring of each teardrop.
4. Pipe a small amount of whipped honey next to the beehive.
5. Place a fennel plouche and mustard blossom into the honey.
6. Place a fennel blossom on top of the beehive and garnish with a red onion chip.
7. Serve immediately.

CONSOMMÉ ROYALE

BRAISED OFFAL RAGOÛT | CUSTARD | BLACK TRUFFLE CONSOMMÉ

MAKES 16 CONSOMMÉ ROYALES

INGREDIENTS

CONFIT

8 guinea hen gizzards
2 each guinea hen hearts, necks,
   and wings
Curing Mix (2%, see Base Recipes,
   page 304)
1 thyme sprig
1 bay leaf
1 garlic clove
160 grams duck fat, rendered

RAGOÛT

15 grams unsalted butter
17 grams chopped black truffle
2 grams finely chopped shallot
20 grams Madeira
2 grams sherry vinegar

100 grams Guinea Hen Jus
   (see Base Recipes, page 305)
Kosher salt
Truffle oil
20 grams unsalted butter

SPECIALIZED EQUIPMENT

• Sixteen 2-piece consommé glasses
   by Crucial Detail

CUSTARD

75 grams eggs
94 grams whole milk
94 grams heavy cream
3 grams kosher salt

SPECIALIZED EQUIPMENT

• Combi oven, for steaming

CONSOMMÉ

200 grams black truffle and chicken
   consommé
0.13 grams low acyl gellan
1 thyme sprig
1 bay leaf

CONSOMMÉ GARNISH

2 leeks, tender light green tops only
2 carrots
1 black truffle, cleaned and dried

SPECIALIZED EQUIPMENT

• 1 punch tool cutter by Crucial Detail

FINISH

16 flowering watercress tops
16 carrot leaves

>>>

FOR THE CONFIT

① Weigh the gizzards, hearts, necks, and wings. Measure 2% of the total weight in curing salt and season them.

② Spoon into a Mason jar and add the thyme, bay leaf, garlic clove, and duck fat.

③ Place a towel in the bottom of a pressure cooker and add 1-inch of water.

④ Put the jar in the pressure cooker and secure the lid.

⑤ Bring the pressure cooker to 15 psi and cook for 60 minutes.

⑥ Let cool until the pressure has fully dissipated, about 10 minutes.

⑦ Remove the guinea hen parts from the duck fat.

⑧ Pick the meat from the wings and coarsely chop along with the heart and neck. Reserve 50 grams for the ragoût.

⑨ Cut the gizzards into halves or quarters depending on size.

FOR THE RAGOÛT

① Heat the butter in a small saucepan over medium heat. Add the black truffle, shallot, and the reserved 50 grams of confit. Cook until tender, about 2 minutes.

② Deglaze with the Madeira and sherry vinegar, scraping any bits from the bottom, and reduce until almost dry.

③ Pour in the guinea stock and season with salt and truffle oil.

④ Whisk in the butter until melted and emulsified. Continue to cook over medium heat until the sauce has reduced to a ragoût consistency.

⑤ Spoon a small amount of the ragoût over the gizzards to lightly glaze. Divide the remaining ragoût evenly between the bottom of the consommé glasses.

⑥ Put in the freezer until firm.

FOR THE CUSTARD

① Put the eggs in a high-powered blender, preferably a Vita-Prep.

② Whisk the milk, cream, and salt together in a medium saucepan and bring to a simmer.

③ Slowly with the blender running, add the milk-cream mixture to the eggs.

④ Portion the custard through a funnel into the consommé glasses over the ragoût.

⑤ Immediately, steam the custards, in a combi oven, being sure they are covered, at 185°F (85°C) for 15 minutes.

⑥ Remove and let cool.

FOR THE CONSOMMÉ

① Combine consommé, gellan, thyme sprig, and bay leaf in a medium saucepan and bring to a boil. Boil for 1 minute to hydrate the gellan.

② Pour the consommé into a bowl over an ice bath and cool.

③ Strain through a fine-mesh strainer and set aside.

FOR THE CONSOMMÉ GARNISH

① Thoroughly wash the leek tops and dry with a kitchen towel.

② Lay each of the tops on a silicone baking mat and, using the small punch, punch small circles, alternating the tool as necessary to get the best yield.

③ Peel the carrots and slice 2 mm thick on a mandoline. Cut into small circles with the punch tool.

④ Slice the truffle 2 mm thick on a mandoline. Cut into small circles with the punch tool.

⑤ Bring a saucepan of salted water to a boil. Fill a bowl with ice water.

⑥ Blanch the leek and carrot punches until just cooked, about 20 seconds, and immediately transfer to the ice water. Let cool completely.

⑦ Drain the carrots and leeks and dry completely.

⑧ Combine the carrots, leeks, and truffles and set aside.

TO SERVE

① Put a truffle punch down in the center of each of the custards.

② Place a glazed gizzard on top, garnish with carrot leaves and flowering watercress as well as some of the punched vegetables and truffle.

③ Mix the remaining leek, carrot, and black truffle punches into the consommé.

④ Pour the consommé into the glass tops and place over the custard glass.

⑤ Pour the consommé into the custard cups at the table.

MATHEW PETERS AND HARRISON TURONE

SLOW-POACHED CARROTS

SWEET CARROTS | ONION SOUBISE
PRETZEL CRISP | WATERCRESS

MAKES 16 CARROT GARNISHES

INGREDIENTS

CARROT COOKING CUISSON

16 sweet carrots

400 grams carrot juice

10 grams kosher salt

10 grams champagne vinegar

50 grams unsalted butter

SPECIALIZED EQUIPMENT

• 1 carrot peeler set by Crucial Detail

• Combi oven, for steaming

LAVASH DOUGH AND PRETZEL TUILE

300 grams all-purpose flour, plus additional for rolling the dough

20 grams granulated sugar

5 grams kosher salt, plus additional for seasoning

1 gram ascorbic acid

90 grams whole milk

32 grams extra-virgin olive oil

1 large egg

100 grams powdered, food-grade lye

3 liters cold water

Fennel pollen

SPECIALIZED EQUIPMENT

• Pasta roller attachment for stand mixer

• Capellini attachment for stand mixer

• 16 cornet cones by Crucial Detail

• 1 tuile rack by Crucial Detail

PICKLED PURPLE CARROTS

5 baby purple carrots

60 grams white distilled vinegar

40 grams distilled water

30 grams granulated sugar

3 grams kosher salt

1 gram celery leaves

1 gram black peppercorns

1 gram dill fronds

.5 gram garlic clove

.5 gram coriander seed

.5 gram crushed red pepper flakes

.3 gram bay leaf

SOUBISE CUSTARD

15 grams unsalted butter

400 grams Vidalia onions

50 grams dry white wine

200 grams chicken stock

75 grams heavy cream

5 grams kosher salt

5 grams freshly squeezed lemon juice

198 grams whole milk

1.2 grams iota carrageenan

1.2 grams kappa carrageenan

1.2 grams low acyl gellan

.6 grams agar agar

CARROT GLAZE

450 grams carrot juice

4 grams kosher salt

6 grams champagne vinegar

7 grams agar agar

FINISHING

Flowering watercress

Extra-virgin olive oil

Fleur de sel

FOR THE CARROT COOKING CUISSON

1. Peel the carrots and trim until about 8 inches in length.
2. Attach the two-piece carrot chuck to a Kitchen-Aid stand mixer and lock into place.
3. Press the carrot firmly into the chuck, and turn to full speed.
4. Press the peeler over the carrot until a conical shape has been achieved.
5. With a chef's knife, trim the top and bottom of the carrot to flatten to keep the carrot from rocking back and forth.
6. Channel and hollow out the carrot leaving about .5 cm on the sides. Remove any trim.
7. Lay the carrot in a Cryovac bag.
8. Repeat with the remaining carrots.
9. Combine the remaining ingredients in a medium saucepan and warm slightly over medium heat, stirring until the salt has dissolved.
10. Pour the liquid into the bag over the carrots. Seal the bag and place in a combi oven set to 212°F (100°C) until the carrots are cooked through, 45 to 50 minutes.
11. Keeping the carrots in the bag, let them cool in the liquid at room temperature.

FOR THE LAVASH DOUGH

1. Mix the flour, sugar, salt, and ascorbic acid in the bowl of the stand mixer fitted with the dough hook attachment on low speed.
2. Add the milk, oil, and egg, and mix until just incorporated. Increase the speed to medium and continue to mix for 3 minutes.
3. Wrap the top of the bowl with plastic wrap and let rest at room temperature for 30 minutes.

FOR THE PRETZEL TUILES

1. Preheat the oven to 300°F (148°C).
2. Line a half sheet pan with parchment paper.
3. Being careful not to touch the lye, preferably wearing gloves, whisk the lye into the cold water in a large storage container. Cover and set aside.

4. Attach a pasta roller attachment to the stand mixer. Set to the largest opening and dust with flour. Roll the lavash dough through each attachment, dusting with more flour as needed, until the dough is about 1 mm thick (number 5 on the attachment).
5. Lay the dough on the work surface.
6. Switch to the capellini cutter on the stand mixer.
7. Spray the cornet molds with nonstick cooking spray.
8. Run the lavash dough through the cutter and then lay the pieces on the work surface.
9. Wrap a single piece (thread) around a sprayed cornet mold. Repeat the wrapping to make 16.
10. One at a time, carefully dip the cornets into the lye solution for two to three seconds and transfer to the lined baking sheet.
11. Season with salt and fennel pollen.
12. Bake for 4 minutes. At this point the tuile is not yet cooked all the way. Loosen the tuiles to keep from sticking, but don't remove from the molds. Bake until golden brown and crispy, 3 to 4 minutes.
13. Unmold from the cornet molds, transfer to a cooling rack, and let cool completely.

FOR THE PICKLED SHAVED PURPLE CARROT

1. Shave rounds from the purple carrots on a mandoline into a small storage container.
2. Put all of the remaining ingredients (the pickling liquid) in a small saucepan and bring to a boil.
3. Strain the liquid through a small fine-mesh strainer into the container with the carrots and let cool.

FOR THE SOUBISE CUSTARD

1. Melt the butter in a large saucepan over medium-low heat. Add the onions and lightly sweat until the onions are translucent and all of the water has evaporated.

>>>

② Pour in the white wine to deglaze and cook rapidly until dry.

③ Add the chicken stock, bring to a simmer, and cook until the liquid has reduced by three-quarters.

④ Add the heavy cream and cook at a simmer to reduce until large bubbles appear.

⑤ Transfer all of the onion mixture to a high-powered blender, preferably a Vita-Prep, and season with the salt and lemon juice. Blend until smooth.

⑥ Strain through a chinois into a mixing bowl. You will need 200 grams. Reserve any remaining for another use.

⑦ Stir the milk into the onion mixture and let cool.

⑧ Pour the mixture into a small saucepan and add the remaining ingredients.

⑨ Set over medium-high heat and, constantly whisking, bring to a boil.

⑩ Strain through the small fine-mesh strainer and immediately pour into a large squeeze bottle.

⑪ Let cool for about 3 minutes and then, squeeze into the channels in the carrots.

⑫ Refrigerate until the custard is fully set up.

⑬ Using a small paring knife, trim away the excess custard leaving a flat, clean surface on top of the carrot.

⑭ Set aside until ready to glaze.

FOR THE CARROT GLAZE

① Set a rack over a quarter sheet pan.

② Put the carrot juice in a small saucepan and bring to a simmer.

③ Once the juice has simmered for about 1 minute, strain through a fine-mesh strainer lined with a large coffee filter.

④ Put 360 grams of the carrot juice, the salt, and champagne vinegar in a medium saucepan.

⑤ Slowly, while whisking, feather (sprinkle) in the agar agar.

⑥ Bring to a boil over medium-high heat.

⑦ Strain the carrot juice mixture through a small fine-mesh strainer into small bowl and let cool at room temperature for a few minutes.

⑧ Poke the side of one of the carrots with the glazing fork and dip the custard-filled side of the carrot into the glaze. Pull out of the glaze and let cool slightly.

⑨ Dip the carrot in again, coating evenly, pull out again, let cool slightly, and then put on the rack, glazed-side up.

⑩ Repeat with the remaining carrots.

TO ASSEMBLE AND SERVE

① Warm the carrots in a 175°F (80°C) oven for 6 to 8 minutes.

② Slide the tuile around each carrot with the flat side sitting flush to the tray.

③ Arrange 3 sliced pickled purple carrots on each filled and glazed carrot, starting from the back.

④ In a small mixing bowl, lightly dress and season the flowering watercress with olive oil and kosher salt. Place 2 pieces on each carrot, one on the back and the other halfway down the carrot.

⑤ Finish with a light drizzle of olive oil and season with fleur de sel.

SNAP PEA CRISP

INGREDIENTS

PEA CHIPS
22 snow peas
300 ml water
210 grams glucose

SPECIALIZED EQUIPMENT
• 1 pea chip kit by Crucial Detail

POTATO CRUMBLE
250 grams peeled Kennebec potatoes
600 grams distilled water
2.5 grams freeze dried pea powder
.75 grams kosher salt

PEA PURÉE
100 grams frozen petite peas
18 grams pea leaves

BLACK TRUFFLE AND
PEA AÏOLI
170 grams hardboiled egg yolks
8.5 grams kosher salt, plus additional
    as needed
9 grams Meyer lemon juice
45 grams canola oil

6 grams Ultra-tex
9 grams black truffle,
    grated with a rasp grater
12 drops truffle oil

FINSHING
64 individual peas,
    from shucked sugar snaps
Extra-virgin olive oil
Fleur de sel
Sorrel blossoms
Sorrel leaves
Pea wisps

>>>

PEA CHIPS | POTATO CRUMBLE |
BLACK TRUFFLE AND PEA AÏOLI |
WOOD SORREL
MAKES 16 PEA GARNISHES

FOR THE PEA CHIPS

1. Bring a large pot of salted water to a boil. Fill a medium bowl with ice water.
2. Blanch the snow peas until tender, about 2 minutes and immediately transfer to the ice bath. Let cool completely.
3. Drain and pat dry on towels.
4. Put the 300 ml of water and the glucose in a medium saucepan and heat just until the glucose is dissolved. Allow to cool completely.
5. Spray the pea chip molds and clamps with non-stick cooking spray.
6. Cut the seam end of the pea pods and remove the seeds. Place the pea pods in a Cryovac bag with the glucose solution and compress under vacuum.
7. Drain the pea pods and pat dry on a towel-lined tray.
8. Place the pods into the mold and clamp the metal wire around the pod.
9. Set on the rack of a dehydrator and dehydrate at 155°F (68°C) until crispy, about 3½ hours.

FOR THE POTATO CRUMBLE

1. Preheat a deep-fat fryer to 315°F (157°C).
2. Cut the potatoes into 1-inch cubes and put in a high-powered blender, preferably a Vita-Prep with the water. Blend on medium-low just to break the potatoes into small pieces.
3. Drain the potato crumble into a fine-mesh strainer, pressing out as much water as you can.
4. Transfer the potato crumble to a piece of fine-mesh cloth and ring out more water.
5. Continue this process until all of the water is removed.
6. Line a quarter sheet pan with paper towels.
7. Using a fine-mesh basket strainer, fry the potato crumble until lightly golden brown. Transfer to the towels to drain. After 1 to 2 minutes drain on a new set of towels. Repeat a few more times until the potato crumble is completely drained of oil.
8. Combine 25 grams of the potato crumble with the pea powder and season with the salt.

FOR THE PEA PURÉE

1. Bring a large pot of salted water to a boil. Fill a medium bowl with ice water.
2. Blanch the peas for 6 minutes. Add the pea leaves and continue to blanch for 2 more minutes. Immediately transfer to the ice bath. Let cool completely. (Keep the pea blanching water.)
3. Drain, pat dry on the towels, and let dry completely.
4. Transfer the peas and leaves to the high-powered blender with 37 grams of the pea blanching water, reserving the remaining blanching water. (The water will also be used for the pea aioli.) Blend for 3 minutes.
5. Strain through a small fine-mesh strainer into another bowl. Set over ice to chill.

FOR THE BLACK TRUFFLE AND PEA AÏOLI

1. Put the hardboiled egg yolks, 100 grams of the pea purée, 20 grams of the pea blanching water, salt, and lemon juice into the blender, and blend on high speed until smooth and homogenous.
2. Slowly, with the blender running, pour in the canola oil. Lightly dust in the Ultra-tex and add more salt to taste.
3. Pass through a small hole tamis into a small mixing bowl, cover with plastic wrap, and refrigerate.
4. Mix in the truffle and truffle oil and transfer to a piping bag. Refrigerate until ready to use.

TO ASSEMBLE

1. Align the pea chips on the stand and fill halfway with the pea crumble.
2. Pipe in the pea aïoli, filling from tip to tip, trying to avoid touching the sides of the chip. (This will cause the chip to sog out quickly.)
3. Lightly dress the shucked peas for garnish with olive oil and season with fleur de sel.
4. Place 4 peas on top of the aioli on each.
5. Finish with sorrel blossoms, sorrel leaves, and pea wisps.

FOIE GRAS QUENELLE

FOIE GRAS MOUSSE | YELLOW
CORN CUSTARD | CELERY ROOT
GASTRIQUE | BLACK TRUFFLE

MAKES 16 QUENELLES

INGREDIENTS

CHICKEN MOUSSE

175 grams chicken meat
    (preferably chicken breast)
25 grams egg whites
4 grams potato starch
4 grams Curing Mix
    (see Base Recipes, page 304)
1.6 grams polyphosphate
75 grams heavy cream
35 grams crème fraîche

FOIE GRAS MOUSSE

Grapeseed oil
100 grams foie gras, preferably
    Hudson Valley
50 grams chicken livers
40 grams thinly sliced shallot
30 grams brioche (without
    the crust)
10 grams port wine
10 grams Madeira
100 grams heavy cream
5 grams kosher salt

2.5 grams pink salt
25 grams unsalted butter
30 grams egg whites

SPECIALIZED EQUIPMENT
• 1 Paco Jet with one canister

CHICKEN LIVER AND
FOIE GRAS QUENELLE

35 grams crème fraîche
1 gram minced shallot
15 turns freshly cracked
    black pepper
1 gram kosher salt

SPECIALIZED EQUIPMENT
• One 16-cavity quenelle mold by
    Crucial Detail
• Combi oven, for steaming

CORN CUSTARD

10 grams freeze dried yellow
    corn powder
250 grams whole milk
7 grams brown butter

7 grams kosher salt
1 large egg

SPECIALIZED EQUIPMENT
• 16 barquette bowls by
    Crucial Detail

CELERY ROOT
GASTRIQUE

150 grams celery root vinegar
75 grams glucose
15 grams black truffle trim
15 grams celery heart
.7 grams kosher salt
8 drops truffle oil

FINISHING

16 thin slices black truffle
16 clusters miner's lettuce
16 chive blossoms
Black-eyed peas, quickly blanched
Chopped toasted pistachios

>>>

FOR THE CHICKEN MOUSSE

1. Dice the chicken meat into 1-inch pieces and refrigerate.
2. When making and working with the mousse always be aware of the temperature of the meat and the equipment. Working the mousse too long will develop heat and cause the mousse to break.
3. In an ice cold Robot Coupe, process the chicken until smooth. Add the egg whites and process until emulsified. Scrape down the sides and lid.
4. Add the potato starch, curing mix, and polyphosphate, and process until it begins to look smooth. Scrape down the sides and lid.
5. Slowly, with the Robot Coupe running, add the cream until emulsified. Scrape a final time.
6. Add the crème fraîche and process until the mousse is smooth with a nice sheen.
7. Fill a medium mixing bowl with ice.
8. Pass the mixture through a fine-mesh tamis into a bowl. Immediately chill the bowl in the ice.

FOR THE FOIE GRAS MOUSSE

1. Line a quarter sheet pan with paper towels.
2. Fill a large bowl with ice water.
3. Heat a film of oil in a small sauté pan. Working in batches, sear the foie gras livers, followed by the chicken livers, over medium-high heat, adding small amounts of oil, only as needed. Remove to the lined sheet pan, keeping the livers separated.
4. Add the shallot and brioche to the pan and cook until lightly golden, about 1 minute.
5. Pour in the port wine and the Madeira, scraping any bits from the bottom and deglazing the pan. Continue to cook until the liquid has reduced by half.
6. Combine the remaining mousse ingredients and add to the pan, along with the livers. Reduce the heat and simmer gently for 5 minutes.
7. Put the mixture into the Paco Jet canister. Freeze until just frozen. Then, blend in the Paco Jet.
8. Pass through a fine-mesh tamis.
9. Put 125 grams of the foie gras mousse and 75 grams of the chicken mousse in a medium mixing bowl for the quenelles. Reserve the extra mousse for another use.

FOR THE QUENELLES

1. Set the quenelle mold on the work surface.
2. Fold the crème fraîche, shallot, salt, and pepper into the combined mousse and transfer to a piping bag.
3. Pipe the mixture into the molds.
4. Steam in a combi oven set to 147°F (64°C) until cooked through, 20 to 24 minutes.
5. Trim and set to the side until ready to assemble.

FOR THE CORN CUSTARD

1. Set the barquette bowls on a half sheet pan.
2. Mix the corn powder, milk, and brown butter in the medium saucepan over low heat until the powder has all dissolved, then increase the heat to medium-high and bring to a gentle boil. Season with the salt.
3. Put the egg in a blender and turn to low.
4. Very slowly, add the hot corn mixture into the egg and continue to blend until the mixture is fully emulsified.
5. Pour the custard into the barquette bowls, cover and steam in the combi oven set to 194°F (90°C) for 15 minutes.
6. Set to the side until ready to assemble.

FOR THE CELERY ROOT GASTRIQUE

1. Combine the celery root vinegar, glucose, black truffle, and celery heart in a small saucepan. Set over medium heat and cook until reduced to a thick syrup (gastrique) consistency.
2. Strain through a fine-mesh strainer into a small bowl and season with the salt and truffle oil. Reserve in a warm place until needed.

TO ASSEMBLE

1. Unmold the quenelles, setting one in each of the corn custards.
2. Warm the foie quenelles and custards in a combi oven set to 140°F (60°C) until warmed through.
3. Drizzle the gastrique over the custards.
4. Set a truffle slice on the top of each quenelle, followed by the miner's lettuce and chive blossoms.
5. Arrange black-eyed peas and pistachios around the quenelles.

POTATO

CHARRED SCALLIONS

POMMES PURÉE | BLACK TRUFFLES

POTATO GLASS

MAKES 16 POTATO GARNISHES

INGREDIENTS

POTATO PURÉE

165 grams peeled La Ratte fingerling
  potatoes

65 grams heavy cream

16 grams chicken stock

65 grams unsalted butter,
  preferably Strauss

30 grams crème fraîche

3.5 grams kosher salt

POTATO GLASS

475 grams Kennebec potato, peeled
  and diced into 1-inch cubes

350 grams distilled water

16 grams white distilled vinegar

12 grams kosher salt

SPECIALIZED EQUIPMENT

• 1 set silicone potato glass molds and
  stand by Crucial Detail

• 1 set frying baskets for potato glass
  by Crucial Detail

POTATO SHELLS

220 grams Kennebec potato, peeled

1 gram kosher salt

450 grams clarified butter

SPECIALIZED EQUIPMENT

• 1 potato cup press kit by
  Crucial Detail

• Combi oven, for steaming

PETITE POTATOES

18 petite potatoes, preferably
  from The Chef's Garden

30 grams unsalted butter,
  preferably Strauss

.6 grams kosher salt

CARAMELIZED SCALLIONS

6 bunches scallions

2 grams kosher salt

3 grams sliced chives

10 grams minced black truffle

FINISHING

1 black truffle

Calvin pea tendrils

FOR THE POTATO PURÉE

1. Seal the potatoes in a 5 x 8-inch Cryovac bag.
2. Put the bag in a medium saucepan with enough water to submerge the potatoes.
3. Set an induction burner to number 4 (or on the stovetop over medium-low heat) and simmer the potatoes until they are fully cooked, 25 to 30 minutes.
4. Set a fine-mesh tamis over parchment paper.
5. Remove the potatoes from the bag, and while still hot, press through the tamis onto the parchment paper.
6. Meanwhile, in a small saucepan combine the cream and chicken stock and bring just to a simmer, keeping a watchful eye that it doesn't boil over.
7. Put the potatoes into a medium saucepan and turn the induction burner to 2 (or on the stovetop over low heat).
8. Slowly mix in the cream mixture until completely incorporated.
9. Next, stir in the butter, continuing to stir until completely smooth. Lastly add the crème fraîche and the salt.
10. Transfer to a piping bag fitted with a #803 tip.

FOR THE POTATO GLASS

1. Cover the diced potato with water in a large saucepan and bring to a boil.
2. Turn off the heat and let sit for 30 seconds.
3. Strain the cooking water. Put 375 grams in a high-powered blender, preferably a Vita-Prep.
4. Add the potatoes, salt, and vinegar to the cooking water in the blender and blend on high-speed until smooth.
5. Pass the purée through a chinois into a medium mixing bowl.
6. Transfer to a Cryovac bag and compress under full vacuum until there are no air bubbles.
7. Line a quarter sheet pan with a silicone baking mat. Set the custom stand on the pan. Assemble the silicone potato glass molds and put into the stand.
8. Coat the potato glass molds with the mixture. Transfer to the dehydrator and dehydrate at 167°F (75°C) for 10 minutes.

9. Remove the tray from the dehydrator, add a second coat to the molds, and return to the dehydrator for 10 more minutes.
10. Transfer the tray with the molds to the work surface. With scissors, trim the bases. Return to the dehydrator, rotating the pan, and continue to dry until the mixture is completely crispy, about 30 minutes.
11. Meanwhile, bring a deep-fat fryer to 315°F (157°C).
12. Set a rack on a quarter sheet pan.
13. Remove the glass from the dehydrator, unmold, and put in the custom frying baskets.
14. Fry until just crisp, but without color, about 30 seconds. Transfer to the rack and let sit to cool slightly and firm up, about 2 minutes.

FOR THE POTATO SHELLS

1. Seal the potatoes in a 8 x 12-inch Cryovac bag.
2. Steam in the combi oven set to 212°F (100°C).
3. Remove the potatoes from the bag, and while still hot, press through a fine-mesh tamis.
4. Weigh the passed potato. You will need about 180 grams.
5. Season with the salt and stir to distribute evenly.
6. Weigh 8 grams of the seasoned potato mix into each potato base cup.
7. Press each to form the cup shape. The potato should adhere to the metal press piece.
8. Set on the rack of the dehydrator and dehydrate at 155°F (68°C) until they form a skin, about 35 minutes.
9. Preheat the oven to 350°F (175°C).
10. Pour 5 grams of clarified butter into each metal potato base and invert the potato cups into each base.
11. Bake for 10 minutes.
12. Remove from the oven. Pop each cup off and place back in the metal cups. Fill with clarified butter and return to the oven for 5 minutes.
13. Remove the potatoes from the metal cups and set on a quarter sheet pan lined with a rack to drain.

FOR THE PETITE POTATOES

① Seal the potatoes with the butter and salt, in a 4 x 6-inch Cryovac bag.

② Steam at 212°F (100°C) in the combi oven until the potatoes are fully cooked, about 30 minutes.

③ Keep warm.

FOR THE CARAMELIZED SCALLIONS

① Trim the scallions so that only the tender green tops remain.

② Cook in a large nonstick sauté pan over medium-high heat until the scallions are evenly browned and tender.

③ Remove to a cutting board and finely chop. You will need 100 grams. Reserve the rest for another use.

④ Mix the scallions, salt, chives, and truffle, and keep warm.

TO ASSEMBLE

① Fill each of the potato cups with about 5 grams of the scallion mixture.

② Pipe potato purée over the top and smooth with an offset spatula, creating a smooth surface.

③ Shave the black truffle into 1.5 mm (1⁄16-inch) slices and punch out 50 nickel sized coins.

④ Slice each coin in half and place around the perimeters of the potato cups, lightly pressing the into the purée, to give the cups a flowering look.

⑤ Put one small potato in the center of the purée along with a small cluster of pea tendrils.

⑥ Finish by setting the potato glass dome over the top, centering it between the shaved black truffle slices.

ASPARAGUS

CALIFORNIA ASPARAGUS | CREMINI MUSHROOMS
LA RATTE POTATOES | BORDELAISE

MAKES 16 ASPARAGUS GARNISHES

INGREDIENTS

BLANCHED ASPARAGUS

4 liters water
180 grams kosher salt
16 jumbo green asparagus spears

CARAMELIZED SCALLIONS

6 bunches scallions
2 grams kosher salt

CRUSHED POTATOES

350 grams peeled La Ratte
   fingerling potatoes
25 grams extra-virgin olive oil
20 grams freshly squeezed
   lemon juice
10 grams Burgundy mustard
7 grams kosher salt
10 grams chopped chives

SPECIALIZED EQUIPMENT

• Combi oven, for steaming

CREMINI MUSHROOM SHEETS

28 cremini mushroom caps

ASPARAGUS GLAZE

420 ml water
25 grams freshly squeezed
   lemon juice
25 grams champagne vinegar
2 strips lemon zest
2 tarragon sprigs
20 grams cornstarch
5 grams kosher salt
50 grams Pickled Mustard Seeds
   (see Base Recipes, page 304)

VEGAN BORDELAISE

450 grams thinly sliced shallots
250 grams diced sweet carrots
150 grams sliced button mushrooms
125 grams garlic cloves
30 grams flat-leaf parsley stems
25 grams peeled, small diced
   red beet

4 grams black peppercorns
1 gram thyme leaves
.5 gram bay leaf
1.5 liters Cabernet Sauvignon wine
1 liter Mushroom Stock
   (see Base Recipes, page 305)
.6 grams xanthan gum
4 grams Ultra-tex
Red wine vinegar
Kosher salt

PUFFED QUINOA

30 grams red quinoa
130 ml water
Kosher salt

FINISHING

Fleur de sel
Extra-virgin olive oil
Pea Shoots
Mustard Blossoms

>>>

FOR THE BLANCHED ASPARAGUS

1. Bring the water and salt to a boil in a 6-quart pot. Fill a large bowl with ice water.
2. Dethorn the asparagus and smooth with a green scrub pad.
3. Tie the asparagus into bundles of 4 with a 6-inch piece of kitchen twine.
4. Blanch the whole asparagus until tender, 4 to 5 minutes, and immediately transfer to the ice water. Let cool completely.
5. Drain the asparagus, pat dry on paper towels, and refrigerate until ready to use.

FOR THE CARAMELIZED SCALLIONS

1. Trim the scallions so that only the tender green tops remain.
2. In a large nonstick sauté pan, cook over medium-high heat until evenly browned and tender. Season with the salt.
3. Remove to a cutting board and finely chop the scallions. You will need 100 grams. Reserve the rest for another use.

FOR THE CRUSHED POTATOES

1. Put the potatoes in a Cryovac bag and steam in a combi oven set to 212°F (100°C) for 45 minutes.
2. Using a plastic bowl scraper, pass the potatoes through a tamis into a small mixing bowl.
3. Add the remaining ingredients and the caramelized scallions. Mix until fully incorporated.
4. Put in a storage container until ready to use.

FOR THE CREMINI MUSHROOM SHEETS

1. Slice the mushroom caps to 1 mm thick on a mandoline.
2. Arrange the mushrooms, facing down in 7 overlapping rows of 3 on a silicone baking mat. Top with another mat.
3. Repeat with the remaining slices and mats for a total of 16 sets.

4. Set 4 sets on a plastic wrapped quarter tray. Repeat to make a total of 4 plastic-wrapped trays.
5. Cryovac each tray in a 12 x 16-inch bag
6. Steam in the combi oven set to 212°F (100°C) for 9 minutes.
7. Refrigerate until cold.

TO ASSEMBLE THE MUSHROOM-WRAPPED ASPARAGUS

1. Set a rack on a quarter sheet pan.
2. Remove the mushroom sets from the Cryovac bags.
3. Working with 1 set at a time, remove the top mat, making sure the mushrooms are facing down on the mat.
4. Spread a ¼-inch layer of potato over the top of the mushrooms.
5. Lay an asparagus spear in the middle of the potato layer, running the length of the mushrooms.
6. Lift, and wrap the potato and mushroom around the asparagus. Trim as needed.
7. Trim the base to square off the end and discard. Cut a 1-inch piece from the end of each wrapped asparagus, on the diagonal.

FOR THE ASPARAGUS GLAZE

1. Put 400 ml of the water, the lemon juice, vinegar, lemon peel, and tarragon in a large saucepan and bring to a boil.
2. Make a slurry with the remaining 20 milliliters of water and the cornstarch.
3. Pour the slurry into the saucepan and bring back to a boil, stirring as the sauce thickens. Season with the salt.
4. Strain into a storage container and mix in the mustard seeds. Set aside until ready to use.

FOR THE VEGAN BORDELAISE

1. Put the shallots, carrots, mushrooms, garlic, parsley stems, beets, bay leaf, thyme, peppercorns, and red wine in a large saucepan.

② Bring to a simmer over medium-high heat and continue to cook until dry.

③ Pour in the mushroom stock, bring back to a simmer, and reduce the heat as needed to maintain the simmer for 45 minutes.

④ Strain the mixture through a chinois into a medium saucepan. Bring back to a simmer and continue to cook until reduced to 400 ml.

⑤ Strain the sauce into a high-powered blender, preferably a Vita-Prep. Add the xanthan gum and the Ultra-tex, and blend on low.

⑥ Transfer to a storage container and season to taste with red wine vinegar and salt. Set aside until ready to use.

FOR THE PUFFED QUINOA

① Put the quinoa and water in a large saucepan. Bring to a light simmer, cover, and cook until all of the water has evaporated, the quinoa is fluffy, and the germ has sprouted out, about 10 minutes.

② Line a dehydrator sheet with a silicone baking mat.

③ Spread the quinoa on the mat and dehydrate on high for 30 minutes.

④ Meanwhile, bring a deep-fat fryer to 400°F (204°C).

⑤ Put the quinoa in a frying basket or heatproof fine-mesh strainer and lower into the fryer until crisp, keeping a watchful eye that the quinoa doesn't burn. Quickly drain, spread on towels, and season with salt.

⑥ Once cooled, the puffed quinoa can be reserved in a storage container lined with a paper towel.

TO ASSEMBLE

① Heat the wrapped asparagus in a 175°F (80°C) oven until warmed through, 6 to 7 minutes.

② Spoon the glaze over the asparagus pieces and sprinkle with the fleur de sel and puffed quinoa.

③ Put one base and one tip piece on each plate. Garnish with mustard blossoms and pea shoots.

④ Reheat the bordelaise and pour tableside.

STAFF MEAL

EVERY DAY OF TRAINING was filled with constant activity from morning to night, so staff meal was always an important time of day for the team. Not only did it provide the necessary sustenance and fuel we needed, it provided pause to help us refocus and bond as a team.

In 2015, we would frequently share The French Laundry's staff meal at lunch, but breakfast was largely on us. Often the menu was scrambled eggs with bacon and toast, but on occasion, perhaps inspired by an especially tough workout, one of the boys would step it up with one of their favorites.

As the intensity built and the days grew longer, we would often find ourselves sharing not only breakfast and lunch together but dinner as well. Because of the pressure and the increased demand for our time, dinner was often impromptu. I'm a little ashamed to admit it, but there might have been a few fast food meals that found their way into the Bocuse House. Needless to say, we welcomed with open arms the occasional roast chicken or pasta my wife would bring over.

The recipes that follow are more than just ingredients and methods on a page, they are cherished memories and will always evoke the treasured friends I shared them with.

When I walked into the kitchen to the smell of these corn cakes I knew it was going to be a good day. They were Skylar Stover's favorite and were a sign that he was feeling motivated and inspired beyond the typical scrambled eggs and toast.

BREAKFAST OF CHAMPIONS: SKYLAR'S CORN CAKES

6:00 A.M.—CROSSFIT | 7:15 A.M.—BOCUSE HOUSE | 7:45 A.M.—BREAKFAST

75 grams | ½ cup cornmeal

100 grams | 1 cup all-purpose flour

15 grams | 1 tablespoon granulated sugar

4 grams | 1 teaspoon baking powder

12 grams | 1 teaspoon kosher salt

250 grams | 1 cup buttermilk

2 large eggs

37 grams | 2½ tablespoons unsalted butter
(preferably clarified), melted,
plus additional for the griddle

YIELD: 8 PANCAKES

FOR THE CORN CAKES

1. In a large mixing bowl, combine the cornmeal, flour, sugar, baking powder, and salt.
2. In a separate bowl mix the buttermilk and eggs until well incorporated.
3. Stir the buttermilk mixture into the dry ingredients. A few lumps are desirable
4. Quickly, whisk in the butter.
5. Heat a griddle or sauté pan over medium heat.
6. Melt enough butter to lightly coat the griddle or the bottom of the sauté pan.
7. Using a 4-ounce ladle, pour the batter into the pan in batches. Cook on the first side until the bottom is set, about 2 minutes.
8. Flip and cook on the second side until cooked through, about 45 seconds.
9. Transfer to a plate and keep warm.
10. Repeat as needed with the remaining batter.
11. Serve immediately.

This was Will Mouchet's go-to workout recovery staple. Passed down from his grandmother, this recipe is second to none.

COMPETITION DAY BISCUITS AND GRAVY

BISCUITS

280 grams | 2 cups all-purpose flour, plus additional for the work surface

12 grams | 1 tablespoon granulated sugar

4.5 grams | 1½ teaspoons kosher salt

7.2 grams | 1½ teaspoons baking powder

2.5 grams | ½ teaspoon baking soda

113 grams | 8 tablespoons cold unsalted butter, cut into ½-inch pieces

110 grams | ½ cup crème fraîche

118 grams | ½ cup Pilsner-style beer

56 grams | ¼ cup melted butter

SAUSAGE GRAVY

454 grams | 1 pound pork sausage, preferably a breakfast sausage

Unsalted butter, as needed

62 grams | ½ cup all-purpose flour

1 liter milk | 1 quart whole milk

Tabasco sauce

Kosher salt

Freshly ground black pepper

YIELD: 10 BISCUITS

FOR THE BISCUITS

① Preheat the oven to 400°F (204°C). Line a baking sheet with parchment paper.

② In a large bowl mix together the flour, sugar, salt, baking powder, and baking soda.

③ Toss the butter in the flour mixture, and using two knives, cut in the butter until the mixture looks like large crumbs. Make a well in the center. Pour in the crème fraîche and beer and stir just until it comes together.

④ Turn the dough out onto a floured work surface and knead until combined. Roll the dough into a 4 x 10-inch rectangle.

⑤ Cut the dough into 2-inch squares and arrange on the prepared baking sheet leaving about 1 inch between squares. Brush the biscuits with half of the melted butter

⑥ Bake until golden brown, about 20 minutes.

FOR THE GRAVY

① Heat a large frying pan over medium heat. Crumble in the sausage and cook until golden brown, about 10 minutes.

② Using a slotted spoon, transfer the sausage to a plate, reserving and measuring the drippings.

③ Add 62 grams (⅓ cup) of the drippings to a clean saucepan. Add butter to make up any difference. Set over medium heat. Whisk in the flour to make a roux. Switch to a spoon and stir until golden brown, 3 to 4 minutes.

④ Stir in half of the milk, continuing to stir until smooth. Stir in the remaining milk and simmer gently until thickened, about 10 minutes.

⑥ Add the sausage, breaking up any larger lumps and bring back to a low simmer. Cook, stirring often, being careful not to break the gravy, about 20 minutes.

⑧ Season with a dash of Tabasco, salt, and pepper.

TO SERVE

① Brush the warm biscuits with the remaining melted butter and spoon the gravy over the top.

During our 2015 Bocuse d'Or training, we took turns cooking. Greg Schesser would mix it up with this playful toad-in-the-hole recipe. During our last week of training, we found a good use for those extra black truffles!

TOAD-IN-THE-HOLE

BACON AND POTATOES

8 slices thick bacon

8 shallots, thinly sliced

650 grams | 1½ pounds fingerling potatoes, cut into ⅛-inch (3 mm) thick circles

Kosher salt

Black pepper

½ bunch chives, thinly sliced

Sherry vinegar

TOAD-IN-THE-HOLE

Four ½ -inch (13 mm) thick slices brioche

56 grams | 4 tablespoons unsalted butter, at room temperature

10 grams | 2 teaspoons unsalted butter, melted

4 large eggs

100 grams | ½ cup grated Parmesan cheese

Black truffle, optional

YIELD: 4 SERVINGS

FOR THE BACON AND POTATOES

① Preheat the oven to 350°F (176°C). Line a plate with paper towels.

② Heat a cast iron skillet over medium-high heat. Lay the bacon in the pan and cook gently, lowering the heat and turning as needed, until the bacon is crisp and the fat has rendered out, about 10 minutes.

③ Transfer to the paper towels. Leave about 50 grams (4 tablespoons) of bacon fat in the pan, and pour off the rest.

④ Add the shallots to the bacon fat in the pan and cook until golden brown and lightly caramelized, about 3 minutes.

⑤ Remove the skillet from the heat, stir in the potatoes, and sprinkle with salt. Transfer to the oven and roast until the potatoes are crispy and golden brown, about 15 minutes. Stir as needed to evenly brown.

FOR THE TOAD-IN-THE-HOLE

① Meanwhile, spray a sheet pan with nonstick cooking spray.

② Using a ring mold or a cookie cutter, cut a 1½-inch circle in the center of each slice of bread. Butter the bread on both sides.

③ Heat a nonstick griddle or frying pan over medium heat. Add the bread and toast until golden brown. Flip the slices and put 2.5 grams (½ teaspoon) of butter in the center of each hole.

④ Crack an egg in each hole while the second side is toasting.

TO FINISH

① Remove the potatoes from the oven, season with pepper, the chives, and vinegar. Keep warm.

② Turn the oven to broil.

③ Carefully (because only the bottom of the eggs will be cooked), transfer each toad-in-the-hole to the sheet pan. Broil until the whites are just set, being careful not to burn the toast.

④ Put a toad in the hole on each plate. Sprinkle with the cheese and shave some black truffle over, if using.

⑤ Serve with the bacon and potatoes on the side.

LYON: THE BISTRO

IN 2013, a few nights before we watched Richard Rosendale compete at the Bocuse d'Or, I wandered the streets of Lyon with Devin Knell, Thomas Keller Restaurant Group's chef de cuisine, in search of the quintessential bistro. After being turned away by a few packed *bouchons*, we found a promising spot, Chez Hugon, and took our seats at the only available table in a tiny dining room with enough seats for just twenty-five guests.

Over the next two hours, we were introduced to true Lyonnaise bistro culture amidst plates of braised tendon salad with mustard, sweetbreads *en cocotte*, duck confit, tarte Tatin, and plenty of Côtes du Rhône.

Midway through the meal, a man and his wife stepped from behind the curtain that separated the dining room from the kitchen and began serenading the guests with classic French folk songs. The entire room followed suit, joining in with song as Devin and I took in the unexpected festivities and tried to follow along. It didn't take long for the other guests to discover we were Americans. Soon the tables around us were welcoming us in, and by the end of the night we departed with the feeling that we were leaving a gathering of friends.

Cuisine. Culture. Friendship. This is bistro cooking at its best.

This classic is the essence of the cuisine of Lyon—even their salad has some form of pork and an egg on it! This is one of many dishes I can eat every night when I'm in the culinary capital of France.

SALADE LYONNAISE

POACHED EGGS

17 grams | 1½ tablespoons white wine vinegar

Kosher salt

6 large eggs

PICKLED RED ONIONS

½ red onion, peeled, root end removed

83 grams | ⅓ cup champagne vinegar

83 grams | ⅓ cup water

83 grams | ⅓ cup granulated sugar

FRISÉE SALAD AND BRIOCHE CROUTONS

33 grams | 3 tablespoons clarified butter

Six ½-inch (12 mm) thick slices brioche, punched
    with a 1½-inch (38 mm) round cutter

Kosher salt

6 heads frisée

7 grams | 1 tablespoon minced shallot

20 grams | ¼ cup picked fines herbes
    (parsley, tarragon, chervil)

Freshly cracked black pepper

Fleur de sel

VINAIGRETTE

140 grams | ⅔ cup bacon lardons

68 grams | ⅓ cup canola oil

14 grams | 2 tablespoons sliced shallots

52 grams | 3½ tablespoons sherry vinegar

26 grams | 1½ tablespoons whole grain mustard

5 grams | 1 teaspoon Dijon mustard

Freshly cracked black pepper

Kosher salt

YIELD: 6 SERVINGS

FOR THE POACHED EGGS

① Fill a large saucepan with 4 to 5 inches of water and bring to a simmer. Add the vinegar and season with kosher salt. Fill a medium bowl with ice water.

② Crack two eggs into a small bowl or ramekin. Transfer to a small fine-mesh strainer, letting the thin egg whites that easily pass through the strainer fall into another bowl. (The thin egg whites will be discarded.)

③ Begin stirring the simmering water until a gentle vortex forms. Gently pour the eggs into the water and let the whites just begin to firm up. Using a slotted spoon, gently move the eggs to keep them from sticking to the bottom of the pan.

④ Poach until the whites are just set and the yolks are still soft, 3 to 4 minutes. Transfer with a slotted spoon to the ice water.

⑤ Repeat two at a time with the remaining eggs. Reserve the poaching water to later reheat the eggs.

⑥ Set aside.

FOR THE RED ONIONS

① Slice the onion lengthwise into ⅓-inch-thick (8 mm) julienne and put in a heatproof bowl.

② Combine the vinegar, water, and sugar in a small saucepan and bring to a boil over medium-high heat.

③ Pour the boiling liquid over the onions and let cool at room temperature.

④ Refrigerate for up to 1 month.

FOR THE BRIOCHE CROUTONS

1. Line a small sheet pan with paper towels.
2. Heat the clarified butter in a medium sauté pan over medium heat.
3. Lay the brioche rounds in the butter and brown evenly on both sides.
4. Remove to the towel-lined tray, season with kosher salt, and set aside.

FOR THE VINAIGRETTE

1. Put the bacon lardons in a medium sauté pan over medium heat. Cook to render out the fat and brown the lardons until just crisp, about 5 minutes.
2. Remove the lardons to a plate with a slotted spoon, leaving the rendered fat in the pan.
3. Lower the heat to medium-low, add the canola oil, followed by the shallots and cook until the onions are translucent, about 2 minutes.
4. Pour in the sherry vinegar, scraping any bits from the bottom of the pan, and deglazing the pan.
5. Remove from the heat and season with the mustards, black pepper, and salt.
6. Set aside.

TO ASSEMBLE

1. Using a pair of scissors, trim away the dark green leaves of the frisée and then trim the root end.
2. Wash the frisée in cold water and spin in a salad spinner until dry. Wash and dry again if necessary.
3. Bring the poaching water for the eggs to a simmer over medium heat.
4. Place the frisée in a large mixing bowl, add the minced shallot and fines herbes. Dress with the vinaigrette and season with pepper and salt to taste.
5. Line a small sheet pan with paper towels.
6. Reheat the eggs in the hot poaching liquid until just warm in the center, 1 to 2 minutes.
7. Remove to the towel-lined tray. Season with pepper and fleur de sel.
8. Set one brioche crouton in the center of each plate.
9. Divide the salad around the croutons.
10. Place an egg on top of each crouton and finish the salad with the lardons and pickled red onions.
11. Serve immediately.

Tarte Tatin is one of my favorite desserts to make at home. This recipe is based on Paul Bocuse's version of the classic. Its simplicity belies the impact it makes at the table. It is a dessert that is as much at home in Paul Bocuse's namesake restaurant as it is in one of his bistros.

TARTE TATIN

SHORTBREAD CRUST

113 grams | 8 tablespoons unsalted butter

1 gram | ¼ teaspoon kosher salt

75 grams | ½ cup plus 1 tablespoon powdered sugar

220 grams | 1½ cups plus 1 tablespoon all-purpose flour, plus additional for dusting

2 grams | ½ teaspoon baking powder

1 large egg, lightly beaten

CARAMEL

200 grams | 1 cup granulated sugar

113 grams | 8 tablespoons unsalted butter

1.2 kilograms | 2 pounds 8 oz. Golden Russet apples

YIELD: 8 PORTIONS

FOR THE SHORTBREAD DOUGH

① Put the butter in a medium heatproof bowl and set over a saucepan of simmering water, whisking often until the butter has melted. Remove from the heat and let cool for a few minutes.

② Whisk in the salt, followed by the powdered sugar.

③ Sift the flour and the baking powder together in a separate bowl.

④ Whisk the butter mixture continuously while adding the flour mixture in a steady stream.

⑤ Once the mixture begins to form a dough, switch to a rubber or silicone spatula and continue to mix for 1 minute.

⑥ Mix in the egg until the dough forms a ball.

⑦ Transfer the dough to a plate, flatten it slightly, cover with plastic wrap, and refrigerate for 1 hour.

FOR THE CARAMEL

① Set an 8-inch tarte Tatin pan or other round, metal baking dish on the work surface.

② Heat the sugar in a small saucepan over high heat until it just begins to brown and starts to foam, about 3 to 4 minutes.

③ Remove the saucepan from the heat and stir with a wooden spoon. Add the butter and continue to stir until the butter has melted.

④ Pour the caramel into the pan and let cool to room temperature.

>>>

FOR THE TARTE

1. Position an oven rack in the bottom of the oven and preheat the oven to 325°F (160°C).
2. Peel and core the apples.
3. Cut the apples lengthwise into quarters.
4. Arrange the apples over the caramel, standing them upright in the pan as tightly as possible. Fill in the center and any gaps. Lay any remaining apple pieces evenly over the top.
5. Bake for 1 hour.
6. Transfer to a cooling rack for 10 minutes, then refrigerate to cool for 1 hour or up to overnight.

TO BAKE THE SHORTBREAD CRUST

1. Preheat the oven to 400°F (200°C).
2. Put the dough on a piece of parchment paper and flour the top of the dough lightly.
3. Roll the dough out into a circle about 3 mm (⅛-inch) thick.
4. Place an 8-inch lid or plate (or use the bottom of the baking dish) upside down on the dough and cut a circle the same size as the baking dish.
5. Prick the surface all over with the tines of a fork.
6. Slide the parchment paper with the dough onto a baking sheet. Trim any excess paper from the edges.
7. Bake until just golden brown, about 10 mintues.
8. Transfer to a cooling rack and let cool completely to firm up.

TO SERVE

1. A few minutes before serving, gently warm a serving plate.
2. Gently warm the bottom of the Tatin pan over a low flame for 1 minute to soften the caramel.
3. Set the shortbread crust on top of the apples and then put the plate on top of it. Holding the plate firmly against the apples invert the pan so that the tart is apple-side up on the plate. Lift the pan away.
4. Let the tart sit for 15 to 20 minutes for the crust to soften.
5. Slice and serve.

I discovered this Rhône-Alpes specialty when I was twenty years old, living in Chambéry, an hour east of Lyon. This rich potato gratin is a meal in itself and is perfect with a simple salad and a glass of Côte du Rhône.

TARTIFLETTE

454 grams | 1 pound thick bacon,
    cut into ½-inch (12 mm) pieces

2 onions, cut into ½-inch | 12 mm dice

2 thyme sprigs

3 parsley stems

1 bay leaf

1 garlic clove

10 peppercorns

2 large russet potatoes, peeled

3.75 grams | 1¼ teaspoons kosher salt

440 grams | 2 cups heavy cream

1½ garlic cloves, finely chopped

454 grams | 1 pound Reblochon* cheese

2 grams | 1 tablespoon thinly sliced chives

*A combination of 2 parts Brie and
    1 part Gruyère can be substituted

YIELD: 4 SERVINGS

FOR THE TARTIFLETTE

1. Preheat the oven to 325°F (160°C).
2. Heat a large saucepan over medium heat. Add the bacon and cook, stirring occasionally to separate the pieces, until the fat has rendered, about 10 minutes.
3. Remove the bacon. Pour off half of the bacon fat.
4. Add the onions, and cook, stirring frequently, until caramelized, about 20 minutes.
5. Gently fold the bacon back into the caramelized onions and then transfer the mixture to a paper-towel-lined plate or tray. Set aside.
6. Make an "herb sachet" by putting the thyme, parsley, bay leaf, garlic clove, and peppercorns in the center of a small piece of cheesecloth. Twist the ends together to form a small bag for the aromatics. Tie with kitchen twine to secure.
7. Using a mandoline, slice the potatoes into ⅛-inch-thick (3 mm) coins.
8. Clean the saucepan and return to the stovetop. Add the cream, herb sachet, and chopped garlic. Bring to a boil and simmer for 5 minutes. Season with salt.
9. Fold the sliced potatoes into the simmering cream. Gently cook, stirring occasionally, until partially tender, about 10 minutes. Remove the sachet and set the pan on a trivet.
10. Carefully shingle one-third of the potato slices in the bottom of a casserole dish. Spoon one third of the bacon and onion mixture over the top until evenly coated. Break one-third of the cheese into nickel-sized pieces over the onions and bacon. Repeat the layering with the remaining ingredients, ending with a layer of cheese.
11. Bake until the potatoes are tender and the casserole is bubbling, about 45 minutes.
12. Sprinke with the chives to serve.

BRINGING IT HOME

ONE OF THE CONSTANT CHALLENGES we faced as we prepared for the Bocuse d'Or was time, or the lack thereof. Some of our greatest discoveries came through the need to find ways to shave precious time off of the traditional preparations we were looking to use.

An indispensable time-saving tool was the pressure cooker, and it soon became our new best friend, opening unexpected doors as we developed methods for gently cooking fish skin or softening previously inedible corn silk. Duck confit, a preparation traditionally cooked overnight in restaurants, yielded identical results after only one hour in the pressure cooker!

Though we ultimately used these preparations to achieve a high level of precision and detail to meet the expectations of the Bocuse d'Or, many of the techniques and recipes are quite simple. I've selected a few here to give you a sense of our competition food and the importance of the most crucial component—taste!

Their simplicity may surprise you.

During my time at Le Bernardin, I was most impressed with the careful attention paid to the balance of each sauce. This brown butter sauce is inspired by those early days and was the sauce we served with our trout pavé at the 2015 Bocuse d'Or competition.

POACHED HALIBUT WITH BROWN BUTTER

MUSSELS AND MUSSEL STOCK

8 grams | 2 teaspoons canola oil

1 medium garlic clove, finely chopped

18 grams | 2 tablespoons finely chopped shallot

354 grams | 1½ cups white wine

3 thyme sprigs

2 flat-leaf parsley stems

1 bay leaf

10 black peppercorns

454 grams | 1 pound mussels, debearded and scrubbed

BROWN BUTTER SAUCE

20 grams | 2 tablespoons hazelnuts

11 grams | 1 tablespoon lemon juice

52 grams | 4 tablespoons unsalted butter

21 grams | 1 tablespoon crème fraîche

1 gram | ⅛ teaspoon kosher salt

14 grams | 2 teaspoons capers, roughly chopped

2 grams | 1 teaspoon finely chopped flat-leaf parsley

>>>

FOR THE MUSSELS

① Heat the oil in a large saucepan or small stock pot over medium heat.

② Stir in the garlic and shallots and gently cook, stirring occasionally until softened, about 1½ minutes.

③ Pour in the wine, and add the herbs and peppercorns.

④ Add the mussels, cover, and let steam for 1 minute. Stir and continue to cook until all of the mussels have opened, 1 to 2 minutes more.

⑤ Remove from the heat. Discard any unopened mussels.

⑥ Set a colander over a bowl and strain the mussels, reserving the cooking liquid. You will need 250 grams of mussel sock (1 cup plus 1 tablespoon) for the brown butter sauce.

⑦ Transfer the mussels to a bowl, cover with plastic wrap, and keep warm.

FOR THE BROWN BUTTER SAUCE

① Preheat the oven to 275°F (135°C).

② Spread the hazelnuts on a parchment-lined baking sheet in a single layer and bake until golden brown, 10 to 15 minutes.

③ Rub the nuts together in a towel to remove the skins.

④ Using the tip of a paring knife, split the nuts in half. Set aside.

⑤ Pour the reserved mussel stock into a small saucepan. Set over medium heat and bring to a simmer. Cook until reduced to 70 grams (⅓ cup), 4 to 5 minutes. Stir in the lemon juice, bring back to a simmer, and cook to reduce again to 70 grams (⅓ cup). Take off the heat.

HALIBUT

Four 1-inch (25 mm) thick pieces, skinless
    halibut, (100 grams, 3½ ounces each)
15 grams | 1 tablespoon kosher salt
250 grams | 1 cup dry white wine
473 grams | 2 cups water
1 lemon, thinly sliced
2 shallots, thinly sliced
2 flat-leaf parsley sprigs
5 grams | 1½ teaspoons kosher salt

FAVA TIPS

30 grams | 2 tablespoons unsalted butter
150 grams | 4 cups fava tips (tender leaves),
    or substitute baby spinach
Kosher salt
1 lemon, cut into wedges

GARNISH

1 lemon, cut into wedges
Arugula blossoms
Fava blossoms

YIELD: 4 SERVINGS

⑥ Melt the butter in a small saucepan over medium heat and continue to cook, swirling the pan occasionally, until a dark brown color. Pour into a bowl.

⑦ Set the reduced mussel stock back over medium-low heat and whisk in the crème fraîche.

⑧ Whisk the reserved brown butter to incorporate the settled browned bits and then slowly whisk into the mussel reduction, whisking constantly to emulsify. Season with the salt and additional lemon juice as needed.

⑨ Set aside.

FOR THE HALIBUT

① Cut a piece of parchment paper to fit the inside of a medium sauté pan to make a parchment lid.

② Set a cooling rack over a sheet pan.

③ Season the halibut on both sides with the salt.

④ In the medium sauté pan, bring the water and wine to a simmer. Add the remaining ingredients.

⑤ Turn the heat to low and gently lay the halibut in the pan.

⑥ Lay the parchment lid over the halibut and slowly cook for 3 minutes. (The poaching liquid must not come back to a simmer.) Turn the pieces of halibut over and cook for another 3 minutes.

⑦ Carefully transfer the halibut to the rack.

FOR THE FAVA TIPS

① Melt the butter in a medium sauté pan over medium heat. Stir in the fava tips.

② Season with a generous pinch of salt and cook until the tips have wilted.

③ Remove from the heat and add a few drops of lemon juice. Divide among the serving plates.

TO SERVE

① With the halibut still on the rack, spoon a small amount of the sauce over each fillet to glaze. Squeeze a small amount of lemon juice over the top and place a fillet on top of the wilted greens on each plate.

② Arrange several mussels around the fish (and feel free to serve the rest on the side!).

③ Combine the remaining sauce with the hazelnuts, capers, and parsley, and spoon around the plate, as well as over the fish and mussels.

④ Garnish with a few arugula and fava blossoms, if using, and serve immediately.

The pressure cooker is one of the most undervalued pieces of kitchen equipment. Not only is it a time-saver, it can transform some of the basic techniques we use in the kitchen every day to produce new and exciting results. This recipe for duck confit is not only easy to follow, it shaves hours off the cooking time and provides what might just become a new kitchen staple in your fridge.

DUCK CONFIT WITH CHERRY ONION MARMALADE

CHERRY ONION MARMALADE

24 grams | 2 tablespoons canola oil

250 grams | 2 cups finely diced red onion

125 grams | ½ cup dry red wine

100 grams | ½ cup red wine vinegar

125 grams | ½ cup port wine

100 grams | ½ cup granulated sugar

58 grams | ¼ cup dried cherries

24 grams | 2 tablespoons canola oil

10 turns fresh black pepper

1 bay leaf

DUCK CONFIT

4 duck legs

20 grams | 2 tablespoons plus
   ½ teaspoon kosher salt

3 grams | 1 tablespoon finely chopped
   flat-leaf parsley

0.5 gram | 1 teaspoon finely chopped thyme

4 thyme sprigs

4 bay leaves

2 garlic cloves

1.4 kilograms | 6 cups duck fat, melted

24 grams | 2 tablespoons canola oil

YIELD: 4 SERVINGS

FOR THE CHERRY ONION MARMALADE

1. Heat a sauté pan over medium heat. Add the oil and onions and cook until the onions are translucent, stirring occasionally, about 6 minutes.
2. Stir in the remaining marmalade ingredients and bring to a simmer. Cook, stirring occasionally, until the marmalade is thick and syrupy, about 20 minutes.
3. Line a sheet pan with parchment paper and pour the marmalade onto it to cool.
4. Transfer the marmalade to a cutting board and using a chef's knife, chop the marmalade until more uniform, but still chunky.
5. Refrigerate in an airtight container until ready to use or up to 2 weeks.

FOR THE DUCK CONFIT

1. Trim the excess fat from the duck legs. Rinse the legs under cold water to remove any excess blood. Using scissors, cut through the tendon attaching the leg meat to the end of the leg.
2. Put the duck legs in a medium bowl with the salt, parsley, and thyme, tossing to evenly coat the duck legs.
3. Transfer to a sheet pan skin-side up. Tightly wrap the pan with plastic wrap and refrigerate to cure for 6 hours.
4. Rinse the legs under cold water to remove the cure. Thoroughly pat dry with paper towels.
5. Divide the duck legs between two 1-quart Mason jars. Add 2 thyme sprigs, 2 bay leaves, and 1 garlic clove to each jar. Fill the jars with enough duck fat to completely submerge the duck legs. Secure the lids.
6. Place a kitchen towel in the bottom of a pressure cooker and add 2 cups of water. Set the jars inside and secure the lid.
7. Bring the pressure cooker to 15 psi. Reduce the heat to maintain a constant pressure, and cook for 1 hour.

8. Let cool until the pressure has fully dissipated. Take off the lid.
9. Carefully remove the legs from the jars and set on a parchment-lined sheet pan. Lay another piece of parchment paper on top, followed by another sheet pan. Put weight on top (large cans or heavy cookware work well) and press in the refrigerator for at least 2 hours or up to 12 hours.

TO FINISH

1. Thoroughly pat the duck legs dry with paper towels.
2. Heat a large sauté pan over medium heat. Add the canola oil.
3. Using tongs, lay the duck legs skin-side down in the pan and cook until golden brown, about 5 minutes.
4. Flip the legs and baste by spooning the rendered fat over the flesh side to warm through, 3 to 4 minutes.
5. Serve the duck legs immediately with some marmalade on the side.

The base for this recipe is soubise, a classic onion cream. It can be made with leeks or onions and provides a depth of flavor for a variety of purées and soups. This soup is essentially a spin on the purée we used for our pea garnish in the 2015 Bocuse d'Or competition.

PEA SOUP WITH MUSTARD

PEA SOUP

42 grams | 3 tablespoons unsalted butter

1 large onion, cut into small dice

2 garlic cloves, peeled

1 thyme sprig

1 bay leaf

96 grams | ½ cup dry white wine

110 grams | ½ cup heavy cream

472 grams | 2 cups water

240 grams | 4 cups baby spinach

147 grams | 1 cup frozen peas, thawed

6 grams | 2 teaspoons kosher salt

GARNISH

85 grams | 1 cup sugar snap peas, shucked

55 grams | ¼ cup whipped crème fraîche,
   lightly seasoned with salt and pepper

Mustard blossoms, optional

Pea blossoms, optional

2 teaspoons Pickled Mustard Seeds
   (see Base Recipes, page 304)
   or whole grain mustard

YIELD: 4 SERVINGS

FOR THE SOUP

① Melt the butter in a large saucepan over medium heat.

② Add the onion, garlic, thyme, and bay leaf. Cook, stirring occasionally, lowering the heat as needed, until the onion and garlic have softened, but are not brown, about 5 minutes.

③ Pour in the wine and cook until reduced by two-thirds, about 3 minutes.

④ Stir in the cream and cook until reduced by half.

⑤ Stir in the water and keep at a gentle simmer until the onion is completely tender, about 20 minutes.

⑥ Stir in the spinach, and cook, stirring often, until completely wilted, about 5 minutes.

⑦ Add the peas and simmer until tender, about 2 minutes.

⑧ Remove the garlic, thyme, and bay. Season with the salt.

⑨ Transfer to a high-powered blender, preferably a Vita-Prep, and purée until smooth.

⑩ Strain the soup through a fine-mesh strainer into a clean saucepan or bowl.

⑪ Adjust the consistency of the soup with hot water as necessary.

⑫ Keep warm or let cool quickly and refrigerate until ready to serve or up to 3 days.

TO SERVE

① Meanwhile, bring a large saucepan of salted water to a boil and fill a bowl with ice water.

② Blanch the peas in the boiling water until tender, 1 to 2 minutes. Immediately put in the ice water. Once cooled, drain the peas and divide among 4 bowls.

③ Spoon a quenelle of whipped crème fraîche onto the peas and garnish with the blossoms, if using.

④ Place a small amount of pickled mustard seeds in the bowl.

⑤ Serve immediately, pouring the soup at the table.

COLLABORATION:
THE CHEFS

I LOVE HOW PERSONAL cooking can be. At The French Laundry and Per
Se, we would change the menu every day, all of the chefs in the kitchen contributing
their thoughts and ideas to help shape the dishes they would be responsible for.
The following day, each chef would not just set up his or her station, but prepare the
dishes he or she had helped to develop. It was a highly personal process that allowed
each of us a personal connection to the food we cooked every day.

When I look at the different styles of cooking expressed by individual chefs—
how they present their food, and even their approach to service and decor—I know
I am seeing a glimpse into who they are as well. This section of recipes is meant to
do precisely that—provide a peek into the world of each chef who offered invaluable support and guidance to make our journey not only successful but deeply
rewarding. Each of the recipes also reflects how many chefs have adopted the met-
ric system in the kitchen. Standard measurements have been provided for some
recipes at each of the chef's discretion.

Sterling Caviar with Avocado Mousse and Brioche "Soldiers"

SERVES 6

CILANTRO OIL

120 grams | 4 cups cilantro,
   leaves and tender stems
25 grams | ¾ cup flat-leaf parsley,
   leaves and tender stems
140 grams | ¾ cup canola oil

AVOCADO MOUSSE

200 grams | 1½ ripe Hass avocados, halved
   and pitted
5 grams | 1 teaspoon lime juice
24 grams | 2 tablespoons cilantro oil
12 grams | 1 tablespoon pistachio oil
2 grams | ½ teaspoon minced shallot,
   rinsed with warm water
.25 grams | ⅛ teaspoon ascorbic acid
3 grams | 1 teaspoon kosher salt
65 grams | ¼ cup crème fraîche

One-quarter loaf brioche
30 grams | 2 tablespoons clarified butter
12 pistachios
60 grams | 2 ounces Sterling Caviar
Garden blossoms and greens

FOR THE CILANTRO OIL

① Bring a large pot of salted water to a boil. Fill a medium bowl with ice water.

② Blanch the cilantro and parsley until tender, about 1 minute. Strain into a colander and immediately submerge in the ice water until cooled.

③ Remove the herbs from the water; lay out on a lint-free towel and wring to dry.

④ Transfer the herbs to a small blender jug for a high-powered blender, preferably a Vita-Prep. Add the oil, and blend on high speed until puréed and steam develops, about 2 minutes.

⑤ Pour the purée into a bowl, nestle in a larger bowl filled with ice, and stir the purée until cool.

⑥ Cover and refrigerate for 24 hours to infuse the color.

⑦ Line a chinois or fine-mesh strainer with a coffee filter. Set over a bowl and spoon in the purée. Let strain.

⑧ You will need 30 grams (2 tablespoons) for the avocado purée.

FOR THE AVOCADO PURÉE

① Combine all of the avocado purée ingredients in the blender except the crème fraîche and purée until smooth and homogenous.

② Once smooth, add in the crème fraîche and pulse the blender until just incorporated.

③ Pass through a fine-mesh strainer and refrigerate.

>>>

FOR THE BRIOCHE

① Cut the crust off the brioche and cut four ½-inch (12 mm) slices. Cut each slice into ½-inch batons.

② Melt the clarified butter in a medium sauté pan over medium heat. Add the brioche batons and brown evenly on all sides.

③ Transfer to a paper-towel-lined tray and set in a warm place.

TO SERVE

① Spoon ½ tablespoon of avocado purée in the bottom of each of 6 wide glasses.

② Using a rasp grater, grate two pistachios over the purée in each glass.

③ Place a quenelle of caviar to the side and dot additional avocado purée in the glass.

④ Garnish with the blossoms and greens.

⑤ Serve with the warm brioche batons on the side.

Quenelles de Brochet

SERVES 6

LOBSTER CREAM SAUCE

60 grams | ¼ cup canola oil

240 grams | 1½ cups carrots, cut into
    ½-inch (12 mm) dice

1 kilogram | 2 pounds lobster bodies,
    cleaned, trimmed, dried

4 liters | 1 gallon water

600 grams | 3½ cups Roma tomatoes,
    cut into quarters

16 grams | ½ bunch tarragon

500 ml | 2 cups heavy cream

COURT BOULLION

2 leeks (dark green portion only),
    cut into ½-inch (12 mm) dice

2 large carrots, cut into ½-inch (12 mm) dice

1 onion, cut into ½-inch (12 mm) dice

1 medium fennel bulb, cut into ½-inch
    (12 mm) dice

1 bouquet garni (thyme, parsley, bay leaf,
    and leek greens)

6 black peppercorns

2 liters | 2 quarts water

250 ml | 1 cup dry white wine

1 lemon, cut in half

PIKE MOUSSE

300 grams | 10.5 ounces clean pike fillet,
    very cold

100 grams | 3.5 ounces scallops, very cold

6 grams | 2 teaspoons kosher salt

2 large eggs

4 large egg yolks

120 grams | ½ cup crème fraîche

100 grams | ¼ cup plus 3 tablespoons
    unsalted butter, at room temperature

4 chives, thinly sliced

FOR THE LOBSTER CREAM SAUCE

1. Place a stockpot over high heat and add the canola oil.
2. Sweat the carrots for about 5 minutes.
3. Add the lobster bodies and sweat for about 3 minutes.
4. Add the water, tomatoes, and tarragon, reserving 2 sprigs of tarragon for the cream.
5. Bring the stock to a simmer, and maintain a simmer for 45 minutes, skimming throughout.
6. Strain the stock through a china cap or other strainer and crush the bodies in the strainer with a spoon or ladle to extract maximum flavor.
7. Pass through a fine-mesh chinois into a large storage container.
8. Pour into a large saucepan and bring to a simmer. Continue to cook at a fast simmer until reduced to 1 liter (4 ¼ cups). (It is recommended that the stock be transferred into a clean pan often to keep the stock clear.)
9. Transfer the stock to a medium saucepan and reduce rapidly to 125 grams (½ cup).
10. Meanwhile, put the cream and the reserved tarragon in a small saucepan and reduce by half.
11. Take both pans off the heat and combine the reduced cream and stock.
12. Return to the heat to reduce slightly, about 5 minutes more.
13. Strain through a fine-mesh strainer and set aside.
14. Reserve in a warm place until ready for use.

>>>

FOR THE COURT BOUILLON

1. Combine the leeks, carrots, onion, fennel, bouquet garni, peppercorns, water, and wine in a stock pot and bring to a boil.
2. Reduce to a simmer and cook for 10 minutes.
3. Squeeze in the lemon juice, stir, and then strain through a fine-mesh strainer.
4. Set aside if using soon or cool and refrigerate until ready to use.

FOR THE PIKE MOUSSE

1. Put the pike and scallops in a Robot Coupe or food processor with the salt and blend for 1 minute.
2. Refrigerate the mixture in the food processor bowl for 10 minutes.
3. Return the bowl to the Robot Coupe and blend again for 1 minute.
4. With the food processor running, slowly add both the eggs and egg yolks. Once added, blend for an additional 30 seconds.
5. Pass the mousse through a tamis. Put in a small bowl and nestle in a larger bowl of ice.
6. Refrigerate until completely chilled, 30 minutes.
7. Bring the court bouillon to a simmer in a large saucepan.
8. Meanwhile, continue with the mousse. Using a rubber or silicone spatula, stir in the crème fraîche, beating it in vigorously to emulsify.
9. Separately, put the butter in a large bowl and soften with a spatula until it has a mayonnaise-like consistency (*beurre pommade*).
10. Adding a tablespoon at a time, beat the butter into the pike mousse base with the spatula until it has all been incorporated.
11. Set the bowl over ice and continue to mix until well chilled.
12. Stir in the chives and reserve.
13. Line a rimmed sheet pan with a lint-free, dry towel.
14. Using two large spoons, and using about one-tenth of the mixture, shape a quenelle of the mousse. There will be extra quenelles.
15. Place the quenelle into the simmering court bouillon and cook for 1 minute. Using a spoon, turn the quenelle over and poach for an additional 2 minutes until cooked through.
16. Remove the quenelle to the towel.
17. Repeat with the remaining mixture to make 9 more quenelles. Remove the towel or transfer the quenelles to a clean tray.

TO SERVE

1. Rewarm the lobster cream sauce and spoon some over each quenelle.
2. Place a quenelle in the bottom of each bowl, divide the cream sauce among the bowls, and serve immediately.

CHEF DANIEL BOULUD

Citrus Cured Fluke,
Shiso Bavarois, Ponzu Gelée

SERVES 6

PONZU GELÉE

100 ml | ½ cup soy sauce

45 ml | 3 tablespoons water, plus additional
    for the gelatin

3 grams | One 2-inch (50 mm) square piece
    dried kombu

5 grams | ½ cup bonito flakes

45 ml | 3 tablespoons mirin

45 ml | 3 tablespoons lemon juice

10 ml | 2 teaspoons orange juice

5 ml | 1 teaspoon sake

6.4 grams | 2½ sheets gelatin

ROASTED BEETS

3 yellow baby beets

3 red baby beets

3 baby Chioggia (candy stripe) beets

Extra-virgin olive oil

Kosher salt

Freshly ground white pepper

SHISO BAVAROIS

210 grams | 7½ ounces shiso leaves,
    stems trimmed

12.8 grams | 5 sheets gelatin

230 ml | 1 cup heavy cream,
    whipped to medium peaks

Kosher salt

>>>

FOR THE PONZU GELÉE

1. In a small bowl, combine all of the ingredients except the gelatin with 45 ml (3 tablespoons) of water and refrigerate for 48 hours.
2. Soak the gelatin sheets in a bowl of ice water for 10 minutes.
3. Meanwhile, strain the cold ponzu liquid into a clean bowl. Pour one-quarter into a small saucepan.
4. Set the saucepan over medium heat and bring to just below a simmer.
5. Remove from the heat.
6. Squeeze out the excess water from the gelatin sheets and stir into the warm liquid. Strain into a flat, rimmed container to reach ½ cm (¼-inch) thickness.
7. Refrigerate until firm, 4 hours.
8. Cut into ½ cm (¼-inch) cubes and refrigerate until ready to use.

FOR THE ROASTED BEETS

1. Preheat the oven to 350°F (177°C).
2. In a medium bowl, toss each variety of beets separately with olive oil, salt, and pepper to coat.
3. Wrap each color in a packet of aluminum foil and set on a sheet pan.
4. Roast in the oven until knife-tender, about 45 minutes.
5. Once cool enough to handle, but still warm, peel and discard the skins.
6. Cut the beets into desired shapes and refrigerate until ready to use.

>>>

EDAMAME PURÉE

300 grams | 2 cups edamame beans

112 grams | ½ cup heavy cream

Tabasco sauce

Kosher salt

Freshly ground white pepper

BEET REDUCTION

240 ml | 1 cup fresh beet juice

0.5 grams | ⅛ teaspoon xanthan gum

SESAME DRESSING

45 ml | 3 tablespoons extra-virgin olive oil

15 ml | 1 tablespoon sesame oil

15 ml | 1 tablespoon sherry vinegar

15 ml | 1 tablespoon lime juice

Kosher salt

Freshly ground white pepper

CURED FLUKE

270 grams | 1 cup kosher salt

100 grams | 2½ cups granulated sugar

Finely grated zest of 2 lemons

Finely grated zest of 2 limes

Two 170 gram | 6-ounce skinless,
      boneless fluke fillets

30 ml | 2 tablespoons extra-virgin olive oil

5 grams | 2 teaspoons grated fresh wasabi

Kosher salt

Freshly ground white pepper

SEAWEED CROUTONS

4 very thin slices white bread

30 ml | 2 tablespoons extra-virgin olive oil

Kosher salt

Freshly ground white pepper

2 sheets nori, finely minced

TO FINISH

57 grams | 2 ounces micro shiso

57 grams | 2 ounces green or red seaweed
      salad (ao-tosaka or aka-tosaka)

FOR THE SHISO BAVAROIS

1. Bring a medium pot filled with salted water to a boil. Fill a medium bowl with ice water.
2. Blanch the shiso leaves for 20 seconds and immediately transfer to the ice water to cool.
3. Meanwhile, soak the gelatin sheets in a bowl of ice water for 10 minutes.
4. Squeeze the cooled shiso leaves until dry and transfer to a high-powered blender, preferably a Vita-Prep, along with 30 grams (2 tablespoons) of the ice water.
5. Purée until very smooth but still thick, adding more water only if needed.
6. Strain through a fine-mesh strainer into a medium bowl.
7. Squeeze out the excess water from the gelatin and stir into the warm shiso purée.
8. While the mixture is still slightly warm, fold in the whipped cream until no streaks remain. Season with salt.
9. Spread the mixture onto a parchment-lined sheet pan in a 1.5 cm (½-inch) layer and freeze, uncovered.
10. Once frozen, cut into six 11.5 cm (4½ inch) by 1.5 cm (1 inch) rectangles. Cover and refrigerate until ready to use.

FOR THE EDAMAME PURÉE

1. Bring a medium pot of salted water to a boil. Fill a medium bowl with ice water.
2. Blanch the edamame until tender, about 1 minute. Immediately transfer to the ice water until cold.
3. Set 30 beans aside for garnish.
4. Put the remaining beans in the blender.
5. Heat the cream to a simmer and, with the blender running, stream in the cream to make a smooth, thick purée.
6. Pass through a fine-mesh strainer and season to taste with Tabasco, salt, and pepper.
7. Put in a squeeze bottle and refrigerate until ready to use.

FOR THE BEET REDUCTION

1. Put the beet juice in a small saucepan and set over medium heat. Reduce to 120 ml (½ cup).
2. Whisk in the xanthan gum until dissolved.
3. Transfer to a small storage container until cold.

FOR THE SESAME DRESSING

1. In a small bowl, whisk all of the ingredients together to combine, and season with salt and pepper.
2. Refrigerate until cold.

FOR THE CURED FLUKE

1. In a non-reactive container, combine the salt, sugar, and zests.
2. Add the fluke fillets, and pack the salt mixture around to coat completely.
3. Refrigerate for 45 minutes.
4. Remove the fluke, rinse off, and pat dry. Discard the salt mixture.
5. With a sharp slicing knife, starting at the tail end, cut the fillets diagonally against the grain into ½ cm (⅛ inch) slices.
6. On a flat surface lined with plastic wrap, arrange the slices in a single layer and season with the olive oil, wasabi, salt, and pepper.
7. Cover with plastic wrap and gently pound with a meat mallet to flatten into thin, translucent petals.
8. Refrigerate until cold.

FOR THE SEAWEED CROUTONS

1. Preheat the oven to 300°F (149°C).
2. Cut the slices of white bread into 13 x 2.5 cm (5 x 1-inch) rectangles.
3. Brush 2 silicone baking mats or sheets of parchment paper with olive oil on one side.
4. Place one baking mat or sheet of parchment on a baking sheet oil-side up.
5. Line the slices of bread on top in a single layer and sprinkle both sides with salt, pepper, and nori.
6. Top with the second baking mat or sheet of parchment, oil-side down.
7. Top with another baking sheet and bake until crispy and lightly browned, 10 to 12 minutes.

TO FINISH

1. Season the beets and fluke separately with the sesame dressing.
2. Place a rectangle of shiso bavarois in the center of each chilled plate and top with a crouton.
3. Arrange 3 or 4 petals of fluke on top of the crouton to resemble waves.
4. Make a line of 5 edamame purée dots, alternating with pieces of diced ponzu gelée.
5. Top the purée dots with the reserved whole edamame.
6. Swipe a line of beet reduction at a right angle to the line of edamame purée and gelée and arrange 3 pieces (one of each color) of beets in front.
7. Garnish the top of the fluke with the micro shiso and seaweed salad.

Pot-au-Feu

SERVES 6

VEAL STOCK

2.7 kilograms | 6 pounds veal bones, cut into
    2-inch (5 cm) slices, fat trimmed, and rinsed

30 ml | 2 tablespoons vegetable oil

2 onions, peeled and quartered

2 small carrots, peeled and cut into
    2-inch (5 cm) pieces

2 celery stalk, cut into 2-inch (5 cm) pieces

16 grams | 1 tablespoon tomato paste

113 grams | 4 ounces button mushrooms,
    trimmed, cleaned, and halved

6 garlic cloves, peeled and smashed

5 sprigs flat-leaf parsley

2 sprigs thyme

2 bay leaves

1 gram | ½ teaspoon white peppercorns

SHORT RIBS

54 grams | ¼ cup extra-virgin olive oil

6 bone-in beef short ribs

Kosher salt

Freshly ground black pepper

1 onion, coarsely chopped

1 large carrot, trimmed and coarsely chopped

Bouquet garni (1 bay leaf, 2 sprigs flat-leaf
    parsley, 2 sprigs thyme, wrapped in a leek
    green and tied with string)

5 grams | ½ tablespoon whole black
    peppercorns

3.8 liters | 1 gallon veal stock

>>>

FOR THE VEAL STOCK

① Place the bones in a large stockpot and cover with cold water. Bring to a boil and then strain the bones and rinse them with cold water; wipe the stockpot clean.

② Meanwhile, in a large sauté pan, heat the oil over medium-high heat and add the onions, carrots, and celery. Cook, stirring, for 5 minutes, or until they start to caramelize.

③ Add the tomato paste and cook, stirring, for 5 minutes. Set aside.

④ Return the bones to the pot, add 6 quarts (5.6 liters) cold water, and simmer for 10 minutes, skimming away any foam that rises to the surface.

⑤ Add the cooked vegetables, the mushrooms, garlic, parsley, thyme, bay leaves, and peppercorns. Simmer, skimming as needed, for 4 hours.

⑥ Strain the stock through a fine-mesh strainer lined with cheesecloth and discard the solids.

⑦ Chill and store, covered, in the refrigerator for up to 1 week, or freeze and use as needed.

FOR THE SHORT RIBS

① Position an oven rack in the bottom of the oven and preheat to 325°F (163°C).

② Warm the oil in a Dutch oven or large pot over medium-high heat.

③ Season the short ribs with salt and pepper. Cook the short ribs, turning to brown on all sides, about 5 minutes per side.

④ Add the onion, carrot, bouquet garni, peppercorns, and veal stock.

>>>

6 egg whites

340 grams | ¾ pound lean ground veal
or chicken

½ carrot, roughly chopped

½ celery stalk, roughly chopped

½ small onion, roughly chopped

½ plum tomato

4 juniper berries

5 coriander seeds

FINISHING

Kosher salt

Freshly ground black pepper

1 head savoy cabbage, cut into 6 wedges

2 carrots, peeled and cut in 5 cm | 2-inch
pieces

1 leek, halved lengthwise, cut in 5 cm |
2-inch pieces, rinsed

1 turnip, peeled and cut into 6 wedges

1 Yukon Gold potato, peeled and cut
into large dice

½ stalk celery, trimmed and cut into
large dice

340 grams | ¾ pound garlic sausage links

2 pieces of marrow bone cut 5 cm | 2-inches
thick

ACCOMPANIMENTS:

Rustic sourdough or country-style bread

Cornichons

Tarragon mustard

Crushed black pepper

Freshly grated horseradish

Coarse sea salt

Huile d'herbes (minced chervil, tarragon,
chives, shallots, and black pepper in
olive oil)

⑤ Bring to a boil, put on the lid, and transfer to the oven to braise until tender, 3 to 3½ hours. Add more stock or water, if needed to keep the ribs covered.

⑥ Let the short ribs cool in the Dutch oven in the broth at room temperature, and then refrigerate overnight.

⑦ The next day, remove any solidified fat from the broth.

⑧ Remove the short ribs, discard their bones and trim each into approximately 5 pieces; reserve.

⑨ Pour the broth through a fine-mesh strainer, discard all the solids, and return the strained broth to a large pot; keep chilled.

FOR THE CLARIFICATION

① In a mixing bowl, whip the egg whites slightly.

② Using a meat grinder, re-grind the ground veal with the carrot, celery, onion, tomato, and spices through a medium die into a large bowl.

③ Mix in the egg whites.

④ In a tall stock pot, using an immersion blender or whisk, blend the cold veal stock with the meat mixture.

⑤ Set the Dutch oven over medium heat.

⑥ Stir the liquid occasionally until the egg whites begin to coagulate and a raft forms. The liquid should reach 160°F (71°C).

⑦ Break a hole in the raft to allow broth to bubble through.

⑧ Simmer the soup for 1½ hours, making sure the raft does not break or sink.

⑨ Line a fine-mesh strainer with 5 layers of cheesecloth.

⑩ Strain the liquid slowly. If the liquid is cloudy, strain the consommé again with fresh cheesecloth.

TO FINISH

① Season the consommé to taste with salt and pepper and bring the broth to a boil.

② Add the cabbage, carrots, leek, turnip, potato, celery, and garlic sausage. Reduce the heat and simmer until the vegetables are tender and sausage is cooked, about 25 minutes.

③ Meanwhile, put the marrow bones on a rack-lined sheet pan and roast at 450°F (232°C) for seven minutes.

④ Add the reserved short ribs and roasted marrow to the consommé and cook an additional 10 minutes, until warmed through.

TO SERVE

① Serve the pot-au-feu family style, passing the meats and all of the accompaniments.

Red Mullet with Potato Scales

SERVES 2

POTATO SCALES AND RED MULLET

2 large potatoes, preferably bintje (or russet)

24 grams | 2 tablespoons clarified butter, melted

3 grams | 1 teaspoon potato starch

2 red mullet fillets, skin on, 350 grams | 14 ounces (total weight)

1 large egg yolk

Kosher salt

26 grams | 2 tablespoons extra-virgin olive oil

30 grams | 2 tablespoons veal stock, warm, optional

ORANGE SAUCE

Juice of 2 oranges, freshly squeezed

3 rosemary sprigs

100 ml | ⅜ cup white dry vermouth, such as Noilly Prat

300 grams | 1¼ cup crème fraîche

Kosher salt

Freshly ground black pepper

TO PREP THE RED MULLET AND POTATO "SCALES"

1. Peel the potatoes, wash them, and cut them into very thin slices, preferably using a mandoline.
2. Cut them into "scales" using an apple corer.
3. Put the potato scales into a large frying pan.
4. Cover the scales with cold water, bring to a boil, and continue to boil for 1 minute.
5. Drain off the water and put the scales into a medium bowl.
6. Drizzle the clarified butter over the scales and carefully mix to coat. Sprinkle in the potato starch and mix again.
7. Cut out two rectangles of parchment paper, slightly larger than the fish fillets.
8. Remove the pin bones from the fillets using a paring knife or tweezers. Lay a fillet, skin-side up, on each piece of parchment paper.
9. Mix the egg yolk with a teaspoon of water and a pinch of salt. Brush the egg mixture over the skin.
10. Starting at the head, arrange the potato scales over the fillets overlapping one another.
11. Refrigerate for 15 minutes. It is important to let the fish rest in the refrigerator for the butter to set and act as an adhesive. During this time, start the preparation of the sauce, which needs successive reductions.

>>>

FOR THE ORANGE SAUCE

1. Put the orange juice and rosemary in a small saucepan over medium heat. Cook until nearly dry.
2. Pour in the vermouth and cook until reduced by half.
3. Slowly add in the crème fraîche and season to taste with 2 to 3 pinches of salt and pepper. Increase the heat to high and continue to cook until reduced by half and thickened.
4. Strain the sauce through a fine-mesh strainer and keep warm.

TO COOK THE RED MULLET

1. Heat the olive oil in a large frying pan over high heat.
2. Working with 1 fillet at a time, lift one of the scaled-fillets while still on the parchment paper and invert scale-side down into the oil. Peel off the paper and salt the flesh side of the fillet.
3. Let the fillets cook until the scales are a deep golden brown, about 6 minutes. The cooking time may vary depending on the thickness of the scales.
4. Turn the fillets over and cook on the flesh side for a few seconds.

TO FINISH

1. Coat the plates with the orange sauce.
2. If you like, with a spoon, draw a few "scales" with warmed veal stock.
3. Arrange the fillets on the plates.

If there is one dish that represents the legend of Paul Bocuse it is the Soup aux Truffes V.G.E. Originally served to French President Valerie Giscard d'Estaing, this soup has greeted numerous guests at the culinary mecca that is L'Auberge du Pont de Collonges, Paul Bocuse's iconic restaurant.

The quality of the truffles is important in this soup. If possible, choose fresh truffles. Out of season, use preserved truffles. Allow 28 grams (1 ounce) of preserved truffles per person, instead of 80 grams (3 ounces) of fresh truffles.

Chef Paul Bocuse's Soup aux Truffes V.G.E.

SERVES 4

500 ml | 2 cups chicken stock

Kosher salt

150 grams | 1 boneless, skinless, chicken breast

100 grams | 4 ounces celery root

100 grams | 4 ounces carrot

8 button mushroom caps, 1¼ inches | 3 cm
   in diameter

80 grams | 3 ounces fresh truffles

60 ml | ¼ cup white dry vermouth,
   such as Noilly Prat

60 grams | 2 ounces cooked foie gras

One 14-ounce package store-bought
   puff pastry, defrosted

1 large egg yolk

FOR THE SOUP

1. Preheat the oven to 400°F (200°C).
2. Bring the stock to a boil in a medium saucepan.
3. Lightly salt the chicken breast on both sides and gently lay in the stock. Bring the liquid back to a simmer and cook for 6 minutes.
4. Take off the heat. Remove the chicken to a cutting board.
5. Peel the celery root and the carrot. Cut the celery root *en matignon* (small dice): First, cut into 13 mm (½-inch) slices, then cut across into 13 mm (½-inch) dice. Cut the carrot and then the mushroom caps in the same manner. Combine all of the vegetables in a bowl.
6. Set four 240 to 300 milliliter (1 to 1¼ cup) ovenproof porcelain bowls on a baking sheet (for ease of moving them around). Measure the diameter of the top of the bowls. (This dimension is needed later.)
7. Pour 15 milliliters (1 tablespoon) of vermouth into each of the bowls.
8. Add 1 rounded soup spoon of the vegetables en matignon to each bowl.

>>>

⑨ Cut the chicken breast into 13 mm (½-inch) slices, then across into 13 mm (½-inch dice). Divide among the bowls.

⑩ Using a truffle slicer, cut the truffles into very thin slices and add to the bowls.

⑪ Cover with the stock, stopping 19 mm (¾ inches) below the rim.

⑫ Roll out the puff pastry on a lightly floured work surface. Using a bowl, saucer, or another like-sized round item, cut 4 circles that are at least 3 centimeters (1¼ inches) larger than the diameter of the bowls.

⑬ Lay a pastry circle across each bowl. Turn the edge down over the brim, pressing lightly to seal it.

⑭ Mix the egg yolk with 1 teaspoon of water and a pinch of salt. Brush it over the pastry discs.

⑮ Transfer the bowls to the oven, and cook for 20 minutes.

⑯ Trim the edge of the pastry with the point of a knife and serve at once.

Striped Bass en Paupiette

SERVES 4

PAUPIETTE

Four 142 gram | 5-ounce portions striped
  bass
Peanut oil, for frying
4 extra-large russet potatoes
Kosher salt
Freshly ground black pepper

LEEK PURÉE AND
LEEK HEARTS

4 liters | 1 gallon water
27 grams | 3 tablespoons kosher salt,
  plus additional as needed
4 leeks
30 grams | ¾ cup baby spinach
Ice water

LEEK BRUNOISE

15 grams | 1 tablespoon unsalted butter
Kosher salt

POMMES PURÉE

½ kilograms | 1 pound (about 6) Yukon Gold
  potatoes, cut into quarters
9 grams | 1 tablespoon kosher salt,
  plus additional as needed
2 liters | 2 quarts cold water
473 ml | 2 cups heavy cream
113 grams | 8 tablespoons unsalted butter

>>>

FOR THE PAUPIETTE

1. Trim each bass fillet as rectangular as possible (about 13 x 5 cm/5 x 2 inches) by cutting a vertical score on the tail end of each fillet a few inches from the end, making sure not to cut all the way through and tucking that end under. Next, slice horizontally through 2½ cm (1 inch) of the thick end of the fillet and fold it over towards the thinner side to flatten the surface.
2. Fit a high-sided pot with a deep-fat/candy thermometer and bring 7.6 cm (3 inches) of oil to 250°F (120°C).
3. Line a sheet pan with parchment paper.
4. Slice the potatoes into long sheets on a Japanese turning slicer.
5. Cut the sheets into 2½ x 15 cm (1 x 6-inch) rectangles.
6. Fry the potatoes in the oil until cooked through and translucent but with no browning. Drain on the lined pan in a single layer and cool to room temperature.
7. On a piece of parchment paper, line up the potato slices overlapping each slice halfway. Group the potato slices to fit each portion of bass, allowing the potatoes to overlap on all sides by 6 mm (¼ inch) once wrapped. Repeat with additional potato slices so that there are a total of 4 overlapping potato sheets.
8. Season the fillets on all sides with salt and pepper.
9. Lay each of the fillets in the center of a potato sheet.
10. Lift and wrap one side of the potato sheet over each fillet, and then tightly wrap the other side over the top, overlapping by 6 mm (¼ inch).

>>>

SAUCE MEURETTE

750 ml | 3 cups dry red wine

350 ml | 1½ cups ruby port wine

1 shallot, thinly sliced

1 bay leaf

8 peppercorns

3 thyme sprigs

480 ml | 2 cups white veal stock

226 grams | 1 cup unsalted butter

Kosher salt

Freshly ground black pepper

FINISHING

Water

Unsalted butter

Clarified butter

FOR THE LEEK PURÉE AND LEEK HEARTS

① Bring the water and salt to a boil in a large pot over high heat. Fill a medium bowl with ice water.

② Trim off the root end of the leek and discard. Remove the dark green leek tops and reserve for another use. Thinly slice the light green portion of the leeks into 6 mm (¼-inch) slices. Rinse slices under cold water to remove any dirt.

③ With the remaining white parts of the leeks, peel off the outer layers until only the heart of the leek remains. Set the outer white part of the leeks aside for the brunoise.

④ Blanch the hearts in the boiling water until tender, 2 to 3 minutes. Immediately transfer to the ice water and let cool completely.

⑤ Transfer to a lint-free towel to drain.

⑥ Next, blanch the sliced leeks until tender, 1 to 2 minutes. Immediately transfer to the ice water and let cool completely.

⑦ Lastly, blanch the spinach until tender, 30 seconds to 1 minute. Immediately transfer to the ice water and let cool completely.

⑧ Wring out the excess water from the sliced leeks and spinach and transfer to a high-powered blender, preferably a Vita-Prep. Blend until smooth, adding ice water, a little at a time, as needed to allow the purée to spin.

⑨ Strain through a chinois or fine-mesh strainer into a bowl. Season with salt and let cool.

FOR THE LEEK BRUNOISE

① Cut the reserved leek whites into a very fine dice. Rinse under cold water to remove any dirt. Dry well.

② Melt the butter in a small saucepan over low heat. Add the diced leek and cook until tender.

③ Season with salt and reserve.

FOR THE POMMES PURÉE

① Put the potatoes in a large saucepan with the kosher salt and cold water. Bring to a simmer over medium heat and cook until the potatoes are tender, 20 to 25 minutes.

② Meanwhile, in a small saucepan, simmer the cream until reduced by half.

③ Stir the butter into the cream until melted. Remove from the heat and keep warm.

④ Strain the potatoes through a colander and return to the pan and set over medium heat, stirring the potatoes until all of the exterior moisture has evaporated.

⑤ Transfer the potatoes to a food mill and pass through back into the pan.

⑥ Set the pan over low heat and stir in the cream mixture until well combined.

⑦ Season with salt.

⑧ Using a plastic bowl scraper, pass the purée through a fine-mesh tamis into another pan or bowl and keep warm.

FOR THE SAUCE MEURETTE

① Combine the red wine, port, shallot, bay leaf, peppercorns, and thyme in a large saucepan. Bring the mixture to a simmer and cook to reduce to 480 ml (2 cups).

② Stir in the stock and reduce until sauce consistency.

③ Strain through a fine-mesh strainer into a medium saucepan.

TO FINISH AND SERVE

① When ready to serve, bring the sauce meurette to a simmer, remove from the heat and whisk in the butter a few pieces at a time, until just melted.

② Season with salt and pepper and then pass through a fine-mesh strainer.

③ Keep warm but do not simmer.

④ Meanwhile, reheat the diced leek brunoise in a small saucepan until warmed through. Stir in enough leek purée to give it a creamy texture.

⑤ Warm the 4 leek hearts in a small sauté pan with a small amount of water and butter, spooning over the leeks to glaze.

⑥ Heat a large sauté pan over medium-high heat. Line a small sheet pan with paper towels.

⑦ Add clarified butter to the pan and lay the potato-encased fillets in the pan spacing them evenly. Cook until golden brown and then flip to color the other side. Lift to evenly brown all the edges. Transfer to the towel-lined tray.

⑧ Place a spoonful of potato purée in the center of each plate and spread in an even circle.

⑨ Spoon the diced leek purée into the center of the potatoes and press down gently.

⑩ Pour the sauce meurette around the potato purée and set a fillet in the center of the plate on the leek purée.

⑪ Arrange a glazed leek heart on each fillet.

⑫ Serve immediately.

Slow-Cooked Carrots

BOCUSE D'OR 2013 | SERVES 12

CARROT JUICE

340 grams carrot juice

10 grams ginger, peeled and sliced

20 grams white wine vinegar

20 grams granulated sugar

Juice of 2 limes

NOODLES

1 gram locust bean gum

1 gram kappa carrageenan

0.5 gram iota carrageenan

0.5 gram calcium lactate

FOR THE JUICE

1. Put all of the ingredients in a large saucepan and bring to a simmer. Maintain the heat to keep at a simmer for 10 minutes.
2. Meanwhile, fill a medium bowl with ice water.
3. Strain the carrot juice into a bowl through a chinois or fine-mesh strainer, and chill in the ice water.
4. Put 300 grams of the flavored carrot juice for the noodles in a high-powered blender, preferably a Vita-Prep.

FOR THE NOODLES

1. Set out 18 pieces of 3 mm (⅛-inch) airline tubing, making sure they are each 60 mm (24 inches) in length.
2. Add the remaining ingredients to the blender with the carrot juice and blend.
3. Let sit for a few minutes to let any bubbles settle.
4. Transfer the mixture to a medium saucepan and heat gently over medium heat, whisking continuously until the mixture reaches 156°F (69°C).
5. Using a syringe, fill the airline tubing.
6. Submerge the tubing in ice water for 10 minutes, making sure the openings stay above water.
7. Using the syringe, blow the noodles out of the tubes. Arrange on a tray and refrigerate.

FOR THE SLOW-COOKED CARROTS

1. Fill a medium bowl with ice water.
2. Peel the carrots and cut them into 50 mm (2-inch) cylindrical shapes using an apple corer.
3. Combine the carrot juice, salt, and coriander in a medium saucepan, then add the carrots.

SLOW-COOKED CARROTS

4 carrots

300 grams carrot juice

2 grams kosher salt

8 coriander seeds

CARROT PURÉE

300 grams carrot trim (or carrots
   if there is no trim available)

470 grams heavy cream

Kosher salt

Ultra-tex or xanthan gum, optional

GARNISH

Carrot top greens

④ Set over medium heat and cook until they are tender.

⑤ Using a slotted spoon, immediately remove the carrots from the pan and put in the ice water. Let cool completely.

⑥ Drain on paper towels.

⑦ Cut out the middle from each cylinder using a 6 mm (¼-inch) metal tube.

⑧ Set aside.

FOR THE CARROT PURÉE

① Thinly slice all of the carrot trim.

② Put the trim in a medium saucepan with the cream over medium heat and cook until tender. Season with salt.

③ Transfer the mixture to the blender and blend until a silky smooth purée forms. Add Ultra-tex or xanthan gum, a little at a time, if necessary, to slightly thicken the purée (it should stand up on a spoon).

④ Transfer to a piping bag.

TO ASSEMBLE

① Preheat the oven to 200°F (95°C).

② Line a large baking dish or casserole (or plan to heat in batches) with parchment paper.

③ Working with 1 at a time, fill all of the carrots: Stand the carrot cylinders up straight and fill with the purée. Clean the edges with a small offset spatula.

④ Hold a carrot noodle in the air and wrap around a filled carrot cylinder from the bottom to the top. Once at the top, trim the noodle on an angle so that it blends into the final loop around the carrot.

⑤ Pipe a drop of purée into the center of twelve small, heat-proof silver dishes or plates. Pipe another drop to the side on each of the dishes.

⑥ Lay the carrots on top of the center dots of purée and place the assembled dishes inside the lined baking dish or casserole. Cover the top of the pan with plastic wrap to prevent drying in the oven.

⑦ Transfer to the oven to slowly warm through, about 6 to 7 minutes.

⑧ Once warmed through, garnish the side dots with a piece of carrot top greens.

⑨ Serve.

Sturgeon and Sauerkraut Tart
Topped with American Sturgeon Caviar

SERVES 6

SAUERKRAUT

300 grams | 11 ounces sauerkraut

13 grams | 1 tablespoon grapeseed oil

15 grams | 1 tablespoon unsalted butter

20 grams | 2 tablespoons chopped onion

½ medium garlic clove, smashed and chopped

150 ml | ½ cup plus 2 tablespoons
   dry white wine

8 juniper berries

1 bay leaf

Kosher salt

Freshly ground black pepper

PHYLLO DOUGH TARTLETS

1 package phyllo dough

125 grams | ¾ cup clarified butter,
   melted but not hot

SABAYON

30 grams | 2 tablespoons grapeseed oil

½ medium shallot, finely chopped

250 ml | 1 cup dry white wine

12 whole black peppercorns, cracked

Juice of ½ lemon

Cayenne pepper

4 large egg yolks

100 grams | ½ cup clarified butter, melted

>>>

FOR THE SAUERKRAUT

1. Put the sauerkraut in a bowl of cold water. Drain. Rinse in cold water again.
2. Drain in a colander and then press out the excess water between your hands.
3. Toss the sauerkraut to break up any clumps.
4. Heat the oil and butter in a large saucepan over medium-high heat. Stir in the onion and garlic and cook until translucent.
5. Stir the sauerkraut into the saucepan and mix well. Toss a couple of times to coat the sauerkraut and then add the wine, juniper berries, bay leaf and a little water if the pan appears dry. Put on the lid and cook over low heat, adding water occasionally to keep the sauerkraut from browning, about 1 hour.
6. Remove the juniper berries and the bay leaf. Season to taste with salt and pepper. Reserve.

FOR THE PHYLLO DOUGH TARTLETS

1. Preheat the oven to 350°F (177°C).
2. Set twelve 6 to 8 cm (2½ to 3 inch) tartlet molds on a sheet pan. Choose a 12 cm (5-inch) cutter.
3. Lay 3 pieces of phyllo dough on the work surface and brush with the clarified butter, laying them on top of each other and pressing them together.
4. Cut out 6 round discs from the layered phyllo dough and put 1 in each of 6 tartlet molds. Put another tartlet mold on top of each and press on top.
5. Bake the tartlets until they are nicely golden brown and crispy, 8 to 10 minutes.

>>>

STURGEON

200 grams | 7 ounces hot-smoked
   sturgeon fillet

GARNISHES

50 grams | 2 ounces white sturgeon caviar

Chopped chives

Chive blossoms, red-veined sorrel,
   or other edible flowers

⑥ Carefully take the shells out of the molds. Turn them upside
   down on a cooling rack and let cool completely.

FOR THE SABAYON

① Heat the oil in a small saucepan over medium-low heat. Add
   the shallot and cook until translucent with no color, about
   2 minutes.

② Add the white wine and peppercorns and cook until reduced by
   three-quarters.

③ Strain through a fine-mesh strainer into a medium bowl. Stir in
   the lemon juice and a small pinch of cayenne.

④ Whisk in the egg yolks until evenly incorporated.

⑤ Place the bowl over a double boiler over medium heat and whisk
   vigorously until a thick ribbon forms. (Be careful the mixture
   doesn't get too hot or the eggs will scramble.)

⑥ Remove the bowl from the heat and slowly stream in the clarified
   butter while whisking to incorporate.

⑦ Transfer the sabayon into a whipped cream dispenser, preferably
   an iSi. Charge once and reserve in a bain marie with warm water.

FOR THE STURGEON

① Clean the sturgeon fillet of any bones, skin, or discoloration. Cut
   into 12 slices to fit in the shells (3 per tartlet), about .4 cm x 4 cm
   (⅛ x 1½-inch) slices.

② Set slices on a small parchment-lined sheet pan, cover with a
   damp paper towel, and plan to heat up "à la minute."

TO FINISH

① Preheat the oven to 400°F (205°C).

② Heat the sauerkraut in a medium saucepan and dry on a paper
   towel.

③ Divide the sauerkraut among the tart shells and press down on it
   slightly. Arrange 3 slices of sturgeon in each of the tartlet shells
   and put in the oven for 1 to 1½ minutes to rewarm.

④ Shake the whipped cream dispenser and expel about 20 grams
   (1 ounce) of sabayon in each tartlet.

⑤ Top each with a quenelle of caviar, chopped chives, and chive
   blossoms.

⑥ Set a tartlet on each plate.

⑦ Using a smoking gun, smoke 4 wine glasses and place them on
   top of each tart.

⑧ Remove the glass in front of the guest.

Cauliflower Custard

SERVES 6

FOIE GRAS

3 grams | 1 teaspoon granulated sugar

9 grams | 1 tablespoon kosher salt

3 grams | 1 teaspoon pink salt

500 grams | 18 ounces foie gras, cleaned

Freshly ground black pepper

CAULIFLOWER CHIPS

3 to 4 large cauliflower florets

Kosher salt

CAULIFLOWER PURÉE

130 grams | 1 cup cauliflower florets

130 grams | ½ cup plus 1 teaspoon
   heavy cream

90 grams | ¼ cup plus 2 tablespoons
   whole milk

3 grams | 1 teaspoon kosher salt

30 grams | 2 tablespoons plus 1 teaspoon
   mini white chocolate chips

2 grams | 1 teaspoon iota carrageenan

ROSE GEL

1 sheet gelatin

140 grams | ½ cup plus 1½ tablespoons
   verjus rouge

1 gram | ¼ teaspoon rosewater

GARNISH

1 block white chocolate

1 organic rose

Liquid nitrogen

FOR CURING THE FOIE GRAS

① Combine the sugar, salt, and pink salt and season the foie gras generously with the mixture. Wrap tightly in plastic wrap and refrigerate for 24 hours.

FOR THE CAULIFLOWER CHIPS

① Bring a large saucepan of salted water to a boil. Fill a small bowl with ice water.

② Using a small knife, trim one side off of each floret, exposing the interior structure of the cauliflower.

③ Carefully slice the cauliflower as thinly as possible, preferably on a mandoline, keeping the floret intact.

④ Blanch the slices for 10 seconds and immediately transfer to the ice water to cool.

⑤ Drain on a lint-free towel.

⑥ Lay on a dehydrator rack *and season lightly with salt.

⑦ Dehydrate at 130°F (54°C) until dry and crispy, about 12 hours.

* *Alternatively, spread on a silicone baking mat and dry in the oven at its lowest setting overnight.*

FOR THE CAULIFLOWER PURÉE

① Combine the cauliflower, cream, milk, and salt in a medium saucepan over medium heat. Cook until the cauliflower is tender, about 15 minutes.

② Remove from the heat and stir in the white chocolate until melted and evenly incorporated.

③ While still hot, transfer to a high-powered blender, preferably a Vita-Prep and blend until a smooth purée forms. Measure the purée. You will need grams 330 grams (1½ cups) in the blender. Reserve the rest for another use.

>>>

④ With the blender running, slowly pour in the carrageenan and blend on high speed for 1 minute.

⑤ Transfer to a small saucepan and rewarm if necessary. It should be hot.

⑥ Divide among 6 serving bowls, tap gently to settle the purée and let sit until set, about 2 minutes.

FOR THE ROSE GEL

① Bloom the gelatin in a medium bowl of ice water. Once softened, wring out the excess water.

② Warm the verjus in a small saucepan over medium to medium-low heat until just simmering.

③ Remove from the heat and stir in the gelatin until completely melted.

④ Strain through a fine-mesh strainer.

TO ASSEMBLE THE CAULIFLOWER CUSTARDS

① Pour a thin layer of the gel on top of each bowl of cauliflower purée, about 15 grams (1 tablespoon) per bowl.

② Refrigerate until cold.

FOR BLANCHING THE FOIE GRAS

① Bring a large pot of water to a boil. Fill a medium bowl with ice water.

② Lay a large piece of cheesecloth, about 1 meter (3 feet) in length, on the work surface.

③ Unwrap the foie gras, set on the cheesecloth, and roll up in the cheesecloth. Twist the ends and tie them tightly with kitchen twine.

④ Lower the boiling water to a very slow simmer and gently blanch the foie gras for 90 seconds. Immediately transfer to the ice water and let cool completely.

TO FINISH THE FOIE GRAS

① Using a small knife, remove any oxidized areas from the outside of the foie gras.

② Cut the remaining foie gras into 2.5 cm (1-inch) cubes and keep very cold.

③ Using a plastic bowl scraper, press through a cold tamis onto a frozen tray to achieve "mini-wheat-like" ribbons of foie gras.

④ Store in the freezer gently wrapped until ready to serve.

TO SERVE

① Using a vegetable peeler, peel curls of white chocolate off of the block. Place on a chilled tray.

② Season the foie gras with black pepper and spoon about 15 grams (2 tablespoons) on top of the gel layer in each dish.

③ Invert the rose in a tall, narrow bowl and add the liquid nitrogen, being sure the rose is fully submerged until frozen.

④ Holding the rose by the stem, shatter the leaves of the rose by "grinding" in a mortar and quickly sprinkle over the top of the foie gras, about 3 grams (2 teaspoons) per dish.

⑤ Top with a white chocolate curl and cauliflower chips.

⑥ Serve immediately.

Roasted Prime Beef Rib Cap with Matsutake Mushrooms, Truffles, and Red Wine Sauce

SERVES 4

ROASTED PRIME BEEF RIB CAP

680 grams | 24 ounces USDA prime beef
   rib cap, trimmed and cleaned
Coarse sea salt
Freshly ground black pepper
Activa GS

15 grams | 1 tablespoon unsalted butter
1 small rosemary sprig
1 small thyme sprig
1 garlic clove, skin on and smashed
Fleur de sel
Assorted micro greens and blossoms

RED WINE SAUCE

15 ml | 1 tablespoon vegetable oil
2 large shallots, diced
1 small carrot, diced
1 small celery stalk, diced
3 white mushrooms, diced
125 ml | ½ cup dry red wine
250 ml | 1 cup veal glace
   (see Base Recipes, note on "Chicken or
   Guinea Hen Jus," page 305)
1 small bouquet garni (bay leaf, peppercorn,
   and thyme sprig, wrapped in cheesecloth)
15 grams | 1 tablespoon unsalted butted
Kosher salt
Freshly ground black pepper

>>>

FOR THE BEEF RIB CAP

① Set up an immersion circulator in a water bath and set to 132°F (55.5°C).
② Season the rib cap on all sides with salt and pepper.
③ Using a small fine-mesh strainer, lightly dust one side of the cap with the Activa GS and leave dusted-side up. Roll the cap, like a roulade/jelly roll and tie with kitchen twine.
④ Put in a sous vide bag and Cryovac to seal.
⑤ Submerge the bag in the water bath and cook for 2 hours.

FOR THE RED WINE SAUCE

① Heat the vegetable oil in a medium saucepan over medium-high heat. Add the shallots, carrots, celery, and mushrooms and cook until translucent.
② Pour in the wine and deglaze the pan, scraping to loosen any bits from the bottom and bring the wine to a boil. Reduce the heat to low and simmer until the wine has reduced by three-quarters.
③ Stir in the veal glace, add the bouquet garni, and continue to simmer on low heat, skimming off any fat and foam that forms on the surface, until reduced by half.
④ Set a cheesecloth-lined fine-mesh strainer over a small saucepan and strain the reduced wine, discarding the vegetables and bouquet garni.
⑤ Set over low heat, stir in the butter, and season to taste with salt and pepper.

>>>

CELERY ROOT PURÉE

500 ml | 2 cups whole milk

450 grams | 1 pound celery root, peeled and
    cut into 2.5 cm (1-inch) cubes

1 small bouquet garni (bay leaf, black
    peppercorn, and thyme sprig wrapped in
    cheesecloth)

1 garlic clove, peeled and smashed

30 grams | 2 tablespoons unsalted butter

Kosher salt

Freshly ground black pepper

ROASTED MATSUTAKE MUSHROOMS

170 grams | 6 ounces matsutake mushrooms,
    cleaned and sliced

Kosher salt

Freshly ground black pepper

5 ml | 1 teaspoon vegetable oil

½ lemon

SAUTÉED SPINACH WITH TRUFFLES

56 grams | 2 ounces black truffle, peeled

6 ml | 1 teaspoon vegetable oil

28 grams | 1 ounce minced shallot

1 very small garlic clove, minced

225 grams | 8 ounces spinach

Kosher salt

Freshly ground black pepper

Pinch freshly grated nutmeg

15 grams | 1 tablespoon unsalted butter,
    divided into 4 pieces

SAUTÉED BABY CARROTS

15 grams | 1 tablespoon unsalted butter

12 baby carrots, peeled and cleaned

50 ml | 3 tablespoons chicken stock

Kosher salt

Freshly ground black pepper

FOR THE CELERY ROOT PURÉE

1. Put the milk, celery root, bouquet garni, and garlic in a medium saucepan. Bring to a simmer and cook until the celery root is very tender.
2. Strain through a fine-mesh strainer, reserving 80 ml (⅓ cup) of the milk and the celery root. Transfer to a high-powered blender, preferably a Vita-Prep.
3. Melt the butter in a small saucepan over medium-high heat and cook until medium brown in color and add to the blender. Purée on high speed until very smooth.
4. Pass the mixture through a fine-mesh strainer or tamis and season to taste with salt and pepper.

FOR THE ROASTED MATSUTAKE MUSHROOMS

1. Season the mushrooms with salt and pepper.
2. Set a medium sauté pan over medium-high heat. Add the oil, followed by the mushrooms. Cook, turning to brown on both sides.
3. Remove from the heat and season with a few drops of lemon juice.

FOR THE SAUTÉED SPINACH WITH TRUFFLES

1. Preheat the oven to 350°F (175°C).
2. Slice half of the truffles thinly, on a mandoline. Using small cutters, punch out different sized disks. Set the disks aside for garnish. Grate the remaining truffles on a rasp grater.
3. Set a medium sauté pan over medium-high heat. Add the oil, followed by the shallot and garlic, and cook for 1 minute. Stir in the spinach until it wilts. Season with salt, pepper, and nutmeg. Remove from the heat.
4. Drain the spinach on a kitchen towel.
5. Divide the spinach into quarters and form each into a small ball. Set on a sheet pan.
6. Put a piece of butter on each patty and put in the oven for 3 to 4 minutes. Remove and set aside.

FOR THE SAUTÉED BABY CARROTS

1. Melt half of the butter in a small sauté pan over medium heat. Add the carrots and stock, bring to a simmer, and cook until the carrots are tender and the liquid has reduced to a glaze.
2. Remove from the heat, stir in the remaining butter, and season to taste with salt and pepper.

BRAISED CIPPOLINI ONIONS

40 grams | 3 tablespoons unsalted butter

4 small cippolini onions

125 ml | ½ cup chicken stock

2.5 grams | ½ teaspoon kosher salt

Freshly ground black pepper

CRISPY SHALLOT RINGS

Vegetable oil

1 shallot, peeled and thinly sliced on a
    mandoline and gently separated
    into rings

All-purpose flour

Kosher salt

Freshly ground black pepper

PARSLEY OIL

1 bunch flat-leaf parsley, leaves removed

125 ml | ½ cup vegetable oil

FOR THE CIPPOLINI ONIONS

1. Melt the butter in a small sauté pan over medium heat. Add the onions and sauté until golden brown.
2. Pour in the stock and season with the salt and some pepper. Simmer uncovered until the onions are tender and glazed.

FOR THE CRISPY SHALLOT RINGS

1. Fit a high-sided pot with a deep-fat/candy thermometer and bring 50 mm (2 inches) of oil to 350°F (175°C).
2. Dust the sliced shallots with flour, shaking off any excess.
3. Fry the shallots in the oil until golden brown, drain on paper towels, and season with salt and pepper.

FOR THE PARSLEY OIL

1. Combine the parsley leaves and oil in the blender. Blend on high speed until a fine purée is achieved, 6 to 8 minutes.
2. Strain through a fine-mesh strainer lined with cheesecloth. Transfer the oil, discarding the water-based liquid, into a small bottle with an eyedropper.

TO FINISH THE BEEF RIB CAP AND SERVE

1. Remove the rolled cap from the bag and pat dry.
2. Melt the butter in a medium sauté pan over medium-high heat and add the rolled cap, rosemary, thyme, and garlic. Cook, turning as needed, to brown the cap on all sides.
3. Remove from the pan and let rest for 10 minutes.
4. Reheat the vegetables, as needed.
5. Slice the rolled cap into 4 even portions. Season with fleur de sel and freshly cracked black pepper.
6. Spoon a dollop of celery root purée in the center of each plate and place a slice of the rolled cap on top.
7. Spoon small dollops of the purée around the plate at 2, 6, and 10 o'clock. Set a slice of mushroom on each of the small dollops, and garnish with the truffle discs and microgreens.
8. Put the spinach at 12 o'clock and arrange the grated truffle in a nest pattern on it. Top with a truffle disc.
9. Arrange three carrots on each of the plates at 4 o'clock. Set a cippolini onion at 8 o'clock and top with the crispy shallot rings.
10. Drizzle the red wine sauce around the plate and add a few drops of parsley oil. Garnish with more microgreens.

Radish Tartlet with Maitre D' Hotel Butter

SERVES 10

**WONDER BREAD
TARTLET SHELL**

10 slices Wonder bread

Unsalted butter, melted

MAITRE D' HOTEL BUTTER

25 grams flat-leaf parsley leaves

25 grams chives, cut into ⅜-inch

   (9.5 mm) pieces

15 grams chervil leaves

15 grams tarragon leaves

15 grams shallot, peeled and roughly chopped

450 grams unsalted butter, preferably Strauss

   or another European-style butter,

   at room temperature

2 grams finely grated lemon zest

9 grams fine sea salt

35 petite breakfast radishes

Fleur de sel

**FOR THE WONDER BREAD
TARTLET SHELLS**

1. Arrange ten 3.5 cm (⅓-inch) tartlet molds on a sheet pan and preheat the oven to 275°F (35°C), preferably with the convection setting.
2. Cut the crusts off all of the slices of bread. Working with 1 piece at a time, carefully roll each piece with a rolling pin to avoid tearing, until a thin, compact layer.
3. Run through a pasta roller until about 1 mm in thickness (about the thickness of a credit card), then cut into a 4.4 cm (1¾-inch) round using a ring mold or round cutter. Brush the rounds with melted butter and gently center in the molds and press in the sides. Set another tartlet mold on top of each, lining them up, covering the bread. Set another sheet pan on top to weigh down the molds.
4. Bake until light brown, about 20 minutes.
5. Transfer to a cooling rack, unmold the tartlets, and let cool completely.
6. If made ahead, the shells can be reserved for up to 5 days in a dehydrator set to 100°F (38°C).

FOR THE BUTTER

1. Roughly chop all of the herbs, then put in a Robot Coupe or food processor and pulse until finely chopped. Add the shallot and pulse again. Then, add the butter and run the machine until the butter is green and the pieces of herb are finely chopped.
2. Season the butter with the lemon zest and salt. Refrigerate until ready to use for at least 4 hours prior to serving or up to 3 days.
3. Bring the butter to 55°F (12°C) to use. You will need about 3 grams (1 teaspoon) per tartlet.

TO PREPARE THE RADISHES

① Slice the radishes on a mandoline and put in a bowl of ice water to crisp.

② Drain and pat dry on paper towels.

TO ASSEMBLE THE TARTS

① Place 3 grams (1 teaspoon) of the butter into each tartlet mold and spread to an even layer.

② Working from the center, arrange the radish slices in concentric circles, overlapping each halfway over the previously placed slice. Continue until the mold is filled and the radishes look like a flower in the shell. Set on a sheet pan.

③ Repeat with the remaining shells. Refrigerate for 15 minutes to firm up the butter.

④ Using an offset spatula, remove the radish flowers in the butter from the molds and transfer them to the wonder bread shells.

⑤ Sprinkle with fleur de sel and serve.

BASE RECIPES

PICKLED MUSTARD SEEDS
Makes about 500 grams

1 liter champagne vinegar
500 grams granulated sugar
10 grams kosher salt
500 ml water
100 grams yellow mustard seeds
100 grams brown mustard seeds

- Put the vinegar, sugar, water, and salt in a small pressure cooker and bring to a simmer.
- Remove half of the liquid and reserve.
- Add the mustard seeds to the remaining liquid in the pressure cooker and secure the lid.
- Bring the pressure cooker to 15 psi (full pressure) and cook for 30 minutes.
- Let cool until the pressure has fully dissipated, and then take off the lid.
- Strain the mustard seeds and discard the cooking liquid.
- Put the cooked seeds in an air-tight storage container with the reserved pickling liquid.
- Refrigerate for at least 24 hours or up to 2 months.

CURING MIX
Makes 55 grams

35 grams kosher salt
15 grams pink salt
5 grams granulated sugar

- Whisk all of the curing mix ingredients together in a small bowl or storage container.
- The curing mix can be used for curing foie gras or as a seasoning blend for meat and fish forcemeats.

PASTRAMI SPICE
Makes 200 grams

50 grams black peppercorns
50 grams coriander seeds
50 grams juniper berries
50 grams mustard seeds

- Put all of the pastrami spices in a high-powered blender, prefereably a Vita-Prep, or a spice grinder and blend at medium-high speed until a powder forms.
- Press the mixture through a fine-mesh tamis and reserve.

PASTRAMI BRINE
Makes 1 liter

1 liter water
100 grams granulated sugar
95 grams kosher salt
6.5 grams pink salt
4 grams thinly sliced garlic
3 grams black peppercorns
1.5 grams coriander seeds
1.2 grams mustard seeds
1.2 grams juniper berries
1.2 grams ground ginger
.5 gram cloves
1 bay leaf

- Bring the water to a boil in a medium saucepan.
- Take off the heat. Add the remaining ingredients, stirring constantly until the sugar and salts have dissolved.
- Let cool to room temperature.
- Refrigerate or set in a bowl of ice water until cold. (The brine needs to be cold before using.)

TO BRINE FOIE GRAS
- Put the foie gras lobes in the brine and cover with a clean kitchen towel to keep submerged.
- Refrigerate in the brine for 6 hours.
- Remove from the brine and pat dry with a clean towel.

TO SMOKE FOIE GRAS
- Fill a 4-inch hotel pan with a layer of ice.
- Put a 1-inch piece of compressed smoke wood in a shallow, heatproof container lined with aluminum foil and set on one side of the hotel pan.
- Light the smoke wood on all sides to generate a slow burn, extinguishing any flames that may start.
- Working quickly place a 2-inch, perforated hotel pan on the ice, lay the foie gras on the side opposite the smoke wood, and cover the pan with aluminum foil. Let smoke for 30 minutes.
- Remove the foil and transfer the foie gras to the refrigerator until completely cold.
- Vacuum seal the foie gras in a Cryovac bag.
- The smoked foie gras can be refrigerated for up to 2 weeks or frozen for up to 1 month.

MUSHROOM STOCK
Makes 1 liter

1.25 kilograms button mushrooms, thoroughly washed
250 grams water

- Using a meat grinder fitted with the smallest die, grind the mushrooms into a large saucepan.
- Add the water, set the pan over high heat, and bring to a boil. Lower the heat and simmer until the mushrooms are cooked, about 5 minutes.
- Cover the pan, take off the heat, and let steep for 30 minutes.
- Line a colander with a clean kitchen towel or cheesecloth and put over a large bowl or pot.
- Pour the mushroom mixture into the lined colander and let drain for 20 minutes.
- Squeeze out any remaining liquid from the mushrooms.
- The mushroom stock can be refrigerated in an airtight container for up to five days or frozen for up to one month.

CHICKEN OR GUINEA HEN JUS
(Demi-glace)
Makes 425 milliliters

1-inch veal neck bones can be substituted for the poultry bones to make a veal jus.

1.8 kilograms bones (poultry wings, carcass, and legs, cut into 1-inch pieces)
60 grams duck fat
450 grams onion, cut into medium dice
300 grams carrot, cut into medium dice
150 grams leek, cut into medium dice
350 grams small tomatoes, cut into medium dice

4 liters chicken stock
600 grams veal tendons
25 grams garlic cloves, skin on and cut in half
1.5 grams black peppercorns
1 gram thyme sprigs
1 gram bay leaf
4.2 grams Ultra-tex (1% of reduced stock by weight, see below)

- Preheat the oven to 375°F (190°C).
- Line a half sheet pan with foil and set a rack on top.
- Set the bones on the rack.
- Roast the bones in the oven until golden brown, about 17 minutes.
- Melt the duck fat in a 12-quart pressure cooker over medium-high heat. Add the onion and carrots and cook until lightly colored, 3 to 4 minutes. Stir in the leeks and cook until translucent, about 3 minutes.
- Stir in the tomatoes and cook until dry, about 5 minutes.
- Pour in 250 milliliters of water to deglaze the pan, scraping any browned bits from the bottom. Continue to cook, stirring occasionally, until the mixture has reduced and is dry.
- Pour in 200 milliliters of the chicken stock and reduce until dry again.
- Add the tendons, garlic cloves, black peppercorns, thyme, bay leaf, and the remaining chicken stock.
- Put the lid on the pressure cooker and bring to full pressure (15 psi). Cook for 2 hours.

- Remove from the heat and let cool until the pressure has released.
- Pour off the stock, keeping the bones and remaining ingredients in the pot for a second cooking.
- Add 3 liters of water to the pot, cover, bring back to full pressure (15 psi), and cook for 2 hours again.
- Meanwhile, strain the first stock through a chinois or fine-mesh strainer, 5 to 6 times, or until no sediment remains. Put in a large saucepan.
- Once the second cooking in the pressure cooker is complete, remove the pressure cooker from the heat and let cool until the pressure has released.
- Strain the stock through a chinois, discarding all of the solids. Continue straining until no sediment remains. Add to the first stock in the large saucepan.
- Set the saucepan over the heat, repeatedly skimming the impurities that rise to the top with a ladle. Change the pan occasionally. Keeping the pan clean will keep the stock from getting bitter. Continue to cook until the stock has reduced to 425 milliliters.
- Remove from the heat, whisk in the Ultra-tex, and cook for 2 minutes.
- Strain into a clean saucepan if using soon or into a storage container.
- The reduced stock can be refrigerated for up to 3 days or frozen for up to 1 month.

INDEX

PHOTO CREDITS

ACKNOWLEDGMENTS

When the idea of this book began, my vision for it was twofold. First was to throw open the curtains and give readers behind-the-scenes access to the journey of the Bocuse d'Or, providing a front-row seat to what it takes to compete at the world's highest level. Second was to inspire chefs, supporters, food enthusiasts, and patriotic Americans across the country to be part of the journey and the success of future generations.

The stories, photos, and recipes in this book would never have been possible without the incredible support of so many talented and dedicated individuals. It has been a privilege to work and learn alongside each of you.

To our Number One Fan, Nathan Daulton, one of the most passionate friends one could ask for, and without whose encouragement this book would never have left the ground.

To Joleen and David Hughes at Level, Calistoga, CA, who patiently traveled this journey with me through all its twists and turns. Thank you for meeting impossible deadlines, and for the amazing designs you painstakingly create.

To Jonah Straus, my agent extraordinaire, thank you for believing in me, this project, and our vision. You went above and beyond and transformed this book from a vision to a reality almost overnight. To Holly La Due and the team at Prestel, I can't thank you enough for your flexibility, patience, and the numerous extended deadlines.

To Andrew Friedman and Russ Parsons for guiding me through the world of intrigue that is writing and publishing. I will always value these months together and your patient efforts to try and turn me into a writer. Your knowledge and expertise shine through these pages and I will fondly remember our many phone calls together.

Thank you, Lara Kastner, Meg Smith, and David Escalante for being amazing photographers and doing whatever it takes to capture the moment. Whether standing on top of a 12-foot ladder, jumping over press barricades, or figuring out how to photograph the world's most reflective platter, you were all amazingly dedicated and true professionals.

To Chefs Keller, Boulud, Bocuse, and Kaysen, thank you for your vision to form Ment'or and establish a solid foundation for future generations to build their success upon. To Young Yun, Jaimie Chew, Monica Bhambhani, Tehani Levin, and the team at Ment'or, past and present, thanks for your tireless dedication, vision, perseverance, and support.

Thank you to the numerous sponsors and supporters who kept us moving through every day of training. Special thanks to Aaron Keefer and Kate Olen for every perfect green from The French Laundry Garden and every wild adventure in pursuit of fennel blooms. Thanks to the Hestan team for the incredible kitchen space, staff meals, and patience throughout our training.

To my dear friend, Martin Kastner, the problem solver, mad genius, and not-so-secret weapon who elevates us above the rest. You never cease to amaze me. Thank you for the thousands of hours and sacrifice you, and the Crucial Detail team—Lukas Kastner and Graham Burns have given to make all this possible.

To the heart and core of Team USA—Will Mouchet, Greg Schesser, Vinny Loseto, Daniel Garcia, Chance Schwab, and Mimi Chen—thank you for making this journey so amazing and having a sense of humor along the way! Skylar Stover, my wingman, we made a lot of mistakes, learned many lessons, and I'd do it all over again together in a heartbeat. To the Golden Boys, Matt Peters and Harrison Turone, what a journey! You guys were amazing from start to finish. Thank you for the privilege of being your coach and patiently listening to every critique and suggestion along the way. We did it!

What a privilege it was to work alongside the best talent in America in Gabriel Kreuther, Richard Rosendale, Grant Achatz, Dave Beran, Robert Sulatycky, Matthew Kirkley. We started this journey as colleagues and finished it as friends and compatriots. Thank you for constantly challenging me and making this journey rich and full with your talents, ideas, and encouragement.

To two very special mentors, Claudia Fitzgerald and Hans Schadler, who gave me my first chance in the kitchen at the age of sixteen and never stopped believing in me. Thank you for teaching me to never stop learning and encouraging me to pursue my dreams.

Lastly, and most importantly, to my dearest wife and best friend, Rachel. You are the anchor of my life and keep me steady through every storm. Without your love, patience, sacrifice, and gentle support, this journey would have faltered before it began. God has been faithful through the peaks and valleys and with Him all things are possible.